THE ENCYCLOPEDIA OF
COMBAT TECHNIQUES

THE ENCYCLOPEDIA OF
COMBAT TECHNIQUES

CHRIS McNAB
WILL FOWLER

LEWIS
INTERNATIONAL, INC.

First published in 2002 by Lewis International, Inc.
2201 N.W. 102 Place, #1
Miami, Fl 33172 USA

Tel: 305-436-7984 / 800-259-5962
Fax: 305-436-7985 / 800-664-5095

Library of Congress Cataloging-in-Publication Data available.

ISBN 1-930983-13-1

Editorial and design by
Amber Books Ltd
Bradley's Close
74–77 White Lion Street
London N1 9PF

Project Editor: Chris Stone
Designer: Brian Rust

The authors would like to thank the officers of the Infantry Trials &
Development Unit, Warminster, UK, for their kind assistance in the research
of this book.

Printed and bound in Italy by: Eurolitho S.p.A., Cesano Boscone (MI)

Contents

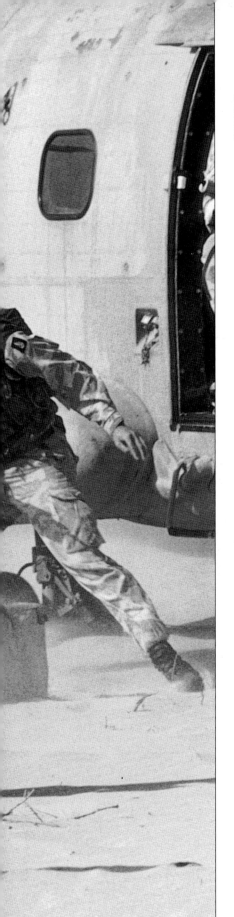

INTRODUCTION

The Four Tactics of Modern Warfare

O ne of the defining characteristics of war is undoubtedly chaos. From the moment that battle is joined, plans disintegrate, communications falter, people die or are wounded, units fragment, logistics are hampered and unpredictability reigns. Tactics are the counterweight to this chaos. Military tactics are the practical means armies use to achieve battlefield objectives. Revealingly, the origin of the word lies in the Greek term *taktos*, meaning 'ordered' or 'arranged'. From this etymology, 'tactics' came to imply the deliberate control of military formation, movement and fire, and the attempt to impose clarity upon the fog of war and achieve ultimate victory over an outclassed enemy.

◄ *A group of British Army soldiers disembarks from a helicopter during deployment in Saudi Arabia, 1990. Following disembarkation soldiers usually adopt defensive positions in a 360 degrees pattern around the helicopter in case of an opposed landing.*

Tactics encompass every method of war-making, but in military theory four elements are central: firepower, mobility, shock and defence. Defence is possibly the most important; upon it depends a soldier's basic survival. Defence tactics are some of the most changeless military principles – soldiers (at least those in the age of firearms) have always appreciated the defensive value of a depression in the ground, even if their leadership disavows such cover. Yet, while cover, concealment and camouflage tactics have remained fairly constant, defence tactics are also the battle between emergent security and counter-security technologies. The weapons of each passing epoch have shaped the nature of defensive warfare. Castles offered formidable defence from the twelfth century until the invention of heavy, wall-smashing siege cannon in the fifteenth century. Fortification designers responded by constructing earthen ramparts to deflect cannon balls, reducing the height of towers and other salient features, and also expanding the quantity and quality of anti-artillery weaponry within the fortification itself. Long-range rifled artillery weapons switched the advantage back to the attackers in the 1860s, after which fortifications countered by sinking into the earth in the form of semi-permanent trenches, bunkers and earthworks (although major permanent fortifications persisted until the early 1940s as tactical options). Today, fighting positions depend on camouflage, concealment and mobility for their defence, as being seen and being static are likely to result in certain destruction. Similar battles between defensive and offensive technologies have occurred in many other fields throughout history, such as the battle between ground-attack aircraft and anti-aircraft defence, and the electronic war between surveillance and counter-surveillance equipment. On a localized scale, every infantryman must conduct his own defence in response to the forces arraigned against him – and adapt his defence accordingly when it becomes inadequate.

Firepower means, simply, the weapons used to inflict casualties upon the enemy. The 5m (15ft) sarissa spears carried by Alexander

▸ *Military tactics hang upon effective leadership, but also on the* esprit de corps *of units. Studies in the Korean War in 1950 found that commitment to the welfare of his unit motivated a soldier to fight more than any other reason.*

▾ *Two US Marines detonate demolitions during an exercise at Camp Pendleton, California. Training using live rounds and munitions prepares a soldier better for actual combat than almost any other training method.*

the Great's army in the third century BC, when presented by units of soldiers 256 men strong and 16 deep (the syntagma), helped his forces carve out a Macedonian Empire from Greece to the Indus. Similarly, but with radically different technology, Allied air power in the Gulf War in 1990–91 killed more than 300,000 Iraqi soldiers and destroyed over 5000 military vehicles with no tactically significant resistance, such was the level of fire supremacy. However, firepower rarely wins battles without mobility. Mobility dictates the speed, tempo and tactical positioning of forces. From at least 1400 BC to the sixteenth century AD, cavalry were the mobile-warfare specialists. In 53 BC, at Carrhae, Parthia, seven Roman

Legions were slaughtered by Parthian mounted archers who surrounded and split the static Roman defence; in 1745, at Hohenfreidberg, Frederick the Great's Prussian Bayreuth Dragoons smashed more than 20 Austrian infantry battalions and captured 2500 prisoners. Cavalry's steady demise, however, began in the 1500s when ranks of longbow- and crossbow-armed infantry inflicted hideous casualties on exposed horsemen (such as in the British victory over French forces at the battle of Crécy in 1346). This problem worsened with the widespread introduction of rifled firearms from the seventeenth century, and, for two centuries, firepower was predominant once more.

Mobility regained supremacy in the twentieth century. Railways and personal vehicles increased the logistical volume of troop and supply movement, which in turn speeded up the operational tempo of the battlefield. Combat movement itself was accelerated by the motorization of armies and a bolder emphasis on shock. Shock is the surprise and violence of an attack. It is the tactical element intended to throw the enemy into disarray. German stormtroopers in late World War I displaced trench-

▼ *US Marines role-play a counter-terrorist operation in the Urban Training Facility, Camp Lejeune. Small-unit tactics have become increasingly central to military training over the last 20 years.*

▸ *A US Air Force Airman attaches a GBU-24 laser-guided bomb to an F15 Eagle at Aviano Air Base, Italy. Laser-guided bombs first made an appearance in warfare during the Vietnam War.*

bound enemies with shock grenade and machine-gun attacks applied through rapid fire-and-manoeuvre assaults. Hitler's blitzkrieg in 1939 and 1940 demonstrated shock on a huge scale, showing how forces mechanized by armoured vehicles and military aviation could surprise and overwhelm huge but static concentrations of enemy soldiers by punching through at weak points and then fanning out in the enemy's rear.

World War II also became the war of combined-arms tactics. The Allied landings on D-Day in 1944 most vividly demonstrated the combined-arms (air force, navy and army) approach to combat that dominates modern military actions. Today, armies are obliged to operate fully in three arenas – land, air and sea – as is seen in actions from the amphibious landings at Inchon to the airborne assaults in Vietnam and the large tanks manoeuvres of the Gulf War. The tactical challenge of the combined-arms operation is to make the logistics, communications and weaponry of previously distinct arms work as one.

This book examines current tactical doctrine as it is taught to soldiers the world over. Chapter One deals with close-quarter battle, looking at techniques of unarmed combat or fighting with knives or improvised weapons. Chapter Two, 'Firearms and Explosives', gives the tactical principles of applying personal weaponry, from the phys-

ical control of an assault rifle to the destructive application of demolitions against major targets. Chapter Three, 'Support Weapons', examines the more powerful instruments in the soldier's arsenal and looks at how he applies or controls support weapons such as anti-tank missiles and heavy artillery to maximize his destructive capability and tactical opportunities. Chapter Four, 'Extreme Terrain Combat', explores in detail how harsh terrains such as arctic landscapes, equatorial jungles and arid deserts affect soldiers, equipment and tactical movement. Chapter Five, 'Unit Tactics', deals with the tactical procedures of military units in standard operational roles, such as conducting an ambush or establishing fighting positions.

Finally, Chapter Six, 'Specialist Skills', looks at the specialist skills of today's armies. These include commonly taught procedures such as the airborne assault, but also those skills which are the preserve of elite forces, such as hostage rescue and parachute infiltration.

Tactics in today's armies have been revolutionized by technology, yet many tactical manoeuvres and actions are rooted in ancient common sense. What will be apparent throughout this extensive study is that, although lethal weaponry and high-tech equipment have transformed the doctrine of military tactics from what it was 100 years ago, personal courage, instinct and moral resources are just as vital today as they have always been to mission success.

CHAPTER ONE

CLOSE-QUARTER BATTLE

Close-quarter battle is the preserve of a very small number of people. With indirect-fire weapons such as mortars and artillery, the target may never be seen or will, at most, be a tiny shape in the landscape. For the infantry, who are the key exponents of close-quarter battle skills, the enemy may be so close that the soldier can feel his opponent's breath on his face. His blood may stain his clothing, and he may bear the bruises and scratches that marked his enemy's last struggles to defeat him and stay alive – even as he extinguished his life. This type of fighting is not the formalized techniques of a martial arts school; it is dirty, violent and with only one rule – kill or be killed.

◄ *A Russian instructor demonstrates a knife disarming technique to a group of recruits. He has not only thrown his assailant, but he will also have taken possession of the bayonet.*

VULNERABLE POINTS ON THE HUMAN BODY

The human body is an enormously complex and versatile organism capable of a vast range of functions. It is tough and resilient, and can withstand modest changes in heat and cold and many of the injuries that occur in the workplace, on the sports field and as a result of day-to-day living. Its complexity, however, makes it vulnerable to more violent blows, especially if these are delivered to crucial parts of the body. In close-combat fighting, a soldier and his opponent may be wearing load-carrying equipment (LCE), as well as helmets and combat boots. These all have the potential to be used as weapons and, equally, to restrict movement and flexibility.

HEAD AND UPPER BODY

Eyes: A slight jab in the eyes causes uncontrollable watering and blurred vision. A powerful jab or poke can cause temporary blindness, or the eyes can be gouged out.

Death can result if the fingers penetrate through the thin bone behind the eyes and into the brain.

Ears: A strike to the ear with cupped hands can rupture the eardrum and may cause concussion. The ears are also vulnerable to tearing.

Nose: Any blow can easily break the thin bones of the nose, causing acute pain and eye-watering. A blow to the nerve centre, which is close to the surface under the nose, can again cause acute pain and watery eyes. If the solder can insert his fingers into his opponent's nostrils, they can be ripped.

Jaw: A blow to the jaw, the classic 'upper cut', can break or dislocate it. If the facial nerve is pinched against the lower jaw, one side of the face will be paralysed.

Chin: A blow to the chin can cause paralysis, mild concussion and unconsciousness. The jawbone acts as a lever that can transmit the force of a blow to the back of the brain where the cardiac and respiratory mechanisms are controlled.

Skull: A moderate blow to the back of the ears or the base of the skull can cause unconsciousness as a result of the jarring effect on the back of the brain. A powerful blow may cause concussion or even brain haemorrhage and death.

The skull is weak where the frontal cranial bones join. A powerful strike causes trauma to the cranial cavity, resulting in unconsciousness and haemorrhage. A severe strike can result in death. A powerful blow can also cause whiplash, while a severe blow can once again cause cerebral haemorrhage and death.

The bones of the skull are particularly weak at the temple, where an artery and large nerve lie close to the skin. A powerful strike can cause unconsciousness and concussion. If the artery is severed, the resulting massive haemorrhage

▾ *The human head is one of the most fragile parts of the body. There are at least eight areas that are highly susceptible to physical force.*

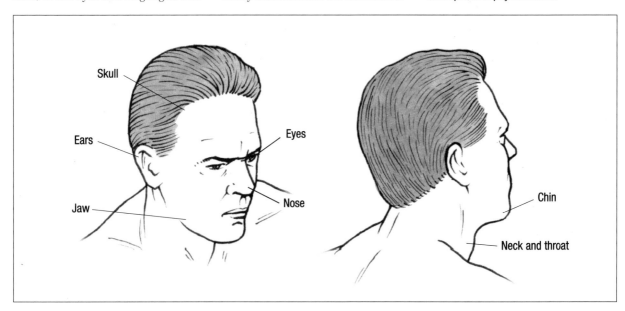

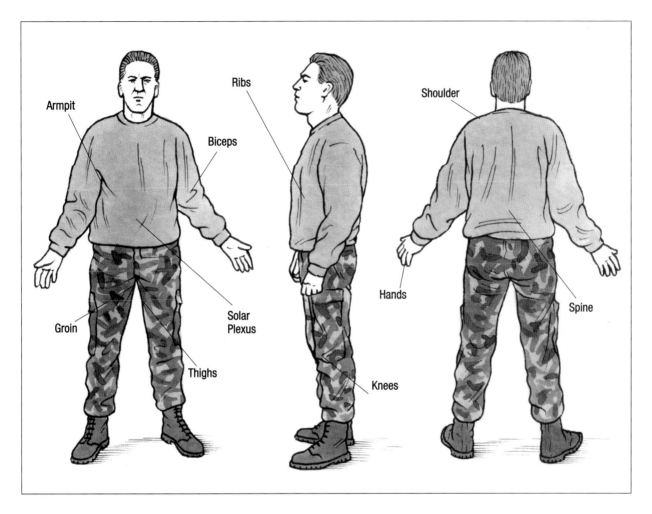

Armpit

Biceps

Ribs

Shoulder

Groin

Solar Plexus

Thighs

Hands

Knees

Spine

▲ *There are a further 10 vulnerable parts of the human body from the neck down. Being aware of these areas helps a soldier to protect himself against attack.*

compresses the brain, causing coma and/or death.

Neck: A sharp blow to the side of the neck causes unconsciousness as a result of shock to the carotid artery, jugular vein and vagus nerve. For maximum effect, the blow should be focused below and slightly in front of the ear. A less powerful blow causes involuntary muscle spasms and intense pain. The side of the neck is one of the

best targets to use to drop an opponent immediately or to temporarily disable him.

A vigorous blow to the back of the neck, often called a 'rabbit punch', can cause whiplash, concussion or even a broken neck and death.

Throat: A powerful blow to the front of the throat can crush the windpipe, resulting in death. At the very least, it causes acute pain and gagging or vomiting.

TORSO

The human torso, or middle section, extends from the shoulders to

the area just above the hips. Most blows to vital points in this region are not fatal, but they can have serious, long-term complications that range from trauma to internal organs to spinal cord injuries.

Shoulder Joint: A large bundle of nerves passes in front of the shoulder joint. A powerful blow causes acute pain and can make the entire arm ineffective if the nerves are struck correctly.

Collarbone (Clavicle): A blow to the collarbone, or clavicle, can fracture it, causing intense pain and rendering the arm on the side of the fracture ineffective. The fracture can also sever the brachial nerve or sub-clavian artery, causing pain and incapacity.

Armpits: A large nerve lies close to the skin in each armpit. A blow to this nerve causes severe pain and partial paralysis. A knife inserted into the armpit is fatal as it severs a major artery leading from the heart.

Biceps and Forearms: A strike to the biceps is very painful and renders the arm ineffective. The biceps are an especially good target when an opponent holds a weapon. The radial nerve, which controls much of the movement in the hand, passes over the forearm bone just below the elbow. A strike to the radial nerve renders the hand and arm ineffective. An opponent can be disarmed by a strike to the forearm; if the strike is powerful enough, he can be knocked unconscious.

Hands: The hands are a sensitive area. As the nerves in the hand pass over the bones, a strike can be intensely painful. The small bones on the back of the hand are easily broken, and such a strike can also render the hand ineffective.

Spinal Column: A blow to the spinal column can sever the spinal cord, resulting in paralysis or death.

Nipples: A large network of nerves and many blood vessels are near the skin at the nipples. A blow here can cause acute pain and haemorrhage, while a jolting blow to the heart can stun the opponent and allow time for follow-up or finishing techniques.

Solar Plexus: The solar plexus is a centre for nerves that control the cardio-respiratory system. A blow to this location is painful and can take away the opponent's breath. A powerful blow causes unconsciousness as a result of shock to the

nerve centre. A penetrating blow can also damage internal organs.

Ribs: A blow to the lower front of the ribs can cause the diaphragm and the other muscles that control breathing to relax. This causes loss of breath and can result in unconsciousness due to respiratory failure.

A blow to the floating ribs can easily fracture them, as they are not attached to the rib cage. If a soldier's fingers can be inserted beneath the ribs, the ribs can be ripped away from their tendons. Fractured ribs on the right side can cause internal injury to the liver; fractured ribs on either side can possibly puncture or collapse a lung.

Kidneys: A powerful blow to the kidneys can induce shock and possi-

▲ The straight punch, shown in two parts above, should be delivered with the body pivoting at the hips. The puncher's arm should twist as he or she throws the punch and the middle knuckle of the fist should remain proud.

bly cause internal injury to these organs. A stab to the kidneys induces instant shock and can cause death as a result of severe internal bleeding.

Abdomen: A powerful blow to the area below the navel and above the groin can cause shock, unconsciousness and internal bleeding.

LOWER BODY

The lower section of the body includes everything from the groin

▲ The elbow strike focuses the attacker's energy into the sharp, bony area of the elbow, which is particularly effective against soft tissue.

area to the feet. Strikes to these areas are seldom fatal, but can incapacitate an opponent.

Groin: A moderate blow to the groin can incapacitate an opponent and cause intense pain. A powerful blow can result in unconsciousness and shock.

Thighs: A large nerve passes near the surface on the outside of the thigh about four fingerwidths above the knee. A powerful strike to this region can render the entire leg ineffective, causing an opponent to drop. This target is espe-

cially suitable for knee strikes and shin kicks.

Another large nerve passes over the bone at about the middle of the inner thigh. A blow to this area also incapacitates the leg, dropping the opponent. Knee strikes and heel kicks are the weapons of choice for this target.

A severe strike to the hamstring can cause muscle spasms and inhibit mobility. Severing the hamstring renders the leg useless.

Knees: The knee is a major supporting structure of the body, so damage to this joint is especially effective. The knee is easily dislocated when struck at an opposing angle to the joint's normal range of motion, especially when it is bear-

ing the opponent's weight. The knee can be dislocated or hyperextended (i.e. extended past its normal range of motion) by kicks and strikes with the entire body.

Calves and Shins: A powerful blow to the top of the calf causes painful muscle spasms and also inhibits mobility. A moderate blow to the shin produces acute pain, especially a blow with a hard object. A powerful blow can possibly fracture the bone that supports most of the body weight.

Ankles and Feet: A powerful strike to the Achilles tendon on the back of the heel can cause an ankle sprain or dislocate the foot. If the tendon is torn or cut, the opponent is incapacitated. If a powerful blow is delivered, the ankle can be sprained or broken, or the victim will suffer acute pain at the very least. The small bones on the top of the foot are easily broken. A strike here will hinder the opponent's mobility.

PUNCHING AND STRIKING

During medium-range combat, punches and strikes are usually short because of the close distance between combatants. Using the entire body mass in motion behind all punches and strikes generates power.

The defender should use a punch to the solar plexus for close-in fighting when the opponent rushes or tries to grab him. He must put his full weight and force behind the punch and strike his opponent in the solar plexus, knocking the breath out of his lungs. The defender can then follow-up with a knee to the groin or other disabling blows.

The thumb strike to the throat is an effective technique when an

opponent is rushing the defender or trying to grab him. In this case, the soldier should thrust his right arm and thumb out and strike his opponent in the throat–larynx area while holding his left hand high for protection. He can follow up with a disabling blow to his opponent's vital areas.

The thumb strike to shoulder joint can be used when the opponent rushes the defender and tries to grab him. The defender strikes the

opponent's shoulder joint or upper pectoral muscle with his fist or thumb. This technique is painful and renders the opponent's arm numb.

In the hammer-fist strike to face, the opponent rushes the defender. The defender counters by rotating his body in the direction of his opponent and striking him in the temple, ear or face. The defender follows up with kicks to the groin or hand strikes to his opponent's

◄ Ducking below his opponent's weapon, which he has pushed to one side, an attacker delivers a stunning blow to the solar plexus. The solar plexus are one of the most tender areas of the human body.

▼ Thai soldiers practice a block and punch move during martial arts training. One arm would deflect an attacker's punch while the fist of the other arm is held back for a counter-attack.

other vital areas. A variant is the hammer-fist strike to the side of the neck. In this, the defender catches his opponent off guard, rotates at the waist to generate power and strikes his opponent on the side of the neck (carotid artery) with his hand clenched into a fist. This strike can cause muscle spasms and may cause his opponent to lose consciousness.

The pectoral muscle can be attacked with a hammer-fist blow. When the opponent tries to grapple with the defender, the defender counters by forcefully striking his opponent in the pectoral muscle with his fist. This blow stuns the opponent, and the defender immediately follows up with a disabling blow.

Punches include the hook punch to solar plexus or floating ribs. In this, the opponent tries to wrestle the defender to the ground. The defender counters with a short hook punch to the solar plexus or floating ribs. A sharply delivered blow can puncture or collapse a lung.

In the classic uppercut to chin, the defender steps between his opponent's arms and strikes with an uppercut punch to the chin or jaw.

The chop with the edge of the hand popular in Asian martial arts techniques includes the knife-hand strike to side of neck. Here, the defender executes a knife-hand strike to the side of his opponent's neck the same way as the hammer-fist strike, except he uses the edge of his striking hand, rather than his fist.

With the knife-hand strike to the radial nerve, the opponent tries to strike the defender with a punch. The defender counters by striking

▲ *The front kick involves two movements: as the attacker moves his upper body back out of range of his attacker, he brings his leg up with the knee bent.*

▼ *The kick is delivered as a flick followed through with the weight of the body and uses the bony outer edge of the foot. Care must be taken to ensure speed and balance with this attack.*

as the attacker moves in. As the defender steps off at an angle of 45 degrees to the side and towards the opponent, he should strike with a short punch to the floating ribs. The defender must then turn his body by rotating on the leading, outside foot and raise the knee of his kicking leg to his chest. He should then drive his kick into the side of the attacker's knee with his foot turned 45 degrees outwards. This angle makes the most of the striking surface and reduces the

◄ *The roundhouse kick uses the strength of not only the leg and knee but also the hips as the attacker pivots and lowers his body to deliver the blow.*

▼ *South American Special Forces split a house tile demonstrating a kick technique. This looks dramatic but is of marginal training value since the unsupported tile is fairly fragile.*

his opponent on the top of the forearm just below the elbow (radial nerve) and uses a follow-up technique to disable his opponent.

KICKING

Kicks during hand-to-hand combat are best directed to low targets and should be simple but effective. Soldiers are usually wearing combat boots and load-carrying equipment that reduces flexibility during combat, and hand-to-hand combat produces high stress. Combatants must rely on gross motor skills and kicks that do not require complicated movement or substantial training and practice to execute.

In the side knee kick, when an opponent launches an attack, for example, with a knife, it is most important for the defender to move his entire body off the line of attack

defender's chances of missing the target.

With the front knee kick as the attacker moves in, the defender should immediately shift off the line of attack and drive his kicking foot straight into the knee of the attacker. His foot should be turned 45 degrees to make the most of the striking surface and to reduce the chances of missing the target. If the kick is delivered correctly, the attacker's advance will stop abruptly, and the knee joint will break.

For the heel kick to inside of thigh, the defender steps 45 degrees outside and towards the attacker to get off the line of attack. He is now in a position where he can drive his heel into the inside of the opponent's thigh (femoral nerve). Either thigh can be targeted, as the kick can still be executed if the defender moves to the inside of the opponent rather than to the outside when getting off the line of attack.

A very effective attack is the heel kick to groin. In this, the defender drives a heel kick into the attacker's groin with his full body mass behind it. As the groin is a soft target, the toe can also be used when striking. The calves and common peroneal nerve are the best striking points with the heel kick. This can also be used to attack the floating ribs.

The shin kick is a powerful one, and it is easily performed with little training. When the legs are targeted, the kick is hard to defend against, and an opponent can be dropped by it.

In the stepping side kick, a combatant starts by stepping either behind or in front of his other foot to close the distance between him and his opponent. The movement

▲ *The front kick develops in two moves. In the fighting stance, the attacker (the figure on the right) brings his leg up with the knee bent and the foot turned at 45 degrees.*

▼ *When his thigh is parallel with the ground he snaps his leg forward. Ideally, the blow should be delivered in boots; in bare feet, use the sole of the foot just below the toes.*

is like that in a skip. The combatant now brings the knee of his kicking foot up and thrusts out a side kick.

For the counter to front kick, the defender traps the kicking foot by meeting it with his own. The defender should turn his foot 45 degrees outwards to increase the likelihood of striking the opponent's kicking foot. This counter requires good timing by the defender, but not necessarily speed. The soldier should not look at his feet when carrying it out, but use his peripheral vision instead. When an attacker tries a front kick, the defender should step off the line of attack of the incoming foot to the

outside. As the attacker's kicking leg begins to drop, the defender kicks upwards into the calf of the attacker's leg. This kick is extremely painful and will probably render the leg ineffective. This technique does not rely on the defender's speed, but on proper timing. The defender can also kick to an opponent's kicking leg by moving off the line of attack to the inside and by using the heel kick to the inside of the thigh or groin.

For the counter to a roundhouse-type kick, the defender moves off the line of attack by stepping to the inside of the knee of the kicking leg. He then turns his body

to receive the momentum of the leg. By moving to the inside of the knee, the defender reduces the power of the attacker's kicking leg. The harder the attacker kicks, the more likely he is to hyperextend his knee against the body of the defender, while the defender remains unharmed. The defender must get to the inside of the knee, however, or an experienced opponent can change his roundhouse kick into a knee strike. The defender receives the energy of the kicking leg and continues turning with the momentum of the kick. The attacker will then be taken down by the defender's other leg with no effort.

◄ *Varying levels of expertise are demonstrated by these Thai soldiers as yelling they deliver a front kick with arms in position to block an attack. Martial arts training not only instils confidence in soldiers, but is also an excellent way to keep them fit and agile.*

▸ *Soldiers practising the Russian martial arts technique called Sambo block punches, while holding their arm back to deliver a counter-attack.*

▾ *Getting it wrong: a French soldier shows how to defeat a front kick, stepping back and catching his attacker's foot – his attacker will be soon be flat on his back on the ground.*

The kick can also be used as a defence against punch. As the opponent on the left throws a punch, the defender should step off the line of attack to the outside. He then turns towards the opponent, brings his knee to his chest and launches a heel kick to the outside of the opponent's thigh. He should

keep his foot turned 45 degrees to ensure the target is struck and to maintain balance.

BLOCKING

When surprised by an opponent armed with a rifle and bayonet, the block is used to cut off the path of his attack by making weapon-to-weapon contact. A block must always be followed immediately with a vicious attack. Strike the opponent's weapon with enough power to throw him off balance.

For the high bloc, extend your arms upward and forward at a 45-degree angle. This action deflects an opponent's slash movement by causing his bayonet or the upper

◄ *The outer block (left) and inner block (right) both use the bony edge of the forearm to strike the soft tissue of an attacker's inner forearm and deflect it.*

It is essential to counterattack each block with a thrust, butt stroke, smash or slash.

GRAPPLING AND LOCKS

Grappling is when two or more combatants engage in close-range, hand-to-hand combat. They may be armed or unarmed. To win, the combatant must be aware of how to move his body in order to maintain the upper hand, and he must know the body's mechanical strengths and weaknesses. The situation becomes a struggle of strength pitted against strength unless the combatant can remain in control of his opponent gaining an advantage in leverage and balance.

In the wristlock from a collar grab when an opponent grasps the defender by the collar, the defender should reach up and grasp the opponent's hand (to prevent him from withdrawing it) while stepping back to pull him off balance. The defender peels off the opponent's grabbing hand by crushing his thumb and bending it back on itself towards the palm in a straight line. To keep his grip on the opponent's thumb, the defender keeps his hands close to his body where his control is strongest. He then turns his body so that he has a wristlock on his opponent. The wristlock is produced by the defender turning his wrist outwards at a 45-degree angle and bending it towards the elbow. The opponent can be driven to the ground by putting his palm on the ground.

part of his rifle to strike against the centre part of the rifle.

In the low block the combatant extends his arms downward and forward about 15º from his body. This action deflects an opponent's butt stroke aimed at the groin by causing the lower part of his rifle stock to strike against the centre part of the combatant's rifle.

Finally for the side block, he extends his arms with the left hand high and right hand low, thus holding the rifle vertical. This block is designed to stop a butt stroke aimed at his upper body or head. Push the rifle to your left to cause the butt of the opponent's rifle to strike the centre portion of his rifle.

The wristlock from an arm grab can be used when an opponent grasps a defender's arm; the defender rotates his arm to grab the opponent's forearm. At the same time, he secures his other hand on the gripping hand of the opponent to prevent his escape. As the defender steps in towards the opponent and maintains his grip on the hand and forearm, a 'Z' shape is formed by the opponent's arm; this is an effective wristlock.

For the elbow lock against the body, the opponent's elbow can be locked against the side of the body

▼ *Grapping during wrestling training: one man has a powerful leg lock on his opponent who is struggling to break free from a throttle.*

by the defender. The defender should turn his body to force the elbow into a position that it was not designed to move in. He can then apply leverage on the opponent's wrist to gain control as the lock causes intense pain. The elbow can easily be broken to make the arm ineffective.

In the elbow lock against the knee while grappling on the ground, a defender can gain control of the situation if he can use an elbow lock against the opponent. He should use his knee as a fulcrum for leverage to break his opponent's arm at the elbow. Once the arm breaks, the defender should follow up with a punch or kick.

An elbow lock can be applied by locking the elbow joint against

the shoulder and pulling down on the wrist. Using the shoulder as a fulcrum, applying force and straightening the knees to push upwards produces leverage. This uses the defender's body mass and ensures more positive control. The opponent's arm must be kept straight so he cannot drive his elbow down into the defender's shoulder.

For the shoulder dislocation, a defender can manoeuvre into position to dislocate a shoulder by moving inside when an opponent launches a punch. The defender should hold his hand nearest the punching arm high to protect his head. The defender continues to move in and places his other arm behind the punching arm. He

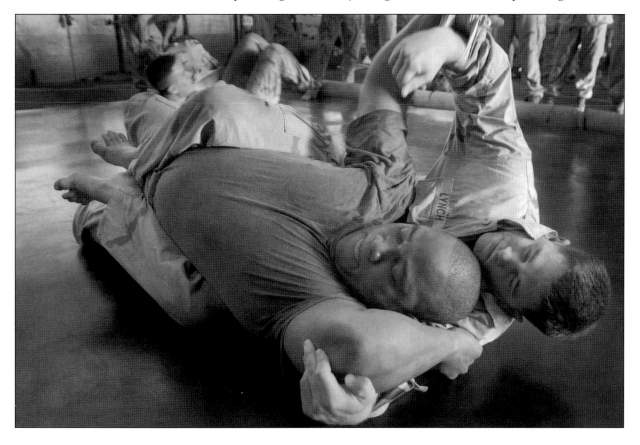

strikes downwards into the crook of the opponent's elbow to create a bend, then clasps his hands and moves to the opponent's outside until the opponent's upper arm is in alignment with his shoulders and bent 90 degrees at the elbow. As he steps, the defender should pull up on the opponent's elbow and direct the wrist downwards. This motion twists the shoulder joint so it is easily dislocated, and the opponent loses his balance.

In the straight-arm shoulder dislocation, the shoulder can also be dislocated by keeping the elbow straight and forcing the opponent's arm backwards towards the opposite shoulder at about 45 degrees. The initial movement must take the arm down and alongside the opponent's body. Bending the wrist towards the elbow helps to lock out the elbow. The dislocation also forces the opponent's head down where a knee strike can be readily made. This dislocation technique should be practised to determine the feel of the correct direction in which to move the joint.

For shoulder dislocation using the elbow, the defender can snake his hand over the crook in the opponent's elbow and move his body to the outside, trapping one of his opponent's arms against his side. The defender can then clasp his hands in front of his body and use his body mass in motion to align the opponent's upper arm with the line between the shoulders. By dropping his weight and then pulling upward on the opponent's elbow, the shoulder is dislocated, and the opponent loses his balance. If the opponent's elbow locks rather than bends to allow the shoulder dislocation, the defender can use the elbow lock to keep control.

Finally, in the knee lock/break, the opponent's knee joint can be attacked to produce knee locks or breaks by forcing the knee in a direction opposite to the way it was designed to move. The knee should be attacked with the body's mass behind the defender's knee, or with his entire body, by falling on the opponent's knee, causing it to hyperextend.

▼ *US Army soldiers practise locks and holds following a throw. Though strength is an advantage in close combat, a man with agility, speed and balance can overcome a more powerful opponent.*

▸ *The sweep uses some of the attacker's energy as he lunges forward – the defender steps back and with this right leg sweeps his assailant's left leg off the ground while simultaneously pulling him down with his arms.*

over-the-shoulder throw can be used. The defender blocks the punch with his left forearm, pivots 180 degrees on the ball of his lead foot and gets well inside his opponent's right armpit with his right shoulder. He should reach well back under his opponent's right armpit and grasp him by the collar or hair. The defender must maintain good back-to-chest, buttock-to-groin contact, keeping his knees slightly bent and shoulder-width apart. He keeps control of his opponent's right arm by holding the wrist or sleeve. The defender bends forwards at the waist and holds his opponent tightly against his body. He locks his knees, thrusts his opponent over his shoulder and slams him to the ground. He can then disable his opponent by kicks or stamping on vital areas.

The throw from rear choke is used when the opponent attacks the defender with a rear strangle choke. The defender should quickly bend his knees and spread his feet shoulder-width apart. (Knees are bent quickly to put distance between the defender and opponent.) The defender reaches as far back as possible and uses his right hand to grab his opponent by the collar or hair. He then forces his chin into the 'V' of the opponent's arm that is around his neck. With his left hand, he grasps the opponent's clothing at the tricep and bends forwards at the waist. The defender locks his knees and, at

should wrap his right arm around his opponent's neck, making sure he locks the throat and windpipe in the 'V' formed by his elbow. He then grasps his left bicep and wraps his left hand around the back of the opponent's head. Pulling his right arm in and flexing it, he pushes his opponent's head forward. The defender should then spread his legs out and back, maintain a choke on his opponent's neck and pull his opponent backwards until his neck breaks.

IMPROVISED WEAPONS

To survive in combat, the soldier must be able to deal with any situation that develops. His ability to adapt any nearby object for use as a weapon is limited only by his ingenuity and resourcefulness. Possible weapons include: pens or pencils; water bottles tied to string to be swung; karabiner snap links at the end of sections of rope; kevlar helmets; sand, rocks or liquids thrown into the enemy's eyes; or radio antennae.

The following are a few expedient weapons that are readily available for defence and counter-attack against the bayonet and rifle with fixed bayonet.

the same time, pulls his opponent over his shoulder and slams him to the ground. He can then spin around and straddle his opponent or disable him with punches to vital areas.

As a technique, the head butt can be applied from the front or the rear. It is repeated until the opponent either releases his grip or becomes unconscious. If the opponent grasps the defender in a bear hug from the front, the defender should use his forehead to smash into his opponent's nose or cheek, stunning him. The opponent

releases the defender, who then follows up with a kick or knee strike to the groin. If the opponent grasps the defender in a bear hug from the rear, the defender should cock his head forward and smash the back of his head into the opponent's nose or cheek area. The defender should then turn to face his opponent and follow up with a spinning elbow strike to the head.

Finally, the rear strangle takedown can be used if the defender strikes the opponent from the rear with a forearm strike to the neck (carotid artery). The defender

In the Soviet Army in World War II, the simple, short-handled entrenching tool had one side of the spade sharpened so that it could be used as a hand axe in combat. Today, almost all soldiers carry a folding entrenching tool. It is a versatile and formidable weapon when used by a trained soldier. It can be used in its straight position, locked out and fully extended, or with its blade folded at right angles.

To use it against an attacker lunging with a bayonet thrust to the defender's stomach along a low angle of attack, the defender moves just outside to avoid the lunge and meets the attacker's arm with the blade of the fully extended entrenching tool. The defender gashes all the way up the attacker's arm with the force of both body masses coming together. The hand gripping the entrenching tool is

given natural protection from the shape of the handle. The defender continues pushing the blade of the entrenching tool up and into the throat of the attacker, driving him backward and downward.

An optional use of entrenching tool against a rifle with fixed bayonet is for the attacker to lunge to the stomach of the defender. The defender steps to the outside of the line of attack at 45 degrees to avoid the weapon. He then turns his body and strikes downward onto the attacking arm (on the radial nerve) with the blade of the entrenching tool. He drops his full body weight down with the strike, and the force causes the attacker to collapse forward. The defender then strikes the point of the entrenching tool into the jugular notch, driving it deeply into the attacker

When the entrenching tool blade is folded at right angles to the

handle and locked into place if the attacker tries to drive the bayonet into the chest of the defender, the defender moves his body off the line of attack by stepping to the outside. He allows his weight to shift forward and uses the blade of the entrenching tool to drag along the length of the weapon, scraping the attacker's arm and hand. The handle protects the defender's hand. He continues to move forward into the attacker, strikes the point of the blade into the jugular notch, and drives it downward.

If the attacker lunges with a fixed bayonet along angle of attack 5 (AoA 5 – see page 37) the defender then steps to the outside to move off the line of attack and turns. He then strikes the point of the blade of the entrenching tool into the side of the attacker's throat.

1m (3ft) stick

Since a stick can be found almost anywhere, a soldier should know its uses as a field-expedient weapon. The stick is a versatile weapon; its capability ranges from simple prisoner control to lethal combat.

Use a stick about 1m (3 ft) long and grip it by placing it in the V formed between the thumb and index finger, as in a handshake. It may also be grasped by two hands and used in an unlimited number of techniques. The stick should not be held at the end, but at a comfortable distance from the butt end.

When striking with the stick,

◀ *Crude bolt-action weapons made by Mau Mau terrorists in Kenya. Often as dangerous to the user as their intended victim, they were only effective over very short ranges.*

achieve maximum power by using the entire body weight behind each blow. The desired point of contact of the weapon is the last 50mm (2in) at the tip of the stick. Effective striking points are usually the wrist, hand, knees and other bony protuberances. Soft targets include the side of the neck, jugular notch, solar plexus and various nerve motor points. Attack soft targets by striking or thrusting the tip of the stick into the area. Three basic methods of striking are:-

Thrusting: Grip the stick with both hands and thrust straight into a target with the full body mass behind it.

Whipping: Hold the stick in one hand and whip it in a circular motion; use the whole body mass in motion to generate power.

Snapping: Snap the stick in short, shocking blows, again with the body mass behind each strike.

When the attacker thrusts with a knife to the stomach of the defender with a low AoA 5, the defender moves off the line of attack to the outside and strikes vigorously downward onto the attacking wrist, hand, or arm.

The defender then moves forward, thrusts the tip of the stick into the jugular notch of the attacker, and drives him to the ground with his body weight, not just his upper body strength.

◀ *A 2m (6ft) pole like a broom handle is an effective improvised weapon. It can be used to sweep an assailant's rifle to one side and then to lunge at vulnerable areas like the throat, stomach or eyes. Even a full size umbrella, which though more fragile, has a steel-tipped point and is therefore a potential defensive weapon, can be used to lunge at an attacker.*

When using a 1m (3ft) stick against a rifle with fixed bayonet, the defender grasps the stick with two hands, one at each end, as the attacker thrusts forward to the chest.

He steps off the line of attack to the outside and redirects the weapon with the stick.

He then strikes forward with the forearm into the attacker's throat. The force of the two body weights coming together is devastating. The attacker's neck is trapped in the notch formed by the stick and the defender's forearm.

Using the free end of the stick as a lever, the defender steps back and uses his body weight to drive the attacker to the ground. The leverage provided by the stick against the neck creates a tremendous choke with the forearm, and the attacker loses control completely.

1m (3ft) rope

A section of rope about one metre (three feet) long can provide a useful means of self-defence for the unarmed combat soldier in a hand-to-hand fight.

Examples of field-expedient ropes are a web belt, boot laces, a portion of a 36.5metre (120ft) nylon rope or sling rope, or a cravat rolled up to form a rope. Hold the rope at the ends so the middle section is rigid enough to serve almost as a stick-like weapon, or the rope can be held with the middle section relaxed, and then snapped by vigorously pulling the hands apart to strike parts of the enemy's body, such as the head or elbow joint, to cause serious damage. It can also be used to entangle the opponent's limbs or weapons he his holding, or to strangle him.

When the attacker lunges with a knife to the stomach, the defender moves off the line of attack 45º to the outside. He snaps the rope downward onto the attacking wrist, redirecting the knife. Then, he steps forward, allowing the rope to encircle the attacker's neck. He continues to turn his body and sinks his weight to drop the attacker over his hip.

When the attacker thrusts with a fixed bayonet, the defender moves off the line of attack and uses the rope to redirect the weapon. Then, he moves forward and encircles the attacker's throat with the rope. He continues moving to unbalance the attacker and strangles him with the rope

The 1m (3ft) rope can also be a useful tool against an unarmed opponent. The defender prepares for an attack by gripping the rope between his hands. When the opponent attacks, the defender steps completely off the line of attack and raises the rope to strike the attacker's face. He then snaps the rope to strike the attacker either across the forehead, just under the nose, or under the chin by jerking his hands forcefully apart. The incoming momentum of the attacker against the rope will snap his head backward, and will probably break his neck, or, at the very least, it will knock him off his feet.

2m (6ft) pole

Another field-expedient weapon that can mean the difference between life and death for a soldier in an unarmed conflict is a pole about 2m (6 ft) long.

The pole could be a broom handle, pry bar, track tool, tent pole or even a small tree or limbs cut to form a pole. A soldier skilled in the use of a pole as a weapon is a formidable opponent. The size and weight of the pole requires him to move his whole body to use it effectively. Its length gives the soldier an advantage of distance in most unarmed situations. There are two methods usually used in striking with a pole:

Swinging: Becoming effective in swinging the pole requires skilled body movement and practice. The greatest power is developed by striking with the last 50mm (2in) of the pole.

Thrusting: The pole is thrust straight along its axis with the user's body mass firmly behind it.

An attacker tries to thrust forward with a fixed bayonet. The defender moves his body off the line of attack; he holds the tip of the pole so that the attacker runs into it from his own momentum. He then aims for the jugular notch and anchors his body firmly in place so that the full force of the attack is felt at the attacker's throat.

The defender then shifts his entire body weight forward over his lead foot and drives the attacker off his feet.

Small targets, such as the throat, may be difficult to hit. In this type of combat, concentrate on good, large targets, such as the solar plexus and hip/thigh joint.

KNIFE FIGHTING

When an unarmed soldier is faced with an enemy armed with a knife, it is vital that he is mentally prepared for being cut. The likelihood of suffering severe cuts is less if the fighter is well trained in knife defence and if the principles of weapon defence are followed. A slash wound is not usually lethal or shock-inducing; however, a stab wound risks injury to vital organs, arteries and veins, and it may also cause instant shock or unconsciousness.

TYPES OF KNIFE ATTACKS

The first line of defence against an opponent armed with a knife is to avoid close contact. Should a soldier come within range, however, the following are the different types of knife attacks that he may encounter:

- The thrust is the most common and most dangerous. It is a strike directed straight into the target by jabbing or lunging.
- The slash is a sweeping surface cut or circular slash. The wound is usually a long cut, varying from a slight surface cut to a deep gash.
- The flick is delivered by flicking the wrist and knife to extended limbs, inflicting numerous cuts. The flick is very distracting to the defender, as he will be bleeding from several cuts if the attacker is successful.
- The tear is a cut made by drag-

ging the tip of the blade across the body to create a ripping-type cut.
- The hack is delivered by using the knife to block or chop.
- The butt is a downward strike with the knife handle.

KNIFE DEFENCE DRILLS

Knife defence drills are used to familiarize soldiers with defence movement techniques for various angles of attack. For training, the soldiers should be paired off; one partner is named as the attacker, while the other is the defender. It is important that the attacker make his attack realistic in terms of distance and angling during training. His strikes must be accurate in hitting the defender at the intended target if the defender does not defend himself or move off the line of attack. For safety, the attacks are delivered first at one-quarter and one-half speed, and then at three-quarter speed as the defender becomes more skilled. Variations can be added by changing grips, stances and attacks. There are six angles of defence (AoD):

AoD 1: In AoD 1, the heck and lift, the attacker delivers a slash along the angle of attack 1 (AoA 1 – see page 37). The defender should meet and check the movement with his left forearm bone, striking the inside forearm of the attacker. The defender's right hand should immediately follow behind the strike to lift, redirect and take control of the attacker's knife arm. The defender should bring the attacking

◄ *Using their knives, British Commando trainees in World War II practise the thrust to the carotid artery. The loss of blood from this type of attack would lead to rapid death.*

arm around to his right side where he can use an arm bar or wristlock to disarm the attacker. He will maintain better control if he keeps the knife hand as close to his body as possible.

AoD 2: In AoD 2, the check and ride, the attacker slashes with AoA 2. The defender should meet the attacking arm with a strike from both forearms against the outside forearm, his bone against the attacker's muscle tissue. The strike checks the forward momentum of the attacking arm. The defender's right hand should then be used to ride the attacking arm clear of his body. He redirects the attacker's energy with strength starting from the right elbow.

AoD 3: For AoD 3, the check and lift, the attacker delivers a horizontal slash to the defender's ribs, kidneys or hip on the left side. The defender should meet and check the attacking arm on his body's left side with a downward circular motion across the front of his own body. At the same time, he should move his body off the line of attack. He needs to meet the attacker's forearm with a strike forceful enough to check its momentum. The defender should then ride the energy of the attacking arm by wiping downwards along the outside of his left forearm with his right hand. He should then redirect the knife hand around to his right side, where he can control or disarm the weapon.

AoD 4: In the check tactic in AoD 4, the attacker slashes the defender with a backhand slashing motion to the right side at the ribs, kidneys or hips. The defender should move his right arm in a downward circular motion and strike the attacking arm on the outside of the body. At the same time, he should move off the line of attack. The strike must be forceful enough to check the attack. The left arm should be held in a higher guard position to protect from a redirected attack or to assist in checking. The defender should move his body to a position where he can choose a proper disarming manoeuvre.

AoD 5: The low parry in AoD 5 is used when an attacker makes a lunging thrust to the stomach along the AoA 5. The defender should move his body off the line of attack and deflect the attacking arm by parrying with his left hand. He deflects the attacking hand toward his right side by redirecting it with his right hand. As he does this, the defender can strike downwards with the left forearm or the wrist onto the forearm or wrist of the attacker. The defender ends up in a position to lock the elbow of the attacking arm across his body if he steps off the line of attack properly.

The high AoD 5 should be used when the attacker lunges with a thrust to the face, throat or solar plexus. The defender should move his body off the line of attack while parrying with either hand. He redirects the attacking arm so that the knife clears his body. He should maintain control of the weapon hand or arm, and gouge the eyes of the attacker, driving him backwards and off balance. If the attacker is much taller than the defender, it may be a more natural movement for the defender to raise his left hand to strike and deflect the attacking arm. He can then gouge his thumb or fingers into the jugular notch of the attacker and force him to the ground. Still another possibility for a high AoA 5 is for the defender to move his body off the line of attack while parrying. He can then turn his body, rotate his shoulder under the elbow joint of the attacker and lock it out.

AoD 6: Finally, in AoD 6, the attacker strikes straight downward onto the defender with a stab. The defender should react by moving his body out of the weapon's path

---

ANGLE OF ATTACK

Knife fighting techniques can be broken down into nine angles of attack (AoA). These angles of attack apply to both bayonet and knife fighting.

- AoA 1 is a downward diagonal slash, stab or strike toward the left side of the defender's head, neck or torso.
- AoA 2 is the same as AoA 1, but delivered to the right.
- AoA 3 is a horizontal attack to the left side of the defender's torso in the ribs, side or hip region.

- AoA 4 is the same as AoA 3, but to the right side.
- AoA 5 is a jabbing, lunging or punching attack directed straight towards the defender's front.
- AoA 6 is an attack directed straight down upon the defender.
- AoA 7 is an upward diagonal attack towards the defender's lower left side.
- AoA 8 is the same as AoA 7, but towards the defender's lower right side.
- AoA 9 is an attack directed straight up, e.g. to the defender's groin.

and parrying or checking and redirecting the attacking arm, as in the movement in the high AoD 5. The reactions may vary according to what is natural for the defender. The defender should then take control of the weapon and disarm the attacker.

FOLLOW-UP TECHNIQUES

Once soldiers are skilled in these basic reactions to attack, follow-up techniques may be introduced and practised. These drills make up the defence possibilities against the various angles of attack. They also enable the soldier to apply the principles of defence against weapons and allow him to feel the

movements. Through repetition, the reactions become natural, and the soldier instinctively reacts to a knife attack with the proper defence. It is important not to associate specific movements or techniques with certain types of attack. The knife fighter must rely on his knowledge of principles and his training experience in reacting to a knife attack. No two attacks or reactions will be the same – memorizing techniques will not ensure a soldier's survival. There are three broad defence follow-up techniques: defend and clear, defend and stun, and defend and disarm.

Defend and clear should be used when the defender has per-

▲ A Russian paratroops instructor shows a knife-disarming technique. By exerting pressure on the back of his attacker's hand, he forces him to drop the bayonet.

formed a defensive manoeuvre and avoided an attack; he can push the attacker away and move out of the attacker's reach.

Defend and stun is employed after the defender performs his first defensive manoeuvre to a safer position; he can deliver a stunning blow as an immediate counter-attack. Strikes to motor nerve points or attacker's limbs, low kicks and elbow strikes are especially effective stunning techniques.

Finally, for defend and disarm,

▸ *In this knife defence technique, the defender grabs the knife hand and, using his entire body weight, and by twisting and bending his knees, he throws the attacker to the ground. He can then follow up using the knife or his boots to kill or disable his attacker.*

the defender also follows up his first defensive manoeuvre by maintaining control of the attacker's weapon arm, executing a stunning technique and disarming the attacker. The stun distracts the attacker and also gives the defender some time to gain possession of the weapon and to execute his disarming technique.

UNARMED DEFENCE AGAINST A RIFLE AND BAYONET

Defence against a rifle with a fixed bayonet involves the same principles as knife defence. The soldier should consider the same angles of attack and the proper response for any attack along each angle.

Regardless of the type weapon used by the enemy, his attack will always be along one of the angles of attack (AoAs) at any one time. The soldier must get his entire body off the line of attack by moving to a safe position. A rifle with a fixed bayonet has two weapons: a knife at one end and a butt stock at the other. The soldier will be safe as long as he is not in a position where either end can strike him during the attack.

Usually, he is in a more advantageous position if he moves inside the length of the weapon. He can then counter-attack to gain control of the situation as soon as possible. The following counter-attacks can be used as defences against a rifle with a fixed bayonet.

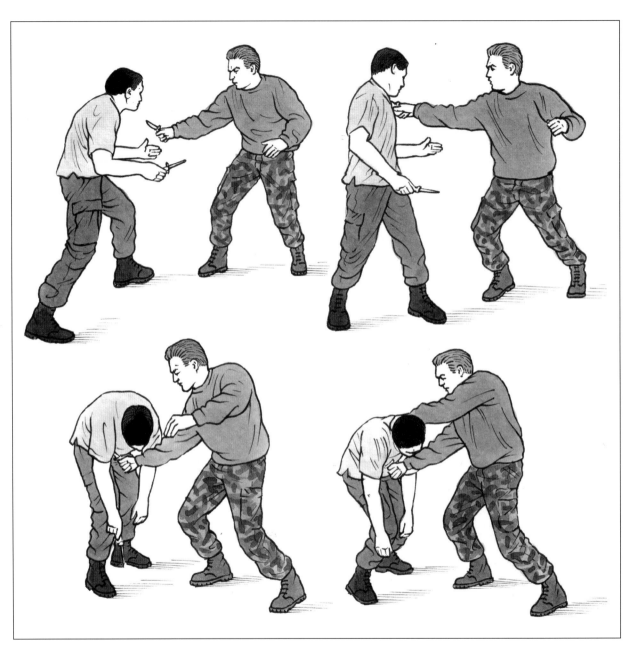

They also provide a good basis for training.

For the defence against AoA 1, the defender should wait until the last possible moment before moving, so that he is certain of the angle along which the attack is directed. This way, the attacker cannot change his attack in response to movement by the defender.

When the defender is certain that the attack is committed along a specific angle (AoA 1), he should move to the inside of the attacker and gouge his eyes with one hand while the other hand redirects and controls the weapon. He should maintain control of the weapon and lunge his entire body weight into the eye gouge to drive the attacker backwards and off balance. The defender now ends up with the weapon, and the attacker is in a poor recovery position.

◄ *Where both combatants are armed with knives and in the On Guard position, the first move by the man in the dark top is to slash at his opponent's upper arm to shock and distract him. Once he has suffered this attack and dropped his guard, he is then vulnerable to a thrust to the abdomen, where a deep, penetrating wound will sever or damage vital organs, resulting in death in a few minutes.*

If the attacker makes a diagonal slash along AoA 2, the defender should wait until he is sure of the attack before moving. The defender should then move to the outside of the attacker and counter-attack with a thumb jab into the right armpit. He should receive the momentum of the attacking weapon and control it with his free hand. He should use the attacker's momentum against him by pulling the weapon in the direction it is going with one hand and pushing with the thumb of his other hand. The attacker is completely off bal-

ance, and the defender can gain control of the weapon.

If the attacker directs a horizontal slash along the AoA 3, the defender should turn and move to the inside of the attacker; he should then strike with his thumb into the jugular notch. His entire body mass should be behind the thumb strike and, coupled with the incoming momentum of the attacker, the strike drives the attacker's head backwards and takes his balance. The defender should turn his body with the momentum of the weapon's attack to strip the weapon from the attacker's grip.

To counter a horizontal slash along AoA 4, the defender should move into the outside of the attacker. He should then turn with the attack, delivering an elbow strike to the throat. At the same time, the defender's free hand should control the weapon and pull it from the attacker as he is knocked off balance from the elbow strike.

If the attacker thrusts the bayo-

net at the stomach of the defender in AoA 5, the defender should shift his body to the side to avoid the attack and to gouge the eyes of the attacker. The defender's free hand should maintain control of, and strip the weapon from, the attacker as he is driven backwards with the eye gouge.

A thrust to the throat of the defender can be countered if the defender shifts to the side to avoid the attack, parries the thrust and controls the weapon with his trail hand. He should then move his entire body mass forward over the lead foot, slamming a forearm strike into the attacker's throat.

Finally, if the attacker delivers a downward stroke along AoA 6, the defender should shift to the outside to get off the line of attack and grab the weapon. He should then pull the attacker off balance by causing him to overextend himself. The defender should shift his weight backwards and cause the attacker to fall, as he strips the weapon from him.

CHAPTER TWO

FIREARMS AND EXPLOSIVES

The development of high explosives and magazine fed rifles made warfare more deadly and the ranges at which it was fought increased. After the invention of gunpowder, gunners no longer stood side by side with the infantry but instead employed indirect fire, while automatic weapons made camouflage, concealment and digging in essential if infantry were to survive. High explosives not only provide the filler for shells, grenades and mortar bombs, but can also be used to make up improvised explosive devices (IED) and for the demolition of key targets such as bridges, culverts and military equipment that might be of use to the enemy.

◄ *Smoke and dust boil up from an exploding charge on a demolition range. The first stage in training is to teach soldiers confidence with explosives, allowing them to make up small charges and detonate them.*

The most basic tool of any soldier is his personal weapon. This may be a pistol, submachine gun, rifle or machine gun. Even the most specialist soldiers, such as electronic warfare troops, begin their training as infantrymen and may be required to serve in this capacity if they are attacked by enemy special forces.

Furthermore, although knowledge of the techniques for employing explosives is normally the preserve of engineers and pioneers, mines and booby traps can present a threat to all troops. Soldiers need not be employed in combat to encounter this potentially lethal hazard; mines are present in war zones where troops may be called upon to act as peacekeepers or to deliver aid. It is essential that soldiers are able to recognize the signs that indicate the presence of mines and also the type that may have been encountered.

COMBAT HANDGUN TECHNIQUES

Pistols are either revolvers that have a cylindrical magazine that revolves and holds six rounds or they are self-loading. These weapons have a detachable box magazine that fits into the handle and may hold up to 14 rounds.

Revolvers are a far older design and date back to the seventeenth century, although the most famous are the nineteenth-century six-shot 'Six Guns' of the United States. In World War I and World War II, British troops used the .455in (11.56mm) Webley MkVI revolver or the .38in (9.65mm) Enfield No. 2Mk1*.

The Germans favoured the Luger self-loading pistol, named after Georg Luger, a designer at the Ludwig Löwe small-arms factory in Berlin. The standard pistol weighed 850g (1.87lb), had an eight-shot box magazine and fired a 9mm (0.35in) Parabellum round.

The US Army carried the big .45in (11.43in) Colt 1911A1 self-loading pistol through two world wars, the Korean War and the Vietnam War. A trained man can engage targets up to 50m (164ft) with this weapon. It is 216mm (8.50in) long, weighs 1.4kg (3.09lb) and has a six-round box magazine feed.

The Italian Beretta Model 92 9mm (0.35in) pistol was adopted by the US Army as the M9, as a replacement for the M1911A1. It has been produced in several versions. The Model 92 is 217mm (8.54in) in length, weighs 850g (1.87lb) and has a 15-round box magazine feed.

The Belgian 9mm (0.35in) Browning Hi Power first manufactured in 1935 has an effective range of between 50m (164ft) and 70m (230ft), and accommodates 13 rounds in two staggered rows in its box magazine – a feature that was copied in many later pistol designs. It is 197mm (7.76in) long and weighs 1.01kg (2.27lb).

HANDGUN FUNDAMENTALS

The main use of the pistol or revolver is to engage an enemy at close range with quick, accurate fire. Accurate shooting results from knowing and correctly applying the elements of marksmanship. The elements of combat pistol or revolver marksmanship are:

- grip
- aim
- breath control
- trigger squeeze
- target engagement
- positions

Grip: The weapon must become an extension of the firer's hand and arm. It should replace the finger in pointing at an object. A firm, uniform grip must be applied to the weapon, as a proper grip is one of the most important fundamentals of quick fire.

For the most common grip, the one-hand grip, the firer holds the weapon in his non-firing hand; a 'V' is formed with the thumb and forefinger of the strong hand (firing hand). The weapon is placed in the V, with the front and rear sights in line with the firing arm. The lower three fingers are wrapped around the pistol grip, with all three fingers exerting equal pressure to the rear. The thumb of the firing hand should rest alongside the weapon without pressure. The firer grips the weapon tightly until his hand begins to tremble; he then relaxes until the trembling stops. At this point, the necessary pressure for a proper grip has been applied. The trigger finger is then placed on the trigger between the tip and second joint, so that it can be squeezed to the rear. The trigger finger must work independently of the remaining fingers.

The two-hand grip allows the firer to steady the firing hand and provide maximum support during firing. The non-firing hand becomes a support mechanism for the firing hand by wrapping the fingers of the non-firing hand around the firing hand. Two-hand grips are recommended for all pistol and revolver firing. Care

should be taken that the recoiling slide does not strike the firer's thumb in this grip.

For the fist grip, the firer holds the weapon as described in the paragraph above. The fingers of the non-firing hand are firmly closed over the fingers of the firing hand, ensuring that the index finger from the non-firing hand is between the middle finger of the firing hand and the trigger guard. The non-firing thumb is placed alongside the firing thumb. Depending upon the individual, a firer may choose to place his index finger of the non-firing hand on the front of the trigger guard of the M9 pistol, as this weapon has a recurved trigger guard designed for this purpose.

The palm-supported grip is commonly called the 'cup-and-saucer grip'. The firer grips the firing hand as described above. The non-firing hand is placed under the firing hand, with the non-firing fingers wrapped around the back of the firing hand. The non-firing thumb is placed over the middle finger of the firing hand.

Finally, the weaver grip is the same as the fist grip. The only difference between these two grips is that the non-firing thumb is wrapped over the firing thumb in the weaver.

Once the grip is correct, the firer raises his arms to a firing position and applies isometric tension. This is commonly known as the

▲ The Beretta Model 92 pistol with its 15-round magazine has been adopted for service in the US Army as the M9. The original Italian pistol is produced in several versions including the stainless steel 92M.

push-pull method for maintaining weapon stability. Isometric tension is when the firer applies forward pressure with the firing hand and pulls rearward with the non-firing hand with equal pressure. This creates an isometric force, but never to an extent that causes the firer to tremble. It steadies the weapon and reduces barrel rise from recoil. The supporting arm is bent with the elbow pulled downwards. The firing arm is fully extended with the

◄ *Recruits in training practice the double handed grip with Colt 1911A1 pistols. The kick from the heavyweight .45in round makes this the most effective way to shoot with the Colt 45.*

he opens his eyes. This enables the firer to determine and use his natural point of aim once he has practised sufficiently. This is the most relaxed position for holding and firing the weapon.

Aiming is sight alignment and sight placement. Sight alignment is positioning the front blade in line with the rear sight notch. The top of the front sight is level with the top of the rear sight and is in correct alignment with the eye. For correct sight alignment, the firer must centre the front sight in the rear sight. He raises or lowers the top of the front sight so it is level with the top of the rear sight.

Sight placement is the positioning of the weapon's sights in relation to the target as seen by the firer when he aims the weapon. A correct sight picture consists of correct sight alignment with the front sight placed centre mass of the target. The eye can focus on only one object at a time at different distances. Therefore, the last focus of the eye is always on the front sight. When the front sight is seen clearly, the rear sight and target will appear hazy. Correct sight alignment can only be maintained through focusing on the front sight. The firer's bullet will hit the target even if the sight picture is slightly off centre, but still remains on the target. This means that sight alignment is more important than sight placement. As it is impossible to hold the weapon completely still, the firer must apply trigger squeeze and maintain

elbow and wrist locked. The firer will need to experiment to find the right amount of isometric tension to apply.

The firing hand should always exert the same pressure as the non-firing hand. If it does not, a missed target could be the result.

Aim: The firer should check his grip for use of his natural point of aim. He grips the weapon and sights properly on a distant target. While maintaining his grip and stance, he closes his eyes for three to five seconds. He then opens his eyes and checks for proper sight picture. If the point of aim is disturbed, the firer should adjust his stance to compensate. If the sight alignment is disturbed, the firer needs to adjust his grip to compensate by removing the weapon from his hand and reapplying the grip. The firer repeats this process until the sight alignment and sight placement remain almost the same when correct sight alignment while the weapon is moving in and around the centre of the target. This natural movement of the weapon is referred to as wobble area. The firer must strive to control the limits of the wobble area through proper breath control, trigger squeeze, positioning and grip.

Sight alignment is essential for accuracy because of the short sight radius of the pistols and revolvers. For example, if a error of 2.5mm (.10in) is made in aligning the front sight in the rear sight, the firer's bullet will miss the point of aim by about 360mm (15in) at a range of 25m (82ft). The 2.5mm (.10in) error in sight alignment magnifies as the range increases; at 25m (82ft), it is magnified 150 times.

Focusing on the front sight while applying proper trigger squeeze will help the firer resist the urge to jerk the trigger and anticipate the actual moment the weapon fires. Mastery of trigger squeeze and sight alignment requires practice.

Breath Control: The firer must learn to hold his breath properly at any time during the breathing cycle if he wishes to attain accuracy that will serve him in combat. This must be done while aiming and squeezing the trigger. While the procedure is simple, it requires explanation, demonstration and supervised practice. To hold the breath properly, the firer should take a breath, let it out, then inhale normally, before exhaling just

enough to be comfortable, holding the remaining breath and firing.

It is difficult to maintain a steady position that keeps the front sight at a precise aiming point while breathing. The firer should therefore be taught to inhale, then exhale normally, and hold his breath at the moment of the natural respiratory pause. The shot must then be fired before he feels any discomfort from holding his breath. When multiple targets are presented, the firer must learn to hold his breath at any part of the breathing cycle. Breath control must be practised during dry-fire exercises until it becomes a natural part of the firing process.

Trigger Squeeze: A poor trigger squeeze causes more misses than any other step of preparatory marksmanship. The aim is disturbed before the bullet leaves the

barrel of the weapon, usually as a result of the firer jerking the trigger or flinching. A slight off-centre pressure of the trigger finger on the trigger can cause the weapon to move and disturb the firer's sight alignment. Flinching is an automatic human reflex caused by anticipating the recoil of the weapon. Jerking is the result of an effort to fire the weapon at the precise time the sights align with the target.

Trigger squeeze is the independent movement of the trigger finger in applying increasing pressure on the trigger straight to the rear, without disturbing the sight alignment until the weapon fires. The trigger slack, or free play, is taken up first, and the squeeze is continued steadily until the hammer falls. If the trigger is squeezed properly, the firer will not know exactly when the hammer will fall; thus he does

▸ *Modern Electric Target Ranges (ETR) have targets that can be operated to appear briefly and randomly. These 'pop up' targets make shooting challenging and realistic.*

not tend to flinch or heel, resulting in a bad shot. Novice firers must be trained to overcome the urge to anticipate recoil. Proper application of the fundamentals will lower this tendency.

To apply correct trigger squeeze, the trigger finger should contact the trigger between the tip of the finger to the second joint (without touching the weapon anywhere else). Where contact is made depends on the length of the firer's trigger finger. If pressure from the trigger finger is applied to the right side of the trigger or weapon, the strike of the bullet will be to the left. This is due to the normal hinge action of the fingers. When the fingers on the right hand are closed, as in gripping, they hinge or pivot to the left, thereby applying pressure to the left. (With left-handed firers, this action is to the right.) The firer must not apply pressure left or right, but instead increase finger pressure straight to the rear Only the trigger finger must perform this action. Dry-fire training improves a firer's ability to move the trigger finger straight to the rear without cramping or increasing pressure on the hand grip.

The firer who is a good shot holds the sights of the weapon as nearly on the target centre as possible and continues to squeeze the trigger with increasing pressure until the weapon fires. The soldier who is a bad shot tries to 'catch his target' as his sight alignment moves past the target and fires the weapon at that instant. This is sometimes called 'ambushing' and causes trigger jerk.

Follow-through is the continued effort of the firer to maintain sight alignment before, during and after the firing of the round. The firer must continue the rearward movement of the finger even after the round has been fired. Releasing the trigger too soon after the round has been fired results in an uncontrolled shot, causing a missed target.

The trigger squeeze of the M9 pistol, when fired in the single-action mode, is 2.49kg (5.49lb); when fired in double-action mode, it is 5.4kg (11.90lb). The firer must be aware of the mode in which he is firing. He must also practise squeezing the trigger in each mode to develop expertise in single-action and double-action target engagements.

Target Engagement: When multiple targets are engaged, the closest and most dangerous multiple target in combat is engaged first and should be fired at with two rounds. This is commonly referred to as a double tap. The firer then traverses and acquires the next target, aligns the sights in the centre of mass, focuses on the front sight, applies trigger squeeze and fires. The firer ensures his firing arm elbow and wrist are locked during all engagements. If the firer has missed the first target and has fired upon the second target, he shifts back to the first and engages it.

When a soldier first learns to shoot, he may begin to anticipate recoil – something that he should be aware of. This reaction may cause him to tighten his muscles during or just before the hammer falls. He may fight the recoil by pushing the weapon downwards in anticipating or reacting to its firing. In either case, the rounds will not hit the point of aim. A good method to show the firer that he is antici-

pating the recoil is the ball-and-dummy method.

Trigger jerk occurs when the soldier sees that he has acquired a good sight picture at centre mass and 'snaps' off a round before the good sight picture is lost. This can become a problem, especially when the soldier is learning to use a flash sight picture.

Heeling is caused by a firer tightening the large muscle in the heel of the hand to prevent the trigger jerking. A firer who has had problems with jerking the trigger will often try to correct the fault by tightening the bottom of the hand, which results in a heeled shot. Heeling causes the strike of the bullet to hit high on the firing hand side of the target. All firers can correct shooting errors if they understand and apply correct trigger squeeze.

Positions: The qualification course is fired from a standing, kneeling or crouch position. All of the firing positions described below must be practised so they become natural movements, during both qualification and combat firing. Although these positions seem natural, practice sessions are essential to ensure correct firing positions are habitually engrained. A soldier needs to be able to assume these positions quickly and without conscious effort. Pistol marksmanship requires him to apply all the fundamentals rapidly with dangerously close targets while under stress. Assuming a proper position to allow for a steady aim is critical to survival.

In the pistol-ready position, the soldier should hold the weapon in the one-hand grip. The upper arm is held close to the body and the forearm at about 45 degrees. The

▲ US Special Forces strike a pose with some of the weapons in their inventory. All weapons, such as pistols, shot guns, assault rifles, submachine guns and machine guns have their own advantages and disadvantages for certain situations.

weapon should be pointed towards target centre as the soldier moves forwards.

For the standing position without support, the soldier faces the target. He should place his feet a comfortable distance apart, about shoulder width. The firing arm is then extended and a two-hand grip used. The wrist and elbow of the firing arm are locked and pointed towards target centre. The body is kept straight, with the shoulders slightly forward of the buttocks.

During combat, there may not be time for a soldier to assume a position that will allow him to establish his natural point of aim. Firing from a covered position may require the soldier to adapt his shooting stance to available cover.

In the kneeling position, the firing side knee only should be grounded as the main support. The foot is placed vertically and used as the main support, under the buttocks. The body weight rests on the heel and toes. The non-firing arm rests just above the elbow on the knee not used as the main body support, and the two-handed grip is used for firing. The firing arm is extended, and the firing arm elbow and wrist are locked to ensure solid arm control.

The crouch position is used when surprise targets are engaged at close range. The soldier should place the body in a forward crouch (boxer's stance), with the knees bent slightly and the trunk bent forwards from the hips to give faster recovery from recoil. The feet are placed naturally in a position that allows another step towards the target. The weapon is extended straight towards the target, and the wrist and elbow of the firing arm are locked. It is important to train consistently with this position, as the body will automatically crouch under conditions of stress such as combat. It is also a better position from which to change direction of fire more quickly.

For the prone position, the soldier should lie flat on the ground, facing the target. The arms are extended in front, with the firing arm locked. The arms may have to be slightly unlocked for firing at high targets. The butt of the weapon is rested on the ground for single, well-aimed shots. The non-firing hand (fingers) should be wrapped around the fingers of the firing hand, and the soldier faces forwards. The head must be kept down between arms as much as possible and behind the weapon.

The standing position with support is used when there is available cover for support, such as a tree or wall. The soldier stands behind a barricade, with the firing side in line with the edge of the barricade. The knuckles of the non-firing fist are placed at eye level against the edge of the barricade. The elbow and wrist of the firing arm are locked. The foot on the non-firing side is moved forward until the toe of the boot touches the bottom of the barricade.

The kneeling supported position is used when there is available cover for support, such as a low wall, rocks or a vehicle. The firing-side knee is placed on the ground, while the other is bent. The soldier kneels and places his foot (non-firing side) flat on the ground, pointing towards the target. The arms are extended alongside and braced against available cover. The wrist and elbow of the firing arm are locked. The non-firing hand should be placed around the fist to support the firing arm, then rested just above the elbow on the knee on the non-firing side.

COMBAT MARKSMANSHIP

After a soldier becomes proficient in the fundamentals of marksmanship, he progresses to advanced techniques of combat marksmanship. The main use of the pistol or revolver is to engage the enemy at close range with quick, accurate fire. In shooting encounters, it is not the first round fired that wins the engagement, but the first accurately fired round. The soldier should use his sights when engaging the enemy, unless this places the weapon within arm's reach of the enemy.

Firing Techniques: Hand—eye co-ordination is not a natural, instinctive ability for all soldiers. It is usually a learned skill obtained by practising the technique of a flash sight picture. The more a soldier practices raising the weapon to eye level and obtaining a flash sight picture, the more natural the relationship between soldier, sights and target becomes.

Eventually, proficiency elevates to a point where the soldier can accurately engage targets in the dark. Each soldier must be aware of this trait and learn how best to use it. Poorly co-ordinated soldiers can achieve proficiency with close supervision. Everyone has the ability to point at an object. As pointing the forefinger at an object and extending the weapon towards a target are much the same, the combination of the two are natural. Making the soldier aware of this ability and teaching him how to apply it when firing results in success when engaging enemy targets in combat.

The eyes focus instinctively on the centre of any object they observe. After the object is sighted, the firer aligns his sights on the centre of mass, focuses on the front sight and applies proper trigger squeeze. Most crippling or killing hits result from maintaining the focus on the centre of mass. The eyes must remain fixed on some part of the target throughout firing.

When a soldier points, he instinctively points at the feature on the object on which his eyes are focused. An impulse from the brain causes the arm and hand to stop when the finger reaches the proper position. When the eyes are shifted to a new object or feature, the finger, hand and arm also shift to this point. It is this inherent trait that can be used by the soldier to engage targets rapidly and accurately. This instinct is known as hand—eye co-ordination.

Usually when engaging an enemy at pistol/revolver ranges, the firer has little time to ensure a correct sight picture. The quick-kill (or natural point of aim) method does not always ensure a first-round hit. A compromise between a correct sight picture and the quick-kill method is known as a flash sight picture. As the soldier raises the weapon to eye level, his point of focus switches from the enemy to the front sight, ensuring that the front and rear sights are in proper alignment left and right, but not necessarily up and down. Pressure is applied to the trigger as the front sight is being acquired, and the hammer falls as the flash sight picture is confirmed. Initially, this method should be practised slowly, gaining speed as proficiency increases.

▲ *Members of a British Army TA Training Team practice with their personal weapon, the 9mm Browning Hi Power pistol. The man in the foreground has expended all his ammunition so the slide on his pistol is now locked to the rear.*

Quick-fire point shooting is for engaging an enemy at less than 5m (16.5ft). It is also useful for night firing. The weapon should be held in a two-hand grip. It is brought up close to the body until it reaches chin level and is then thrust forward until both arms are straight. The arms and body form a triangle, which can be aimed as a unit. In thrusting the weapon forward, the firer can imagine that there is a box between him and the enemy, and he is thrusting the weapon into the box. The trigger is smoothly squeezed to the rear as the elbows straighten out.

Quick-fire sighting is used when engaging an enemy at a range of 5–10m (16.5–33ft). It is used only when there is no time available to get a full picture. The firing position is the same as for quick-fire point shooting. The sights are aligned left and right to save time, but not up and down. The firer must determine in practice what the sight picture will look like and where the front sight must be aimed to hit the enemy in the chest.

Target Engagement: In close combat, there is seldom time to precisely apply all of the fundamentals of marksmanship. When a soldier fires a round at the enemy, he will often not know if he has hit his target. Two rounds should therefore be fired at the target. This is called a double tap. If the enemy continues to attack, two more shots should be placed in the pelvic area to break the body's support structure, causing the enemy to fall.

In close combat, the enemy may be attacking from all sides. The soldier may not have time to change his position constantly to adapt to new situations. The purpose of the crouching or kneeling 360-degree traverse is to fire in any direction without moving the feet.

For the crouching 360-degree traverse, the firer remains in the

▲ *On an improvised range in the desert a US soldier practices a seated two-hand grip shoot with his 9mm M9, the Beretta Model 92 adopted by the US Army. The very stable position adopted by the soldier ensures a high degree of accuracy.*

crouch position with feet almost parallel to each other. (The following instructions are for a right-handed firer). The two-hand grip is used at all times except for over the right shoulder. Turning will be natural on the balls of the feet.

Over the left shoulder: The upper body is turned to the left, with the weapon pointing to the left rear and the elbows of both arms bent. The left elbow will naturally be bent more than the right elbow.

Traversing to the left: The upper body is turned to the right, and the right firing arm straightens out. The left arm will be slightly bent.

Traversing to the front: The upper body is turned to the front as the left arm straightens out. Both arms will be straight forward.

Traversing to the right: The upper body is turned to the right as both elbows bend. The right elbow will naturally bend more than the left.

Traversing to the right rear: The upper body continues to turn to the right until it reaches a point where it cannot go further comfortably. Eventually, the left hand will have to be released from the fist grip, and the firer will be shooting to the right rear with the right hand.

In the kneeling 360-degree traverse (when employed by right-handed firers), the hands are in a two-hand grip at all times. The unsupported kneeling position is used. The rear foot must be positioned to the left of the front foot.

Traversing to the left side: The upper body is turned to a comfortable position towards the left, and the weapon is aimed to the left. Both elbows are bent, the left more naturally bent than the right.

Traversing to the front: The upper body is turned to the front, and a standard unsupported kneeling position is assumed. The right fir-

ing arm is straight, and the left elbow is slightly bent.

Traversing to the right side: The upper body is turned to the right as both arms straighten out.

Traversing to the rear: The upper body continues to turn to the right, as the left knee is turned to the right and placed on the ground. The right knee is lifted off the ground and becomes the forward knee. The right arm is straight, while the left arm is bent. The direction of the kneeling position has been reversed.

Traversing to the new right side: The upper body continues to the right. Both elbows are straight until the body reaches a point beyond which it cannot comfortably go. Eventually, the left hand must be released from the fist grip, and the firer will be firing to the right with the one-hand grip.

RELOADING TECHNIQUES

Reloading was an overlooked training area for many years until it was discovered that soldiers were being killed as a result of dropped magazines, shaking hands, placing magazines in backwards and placing empty magazines back into the weapon. The stressful state induced by a life-threatening situation can cause soldiers to do things they would not otherwise do. Consistent, repeated training is needed to avoid such mistakes.

The soldier should develop a consistent method for carrying magazines in the ammunition pouches. All magazines should face down with the bullets facing forward and to the centre of the body.

It is also important to know when to reload. Where possible, the soldier should count the num-

ber of rounds fired; however, it is possible to lose count in close combat. If this happens, there is a distinct difference in recoil of the pistol when the last round has been fired, and the soldier should learn to discern this difference.

Magazines should be changed when two rounds are left – one in the magazine and one in the chamber. This prevents the soldier being caught with an empty weapon at a crucial time. Reloading is faster with a round in the chamber, as time is not needed to release the slide.

The soldier should always obtain a firm grip on the magazine. This prevents the magazine being dropped or difficulty in getting the magazine into the weapon. The knuckles of the hand must be towards the body while gripping as much of the magazine as possible. The index finger is placed high on the front of the magazine when withdrawing from the pouch. It is also used to guide the magazine into the magazine well.

Every soldier needs to know which reloading procedure to use for any given tactical situation. There are three systems of reloading: rapid, tactical and one-handed. Rapid reloading is used when the soldier's life is in immediate danger, and the reload must be accomplished quickly. Tactical reloading is used when there is more time and the replaced magazine is to be kept because there are rounds still in it or it will be needed again. One-handed reloading is used when the soldier has suffered an arm injury.

For rapid reloading, the soldier places his hand on the next magazine in the ammunition pouch to ensure there is another magazine. The magazine is withdrawn from the pouch while the other magazine from the weapon is released. The replaced magazine is allowed to drop to the ground. The soldier inserts the replacement magazine, guiding it into the magazine accurately with the index finger. The

slide is released, if necessary, and the dropped magazine picked up if time allows. The soldier should then place this in his pocket, not back in the ammunition pouch, where it may become mixed with full magazines.

For tactical reloading, the hand is placed on the next magazine in the ammunition pouch to ensure there is a remaining magazine. The magazine is withdrawn from the pouch. The used magazine is dropped into the palm of the non-firing hand, which is the same hand holding the replacement magazine. The soldier should then insert the replacement magazine, guiding it into the magazine well with the index finger. The slide is released, if necessary, and the used magazine placed into a pocket. It should not be mixed with full magazines.

For one-handed reloading using the right hand, the soldier pushes the magazine release button with the thumb. The safety catch is placed ON with the thumb if the slide is forward. The weapon is then placed backwards into the holster. (Note: If placing the weapon in the holster backwards is a problem, place the weapon between the calf and thigh to hold it.) The replacement magazine is inserted, then the weapon withdrawn from the holster. The safety catch is removed with the thumb if the slide is forward, or the slide release pushed if the slide is back.

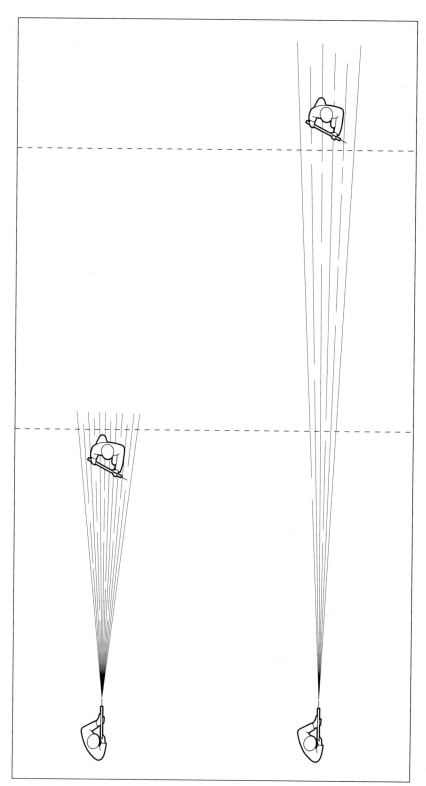

◀ *Automatic fire is most effective at 25m (82ft), but over 50m (164ft), a soldier should use semi-automatic fire to increase his chances of a kill.*

When the left hand is being used for one-handed loading, the magazine release button is pushed with the middle finger. The safety catch is placed ON with the thumb if the slide is forward. With the .45-calibre pistol, the thumb must be switched to the left side of the weapon. The weapon is then placed backwards into the holster. (Note: Once again, if placing the weapon in the holster backwards is a problem, the weapon can be placed between the calf and thigh to hold it.) The replacement magazine is inserted, and the weapon removed from the holster. The safety catch is released with the thumb if the slide is forward or the slide release lever pushed with the middle finger if the slide is back.

POOR VISIBILITY FIRING

Poor visibility makes firing with any weapon difficult, as shadows can be misleading to the soldier, mainly during the 30 minutes before dark and 30 minutes before dawn. Even if the weapon is a short-range one, the hours of darkness and poor visibility further decrease its effect. To compensate, the soldier must use the three principles of night vision:

• Dark adaptation is the process that conditions the eyes to see during poor visibility. The eyes usually need about 30 minutes to become 98 per cent dark-adapted in a totally darkened area.
• When viewing an object in daylight, a person looks directly at it.

M3 "Grease Gun"

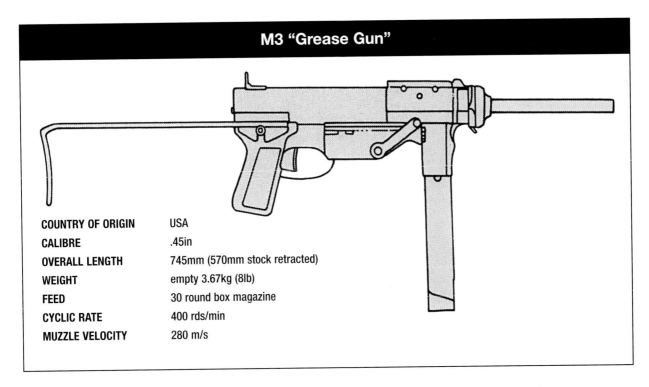

COUNTRY OF ORIGIN	USA
CALIBRE	.45in
OVERALL LENGTH	745mm (570mm stock retracted)
WEIGHT	empty 3.67kg (8lb)
FEED	30 round box magazine
CYCLIC RATE	400 rds/min
MUZZLE VELOCITY	280 m/s

At night, however, he would see the object for only a few seconds. To see an object in darkness, he must concentrate on it while looking six to ten degrees away from it.

• Scanning is the short, abrupt, irregular movement of the firer's eyes around an object or area every four to ten seconds. When artificial illumination is used, the firer uses night-fire techniques to engage targets, as targets seem to shift even though they are not actually moving.

USING SUBMACHINE GUNS

An ultra lightweight machine gun, developed by the Italians at the end of World War I, was the first submachine gun (SMG). In the early years of the 1920s, however, the greatest influence on submachine gun design was the .45in (11mm) Thompson submachine gun, or Tommy gun. J.T. Thompson des-

igned it in 1918, in the United States. Known as the 'Trench Broom', its intended use was for trench fighting in World War I, but it was delivered too late to see service. In the 1920s and 1930s, it was used in the Prohibition gang warfare in the United States. Following the Fall of France in 1940, any reservations that the British War Office may have had about this 'gangster's weapon' were forgotten in the face of the threat of German invasion, and orders were placed for the Model 1928. This gun saw service in North Africa and Italy.

During World War II, the US Army adopted a simpler weapon: the .45in (11mm) M3 'Grease Gun'. The M3 is still in use in remote areas of Central and Southeast Asia and Central and South America.

Many submachine guns have been produced around the world

since the 1920s, but the one most widely used today is the 9mm (0.35in) Heckler & Koch that was first produced in 1970. It is light and reliable, and has been produced in five versions. The most compact is the H & K MP5K, which is only 325mm (12.80in) long and has the remarkable rate of fire of 900 rounds a minute. The SD versions have a very effective silencer. Police, soldiers and counterterrorist forces use H&K weapons.

There are three necessary skills for handling the submachine gun: sighting and aiming, position and trigger manipulation.

SIGHTING AND AIMING

The first step of preparatory marksmanship is sighting and aiming. Sights on the submachine gun are not adjustable. The weapon is primarily intended for firing automatic fire at short

H & K MP5SD1

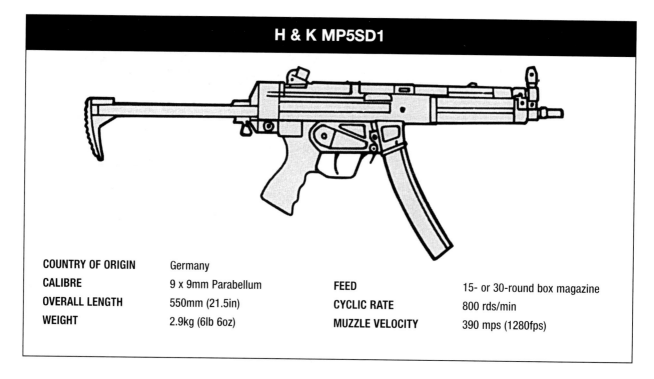

COUNTRY OF ORIGIN	Germany		
CALIBRE	9 x 9mm Parabellum	**FEED**	15- or 30-round box magazine
OVERALL LENGTH	550mm (21.5in)	**CYCLIC RATE**	800 rds/min
WEIGHT	2.9kg (6lb 6oz)	**MUZZLE VELOCITY**	390 mps (1280fps)

ranges, where quick shooting is required. Generally, the sights are used for the initial alignment of the weapon on the target. During firing, the firer can observe the strike of the rounds and 'walk' them onto the target. In a situation where the firer wants to fire single shots or short bursts, and has enough time to obtain the correct sight alignment and sight picture, he should do so. He must therefore understand the correct sight alignment and sight picture:

• The front sight must be accurately centred in the rear sight.
• The bull's-eye should be centred above and appear to barely touch the top of the front sight.
• The last focus of the eye should be on the front sight. The front sight will be seen clearly and sharply, while the bull's-eye will appear to be slightly fuzzy.

POSITION

The second and most important step of preparatory marksmanship is the position exercise. To hit a target and to continue to hold a burst on a target, the firer must have a good position. The submachine gun may be fired from the standing, sitting, kneeling, prone or assault position.

The standing position is the normal firing position. To assume it, the soldier stands facing the target, then makes a half right face. The left foot is moved forward one step, with the left toe pointing towards the target. The soldier should then lean forward; the left knee is bent slightly, while the right leg is kept straight, with about two-thirds of the body weight on the left foot. The magazine guide is grasped with the left hand and the pistol grip with the right hand. The butt of the stock is

placed against the right shoulder, and the body is twisted (at the waist) to the left to bring the right shoulder forward. The left elbow should be under the weapon, and the right elbow should be shoulder-high. The cheek is pressed against the stock. The recoil is slight for one shot; however, in automatic fire, each time the gun recoils, it will tend to push the shoulder backwards. The gun will therefore move off the target if the firer is not well braced and in the proper position.

Sitting is the best position when firing from ground that slopes to the front. To assume this position, the soldier should face the target, half-face to the right, spread his feet a comfortable distance apart and sit down. The feet should be farther apart than the knees. The body is bent forward from the hips, keeping the back

▸ *An Egyptian soldier armed with compact Heckler & Koch MP5K submachine gun. It weighs only 1.99kg (4lb 6oz) and can be fitted with a 15- or, as in this case, a 30-round magazine.*

straight. The right shoulder is pushed slightly forward (towards the target). The soldier should then place the left upper arm on the flat part of the shinbone, so that the tip of the elbow is crossed over the shinbone. There should be several inches of contact between the upper arm and the shinbone. The right elbow is blocked in front of the right knee.

The kneeling position affords a steadier aim than the standing position, and it is useful when the firer can crouch behind a rock, log or other protection. This position is frequently used on level ground or ground that slopes upward. To assume this position, the solder faces the target, half-face to the right, and kneels on the right knee. He sits on the right heel, with the right thigh forming an angle of 90 degrees with the line of aim. The entire surface of the lower right leg, from knee to toe, must be in contact with the ground. The left foot should be placed about 45cm (18in) to the front, with the toe pointing at the target. The left lower leg is vertical when viewed from the front. The weight of the body is moved forward, and the point of the left elbow is placed a few inches forward of the knee. The right elbow is raised to the height of, or slightly below, the right shoulder.

Prone is the steadiest position and should be used whenever time and terrain permit. To assume this

position, the soldier should take a prone position, with the body inclined to the left of the line of aim at an angle of 20 degrees or less. The legs are spread a comfortable distance apart, with the toes pointed outwards. The spine should be kept straight. The soldier places the left elbow under the gun, with his left hand grasping the magazine guide. The right elbow is out from the body so that the shoulders are level. The butt of the stock is placed in the pocket formed by the shoulder, and the cheek is pressed against the stock.

Finally, the assault position, usually called the hip position or

chest position, is used for close combat. When this position is used, there is less tendency for the muzzle to climb. The sights are not used to aim the weapon; the firer simply points the weapon towards the target and commences firing. The soldier needs a great deal of practice before he can shoot accurately. To assume this position, he presses the stock against the side of the hip with the right arm or places the stock under the armpit and presses it against the body. The body should be in a crouched position, and the firer should walk on the balls of his feet so that he can turn or move quickly.

▲ *The Belgian FN 5.7 x 28mm (1in) P-90 submachine gun used by an anti-terrorist squad. The P-90 weighs 2.54kg (5lb 9oz) empty, has a 50-round magazine and is 500mm (19.68in) overall. The P-90 fires a round with a very penetrative power and has a rate of fire of 900 rounds per minute.*

TRIGGER MANIPULATION

The soldier does not squeeze the trigger; he manipulates it to obtain a single shot or burst. In addition, he must be familiar with his weapon, as the trigger pull is not the same on all submachine guns:

• To fire single shots, the firer may press or tap the trigger to the rear

FN MAG

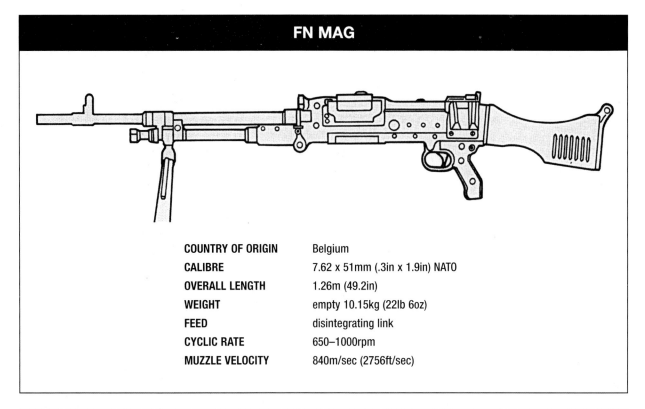

COUNTRY OF ORIGIN	Belgium
CALIBRE	7.62 x 51mm (.3in x 1.9in) NATO
OVERALL LENGTH	1.26m (49.2in)
WEIGHT	empty 10.15kg (22lb 6oz)
FEED	disintegrating link
CYCLIC RATE	650–1000rpm
MUZZLE VELOCITY	840m/sec (2756ft/sec)

BROWNING M2HB .50IN

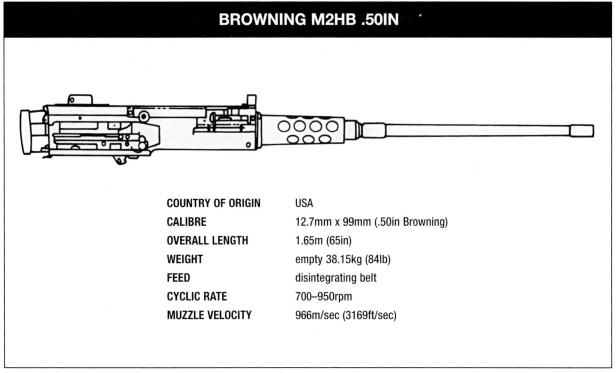

COUNTRY OF ORIGIN	USA
CALIBRE	12.7mm x 99mm (.50in Browning)
OVERALL LENGTH	1.65m (65in)
WEIGHT	empty 38.15kg (84lb)
FEED	disintegrating belt
CYCLIC RATE	700–950rpm
MUZZLE VELOCITY	966m/sec (3169ft/sec)

800m (875yds) and 1800m (1969yds). An optical sight similar to that on a mortar can also be fitted which allows the gun to be fired on pre-registered targets which may be obscured by darkness or smoke.

In the light role, the sights lay flat and are graduated between 200m (219yds) and 800m (875yds) in 100m (109yd) intervals. Experienced gunners can fire short bursts and, even with a short pressure on the trigger, 'double tap' or put two rounds into the target area. The gun is easy to strip and clean in the field, with the piston and bolt assembly in one piece; the only small part is the collets on the gas regulator.

LIGHT MACHINE GUNS

The FN-designed Minimi is an ideal light automatic weapon. It can fire, feeding from the left, either belted disintegrating link SS 109 NATO or US M193 5.56mm (0.22in) ammunition or, from the 30-round box, magazines compatible with the US M16 and most NATO rifles.

A 200-round box of belted ammunition can be clipped directly to the Minimi, making it a formidable close-quarter battle weapon.

Gas operated, the Minimi is normally fired from its bipod, although a sustained-fire tripod is available. The gun handles very much like a baby brother of the MAG; it has a top cover and the cocking handle is on the right, with a gas regulator that has two settings, normal and adverse. The latter ensures a sufficient flow of gas against the piston to clear a malfunction. The adjustment can be made even with a hot barrel. It does not have the recoil forces of a full-size 7.62mm (0.3in) round and so consequently it can be fired with greater accuracy. Like the MAG, it can be fitted with a backplate for use in helicopters and vehicles where a butt would be a hindrance. The standard weapon has a 465mm (18.31in) barrel, but a more compact Para model for airborne forces has a 347mm (13.66in) barrel, which means that, with the wire stock folded, it is only 755mm (29.72in) long. The Para model, at 7kg (15.43lb), is 150g (5.29oz) heavier than the standard weapon, but its compact size means that it is ideal where heavy short-range fire is required, such as in room-clearing operations or anti-ambush drills.

The Minimi has been adopted by the Australian (as the F89), Belgian, Canadian, Indonesian and Italian armed forces, while in US service it is designated the

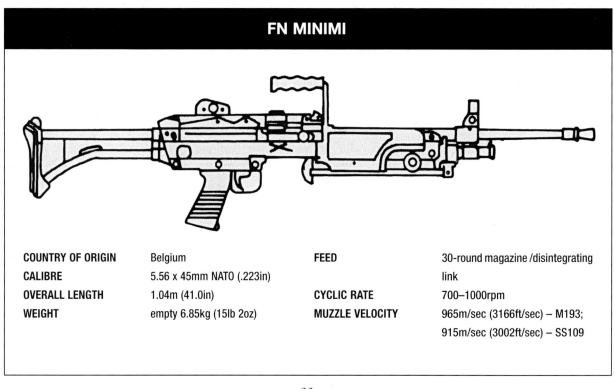

FN MINIMI

COUNTRY OF ORIGIN	Belgium	FEED	30-round magazine /disintegrating link
CALIBRE	5.56 x 45mm NATO (.223in)		
OVERALL LENGTH	1.04m (41.0in)	CYCLIC RATE	700–1000rpm
WEIGHT	empty 6.85kg (15lb 2oz)	MUZZLE VELOCITY	965m/sec (3166ft/sec) – M193; 915m/sec (3002ft/sec) – SS109

M249 Squad Automatic Weapon (SAW).

CLASSES OF FIRE

Fire is classified with respect to the ground and the target. Fire classified with respect to the ground is either grazing fire or plunging fire. Grazing fire is where most of the rounds do not rise more than 1m (3ft) above the ground. Plunging fire is where the path of the rounds is higher than a standing man, except in its beaten zone. Plunging fire is attained when firing at long ranges, when firing from high ground to low ground and when firing into a hillside.

Fire classified with respect to the target is designated as frontal, flanking, oblique or enfilade fire: Frontal fire is where the rounds are fired directly at the front of the target, while in flanking fire the rounds are fired at the flank of the target. In oblique fire, the long axis of the beaten zone is oblique to the long axis of the target. Enfilade fire is where the long axis of the beaten zone is the same as the long axis of the target. It can be either frontal, flanking or oblique. It is the best type of fire with respect to the target, as it makes optimum use of the beaten zone.

Fire directed at the enemy to keep him from seeing, tracking or firing at the target is suppressive fire. It can be direct or indirect fire. Smoke placed on the enemy to keep him from seeing targets is also suppressive fire.

When firing at an enemy position, the section commander will distribute his unit's fire to cover the position. There are two ways to distribute fire on a target: point fire and area fire. Point fire is fire

directed at one point, such as when an entire team fires at one bunker.

Area fire is fire directed to cover an area both laterally and in depth. If the section commander wants fire on a woodline, he may first fire tracers to mark its centre. He may then have the men on his left fire to the left of the tracers and those on his right fire to the right of the tracers. This is the best and quickest way to hit all parts of an area target. In area fire, fire is directed at likely enemy positions, rather than at a general area. The soldier fires first at that part of the target relative to his position in the team. He then distributes his fire over an area a few metres to the right and left of the first shot.

CHARACTERISTICS OF RIFLE AND MACHINE GUN FIRE

Many of the techniques and characteristics of rifle and machine gun fire are similar to those of submachine guns and handguns. The difference that distinguishes rifles is the increased range, while machine guns can put down sustained fire, as they are normally belt fed. The terminology used for both weapons, however, is similar:

• The part of the target that a rifleman or machine gunner can hit depends on his position and the range to the target. When possible, he should cover the entire target. When firing automatic fire, he should aim low at first, then walk the rounds up to the target.
• The trajectory is the path of a projectile from a weapon to the point of impact. At ranges out to 300m (328m), the trajectory of rifle fire is almost flat. For greater ranges, the rifle needs to be raised.

• Danger space is the space between a weapon and its target where the trajectory does not rise above the average height of a standing man (1.8m/6ft). It includes the beaten zone.
• Dead ground is any area within a weapon's sector that cannot be hit by fire from that weapon.
• The cone of fire is the cone-shaped pattern formed by the paths of rounds in a group or burst. The paths of the rounds differ and form a cone because of gun vibration, wind changes and variations in ammunition.
• The beaten zone is the area on the ground where the rounds in a cone of fire fall.
• The casualty radius is the area around a projectile's point of impact in which combatants could be killed or injured by either the concussion or fragmentation of the projectile.

MACHINE GUNNER OR RIFLEMAN

A machine gunner or rifleman fires into the part of the target assigned by the section commander. The noise and confusion of battle may oblige a section commander to use a variety of methods of communication to indicate targets and give fire orders. Among these methods are:

Sound: This includes the use of both voice and devices such as whistles and horns. Sound signals are good only for short distances. Battle noise, weather, terrain and vegetation reduced their range and reliability. Voice communications may come directly from the soldier's section commander or they may be passed from soldier to soldier.

▲ *A former US Army truck explodes as Browning M2HB tracer rounds impact on the cab. The 'Big Fifty' is a weapon with a long pedigree but remains in service throughout the world and is still being modified and improved.*

Prearranged fire: This is where the section commander tells the soldiers to start firing once the enemy reaches a certain point or terrain feature. When using prearranged fire, soldiers do not have to wait for an order to start firing.

Prearranged signal: In this method, the section commander gives a prearranged signal when he wants firing to start. This can be either a visual signal or a sound signal. Firing starts immediately on receipt of the signal.

Soldier-initiated fire: This is used when there is no time to wait for orders from the section commander.

STANDING OPERATING PROCEDURES

Standing operating procedures (SOPs) can reduce the number of oral orders needed to control fire. SOPs must be known and understood by all members of the unit. Three examples of SOPs are the search-fire-check SOP, the return-fire SOP and the rate-of-fire SOP.

The search-fire-check SOP follows these steps: a) search assigned sectors for enemy targets; b) fire at any targets (appropriate to weapons) seen in sectors; and c) while firing at sectors, soldiers should visually check section commander for specific orders.

The return-fire SOP tells each soldier in a unit what to do in case the unit makes unexpected contact with the enemy (such as in an ambush). These instructions will vary from unit to unit and from position to position within those units.

The rate-of-fire SOP tells each soldier how fast to fire at the enemy. The rate of fire varies among weapons, but the principle is to fire at a maximum rate when first engaging a target and then slow the rate to a point that will keep the target suppressed. This helps prevent weapons running out of ammunition too fast.

FIRE ORDERS

To help identify a target for a direct-fire weapon and to control that weapon's fire, a section commander may give a fire command to that weapon. A fire order has the following five parts:

- group
- range
- indication
- type
- command to fire.

Group: This gets the soldier's attention. The section commander may alert soldiers by name or unit designation by giving some type of visual or sound signal, by personal contact or by any other practical way. The order may be 'GUN GROUP', alerting the squad automatic weapon (SAW) or light support weapon crew.

Range: This tells how far away the target is and is given in metres.

Indication: This describes the target. The section commander should describe it briefly, but accurately. For example, 'MACHINE GUN POSITION IN THE WOODLINE', plus an indication of the direction of the target. The following are ways to give target directions:

- The section commander may point to a target with his arm or rifle. This will give the general direction of the target.
- The section commander may fire tracer ammunition at a target to identify it quickly and accurately. Before firing, however, he should show the general direction. He will shout, 'WATCH MY TRACER.'
- During the advance to contact, the section commander may desig-

▼ A GPMG position showing the gun on a sustained fire (SF) tripod used for long-range engagements. The No. 2 on the gun is in position on the left to feed ammunition belts.

nate certain features as target reference points (TRPs). He will shout to the section a description or number to identify it. For example, 'TREE ON LEFT WILL BE KNOWN AS "ROUND TREE".' He may give a target's direction in relationship to a target reference point. For example, 'MACHINE-GUN POSITION IN EDGE OF WOODLINE, FROM ROUND TREE, GO RIGHT 50.' That means that the machine gun is 50m (55yds) to the right of the tree.

Type: This gives the type of fire – single shots, bursts or whether the section commander only wants the M203 grenadier to engage the target. He may also want him to fire only three rounds. In this example, he would say, 'THREE ROUNDS'.

Fire Order: This tells the soldier or group when to fire. It may be an oral command or a sound or visual signal. If the section commander wants to control the exact moment of fire, he may say 'AT MY COMMAND ...' (then pause until he is ready) '... FIRE'. If he wants fire to start upon completion of the fire order, he will simply say 'FIRE' without pausing or 'GO ON'.

Visual signals are the most common means of giving fire commands. Arm-and-hand signals, personal examples and pyrotechnics are some of the things the section commander may use for visual signals. The section commander may use arm-and-hand signals to give fire commands when the soldier can see him. He may use miniflares or smoke grenades to mark

targets in most conditions of visibility. The section commander may also use his weapon to fire on a target as a signal – fire when he fires.

COMBAT DEMOLITIONS – EXPLOSIVES AND PRINCIPLES

Military or commercial explosives come in two forms: low explosive and high explosive.

Low explosives burn as they detonate, and this produces gas that expands. They are used in propellants such as cordite and the world's first explosive, gunpowder or black powder. Black powder is still in use as the slow-burning core in safety fuse.

High explosives turn into gas instantly, and this produces a violent shock that can be used to shatter targets. Unlike low explosives, high explosives will not detonate if exposed to a naked flame, although they may burn. They require a shock from a smaller explosion to detonate. High explosives include plastic explosives (PE) that can be shaped and moulded, and are the most versatile explosive available, and slab TNT, which, although obsolete, is still to be found around the world.

PE 808 plastic explosives, a British invention perfected at the Royal Ordnance Factory at

▲ Lance Cpl Timothy Exley (US Marine Corps) and Sapper Tania Dawson (Australian Army) check the position of plastic explosives on a bridge during Exercise Tandem Thrust 1997 in Shoalwater Training Area, Queensland Australia.

Bridgwater just before World War II, was composed of cyclotrimethylene-tritramine, a powerful but sensitive explosive which the British called Research Department Explosive, or RDX. Mixed as 91 per cent RDX and 9 per cent plasticizing agent, it was a stable, waterproof, shockproof, putty-like material which could be moulded into containers or directly onto a target.

emplaced – a slower but much more reliable method – a hole is dug that ensures that the mine is about 90mm (3.54in) below the surface. The soil at the bottom of the hole is rammed hard to prevent the mine settling, and the sides are cut at an angle. The hole is back-filled after the mine has been armed. If the track of a tank catches the edge of the hole, the angle will ensure that the weight of the

▾ The rubble-strewn streets of Manchester's downtown shopping district following an IRA car bomb attack on 16 June 1996. IRA bombs are generally made from a mixture of fertilizer-based 'home-made' explosive with a plastic explosive booster charge.

vehicle causes it to slip sideways and impact with the pressure plate of the anti-tank mine.

One common mistake with hand emplacing mines is to dig the hole too deep with straight sides. The sides support the tracks and this prevents the weight bearing on the pressure plate. If the depth at which the mine is laid is too shallow, the soil will stand proud as a small mound when the hole is back-filled .

Anti-personnel mines can be blast or fragmentation; the latter may also be omnidirectional or directional command detonated. Blast mines such as the US M14 or former Eastern Bloc PMN will either destroy the victim's foot if he

or she treads on it with their toes, or the leg up to the knee if the heel strikes the mine. This type of anti-personnel mine is intended to inflict a human M Kill. The philosophy behind this is that a wounded man will require assistance from the battlefield, and his injuries will demoralize his comrades and slow their movement.

Bounding fragmentation mines such as the US M16A1, M86 or former Eastern Bloc PMR-1 or POMZ-2 may inflict a K or an M Kill. They are designed to blast ball bearings or chunks of metal rod over a lethal area of 15m (49ft) and a wounding zone of 25m (82ft). The omnidirectional fragmentation mines may simply be a variant of a

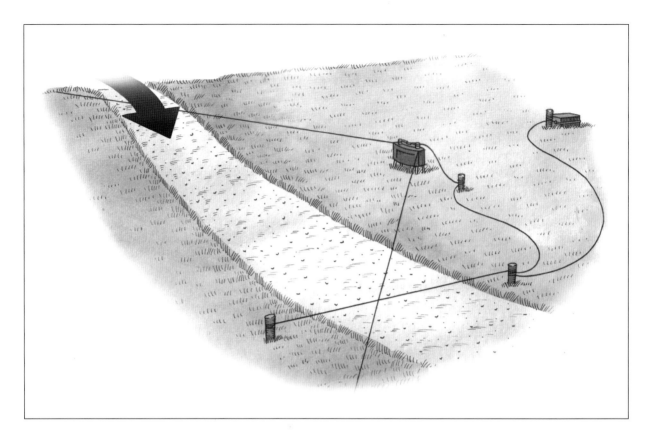

hand grenade on a stake, or more sophisticated bounding mines such as the US M26 or Eastern Bloc PROM-1. The most widely known command-detonated mine is the US M18A1 Claymore, which has a lethal radius of 15–20m (49–66ft).

Most mines today are made from plastic, which makes them almost impossible to detect with older mine detectors. One of the most reliable, if slow, methods of locating mines is prodding, using a sharp 350mm (13.78in) rod that is inserted into the ground at an angle until it strikes the side of a mine. New technology has been developed for detecting and clearing mines, or, in an assault, engineers may simply blast a path through a minefield using explosive-filled,

rocket-propelled hoses that are detonated when they have landed on the minefield.

Tanks and other armoured vehicles can be fitted with rollers to explode mines or with ploughs that dig in and push the mines to the side. Normally, to be effective against a well-laid minefield, it is necessary to use a combination of these breaching techniques to cut a safe lane through the obstacle.

INITIATION

One or a combination of fuses may initiate anti-tank mines.

Pressure fuse: A weight of more than 100kg (220lb) on the pressure plate is transmitted to the fuse in the fuse well. A double-impulse fuse operates after it has twice come under a 100kg (220.5lb) load – this ensures

▲ *An M18A1 Claymore AP mine rigged with a trip-wire and battery. When the patrol trips the wire, this completes the electrical circuit and so fires the Claymore, sending its steel balls across the track.*

that tanks will penetrate a minefield before mines on the outer edge are detonated by follow-up vehicles.

Influence fuse: The close proximity of a metallic mass, often the tank straddling the mine, causes initiation. Shaped charge warheads can cause a K Kill if they penetrate the belly armour. The impulses that will trigger this fuse include vibration, magnetic, electromagnetic frequency and audio frequency.

Tilt rod fuse: A 500mm (19.68in) short rod screwed into the fuse well is pushed out of alignment by the tank's glacis and triggers the mine after about three seconds.

Break wire: An electric circuit is completed by the vehicle snapping a thin wire, and this fires an off-route mine which hits the hull side.

Anti-personnel mines are initiated by the following:

Pull: 3kg (6.6lb) on a trip-wire; some trip wire mines may also be initiated by pressure of 9kg (19.84lb) on the prongs.

Pressure: 9kg (19.84lb) or greater on the prongs or plate.

Electrical: Command detonation.

▾ *The fragmentation grenade in the tin can is an old but effective booby trap. Here, the soldier might be able to take cover or kick it clear – the best location is in vegetation or hidden in rubble.*

CLASSIFICATION

Minefields are classified by the purpose they serve. Types of minefields include: protective, tactical, point, interdiction and dummy.

Protective minefields: These aid units in local, close-in protection. There are two types of protective minefields: hasty and deliberate. Hasty protective minefields are used as part of a unit's defensive perimeter. They are usually laid by units using mines (conventional or scatterable) from their basic loads. If conventional mines are used, they are laid on top of the ground in a random pattern. No anti-handling devices will be used. They are employed outside hand-grenade range, but within small-arms range. The emplacing unit picks up all mines upon leaving the area, unless enemy pressure prevents mine retrieval.

If scatterable mines are used for the purpose of hasty protective mining, the system most likely to be used is the US Modular Pack Mine System (MOPMS). This system is man-portable and can be employed rapidly. The MOPMS container has both anti-tank and anti-personnel mines, and it is placed and aimed in the desired direction. If the unit determines that the mines should be employed due to enemy action, the box is explosively command-detonated and the mines scattered. Once employed, the mines cannot be retrieved. If the minefield is not required, the unit simply picks up the unexploded MOPMS box and moves to a new location. The British Ranger system is vehicle mounted and fires anti-personnel mines into an anti-tank minefield to thicken it.

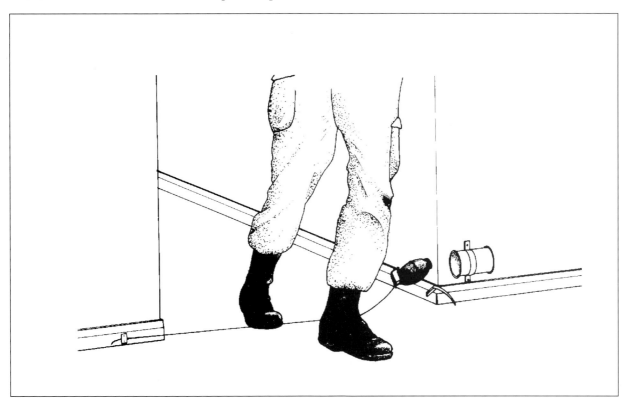

Deliberate protective minefields are used to protect static installations such as depots, airfields and missile sites. Conventional mines are always used and are emplaced in standard patterns, usually by engineers. The field is always fenced, marked and covered by fire. These minefields are usually emplaced for long periods. When these minefields are to be removed, engineers clear them.

▾ *US Marine engineers lift M15 anti-tank mines at the US Naval Station Guantanamo Bay, Cuba. The mines were laid in 1961 at the height of the Cold War but have been replaced by intrusion sensors that detect sound and movement.*

Tactical minefields: These are emplaced as part of the obstacle plan. They:

• canalize, delay and disrupt enemy attacks
• reduce enemy mobility
• block enemy penetrations
• increase effectiveness of friendly fire
• deny enemy withdrawal
• prevent enemy reinforcement
• protect friendly flanks
• destroy or disable enemy vehicles and personnel.

Tactical minefields are emplaced using conventional or scatterable mines. Density and depth of the minefield depend on the tactical situation. All types of mines and anti-handling devices can be used.

Point minefields: These minefields disorganize enemy forces and hinder their use of key areas. Point minefields are of irregular size and shape, and include all types of anti-tank and anti-personnel mines – and anti-handling devices. They can be used to reinforce obstacles, or to rapidly block an enemy counter-attack along a flank avenue of approach.

Interdiction minefields: These are placed on the enemy or in his rear areas to kill, disorganize and disrupt lines of communication and

command and control facilities. Interdiction minefields are used to separate enemy forces and delay or destroy enemy follow-on echelons. They are emplaced using air or fire support delivering scatterable mines.

Dummy minefields: These are used to degrade enemy mobility and preserve the defence's own. They are areas of ground used to simulate live minefields and deceive the enemy and are used when lack of time, personnel or materiel prevents employment of actual mines. Dummy minefields can supplement or extend live minefields, and they may be used as gaps in live minefields. To be effective, a dummy minefield must, naturally enough, look like a live minefield. This is done by either burying metallic objects or making the ground look as though objects are buried. Dummy minefields are of no value until the enemy has become sensitive to mine warfare.

REPORTING, RECORDING AND MARKING

Once emplaced, minefields are lethal and make no distinction between friend and enemy. For this reason, positive control and a continuous flow of information are necessary. Reporting, recording and marking of minefields must be performed using methods that are consistent and well understood. The basic differences between conventional and scatterable mines require that they be treated differently with respect to reporting, recording and marking.

Conventional Minefield Reporting

A minefield report is an oral, electronic or written communication concerning mining activities, friendly or enemy. These reports document information on friendly and enemy minefields. The information is transmitted through operation channels and furnished to intelligence staff officers. It is then processed, integrated with terrain intelligence and disseminated through intelligence channels to affected units. Mandatory conventional minefield reports are:

- Report of Intention
- Report of Initiation
- Report of Completion.

The emplacing unit commander will submit these reports through operational channels to the operations officer of the authorizing headquarters (HQ). That HQ will integrate the reports with terrain intelligence and disseminate them through tactical intelligence. The reports should be sent by secure means.

The Report of Intention is made as soon as it is decided to lay the minefield. It doubles as a request when initiated at levels below those with authority to emplace. In NATO operations, this report, when required, includes the following required data (Standardisation Agreement (STANAG) 2036) on the proposed minefield:

- tactical purpose
- type of minefield
- estimated number and types of mines
- whether mines are surface laid or buried
- whether anti-handling devices are used
- location of minefield
- location and width of lanes and gaps

- proposed date and time for starting and completing.

Conventional minefields that are part of an operation or general defence plan that has been approved by the authorizing commander do not require a Report of Intention. Their inclusion in such a plan implies an intention to lay.

The Report of Initiation is a mandatory report made by the laying unit when installation begins. It informs higher HQ that emplacement has begun and that the area is no longer safe for friendly movement and manoeuvre.

The Report of Completion is usually an oral report to the authorizing commander that the minefield is complete and functional. The Report of Completion is followed as rapidly as possible by the completed Minefield Record. Completion of the minefield records is the responsibility of the laying unit.

The authorizing commander may require additional reports – for example, a Progress Report when, during the emplacing process, he may require periodic reports on the amount of work completed.

A Report of Transfer is a written report that transfers the responsibility for a minefield from one commander to another. Both the relieved and relieving commanders must sign this report. It must include a certificate stating that the relieving commander has been shown – on the ground or otherwise informed of – all mines within the zone of responsibility. It must state that the relieving commander assumes full responsibility for those mines. The Report of Transfer is sent to the next higher

▲ *A simple anti-personnel device that was used at the beginning of the Vietnam War. It consist of sharpened bamboo on a weighted log that swings down onto a track, impaling its victim.*

commander who has authority over both relieved and relieving commanders.

Finally, a Report of Change is made immediately to the next higher commander when the minefield is altered. It is sent through channels to the HQ that keeps the writ-

ten mine record. A Report of Change is made as soon as changes in any friendly minefields occur. The commander responsible for surveillance and maintenance of the minefield makes this report.

Conventional Minefield Recording

All conventional minefields are recorded on standard forms, except for hasty protective minefields, which have their own form.

Preparing the standard minefield record form is the responsibil-

ity of the laying unit. The officer in charge of the laying must sign and forward it to the next higher command as soon as possible. Once the information is entered, the form is classified 'SECRET' or 'NATO SECRET', as required. The number of copies prepared depends on the type of minefield and local procedures. Unit standing operating procedures (SOPs) should provide for information on minefields being passed to higher and lower command levels and laterally to adjacent units. When the record is made, it should be reproduced at the lowest level having the necessary equipment to make copies. Minefield records are circulated on a 'need-to-know' basis. When used for training, they are marked 'SPECIMEN'. Large minefields are recorded on two or more forms.

Whenever any changes are made to an existing minefield, a completely new record must be prepared. This record is marked 'REVISED' and shows the minefield as it is after the changes. The original minefield number remains unchanged. Some changes that require a new record are:

• relocation of mines in safe lanes
• relocation of safe lanes
• changed lane or minefield markings
• inclusion of the minefield into a larger minefield system
• removal or detonation of mines
• addition of mines to the minefield.

An overlay should be used when the minefield is to be related to operational maps. Standard military symbols are used in preparing mine warfare overlays.

Aerial photographs can be used to record minefields if strip centre-line tapes are kept in place until the camera work is done and prominent terrain points can be located. Aerial photographs can be used in conjunction with the completed form.

Any type of angle-measuring device that can be oriented in reference to magnetic North can be used to lay out or plot mines. Conventional minefield records are forwarded through operational channels to theatre Army HQ, where they are maintained on file

by the theatre engineer. Minefield records may be maintained on file with the assistant corps engineer in whose area of operation the minefield is located, if deemed necessary.

Minefields are marked as necessary to protect friendly forces. STANAG 2889 is the authoritative reference for marking conventional minefields emplaced by NATO forces. Normally, protective and tactical minefields will be fenced to protect friendly troops, non-combatants and domestic livestock. In rear areas, minefields

will be fenced on all sides. Two-strand barbed wire or concertina fences with signs are minimum protection.

The US Army Hand Emplaced Minefield Marking Set (HEMMS) may also be used as a marking means. Lanes will be marked using

▼ *Loading a Cluster Bomb Unit (CBU) onto a US Navy F/A-18C Hornet during operations in the Arabian Gulf in November 1977. Though a very effective area weapon, the CBU can produce large quantities of unexploded ordnance if dropped too low.*

▲ *It is mandatory to mark minefields to ensure that civilians are not innocent victims. However, unmarked AP mines have been laid widely in war zones and have claimed huge numbers of civilian casualties.*

standard minefield marking sets. In forward areas, minefields will normally be marked only on the friendly (rear) side or on the friendly side and the flanks. Lanes will be marked inconspicuously using wire, tape, rope or easily identifiable terrain features. Minefield markings may be removed upon withdrawal. Point and interdiction minefields are not normally marked.

Accurate, timely and uniform reporting and dissemination of scatterable minefield emplacement information is a must. Fluid and fast-moving tactical situations require that complete information on scatterable mine employment be known and passed on in a simple

and rapid manner to all units that could be affected. The variety of emplacing systems and emplacing units precludes the use of locally devised reporting and dissemination methods. Scatterable minefields must also be recorded to facilitate clearing operations after the war is over. They need not be recorded in the detail required when emplacing conventional mines.

As the locations of individual scatterable mines are unknown, they cannot and need not be plotted as are conventional mines. The aim points or corner points and the type mines emplaced are basic information which must remain on file for future reference and use. Some systems such as artillery-delivered mines or the US Army Gator and MOPMS are point oriented, with the safety zone calculated from one or more aim points. Other systems such as GEMSS and the M56 have distinct

minefield corner points that must be reported. The basic purpose of this procedure is to provide a uniform method with all basic information required to report and maintain a record of scatterable mine employment. This procedure also contains all the information necessary to warn units that may be affected. Warning information can easily be extracted and disseminated to those units that require it. The unit emplacing the mines will immediately report the pertinent information required by the most expeditious secure means. If the initial report is not a hard copy report, the emplacing unit will prepare the report in hard copy as soon as possible. The report is sent through operations channels to the HQ authorizing the minefield.

The information is posted on operations maps and disseminated to units that are affected. The report is then forwarded in the same manner as the conventional minefield record to the senior engineer in the theatre for permanent retention. Forwarding the hard copy report to the theatre commander is not time-sensitive. Reports can be batched and forwarded when time permits.

BOOBY-TRAPS

Improvised anti-personnel and anti-vehicle devices, either explosive or mechanical, are commonly known as booby-traps.

A booby trap is a cunning contrivance, designed to catch the unwary; it has been called 'a savage practical joke'. It is aimed directly at the reduction of morale and mobility, or terrorizing its victims and creating insecurity. It need not be constructed using high explosive; some of the most effective use materials are easily found in a builder's merchants, garage or even under a kitchen sink.

Physicians have established an international classification of four groups for the lethality of anti-personnel mines, which is also applicable to booby traps:

Pattern A: Small blast injuries Traumatic injury usually below the knee; amputation often required.

Pattern B: Larger mines, e.g. PMN Traumatic amputation of the lower leg and injury to the thighs, genitals and buttocks.

Pattern C: 'Butterfly' mines, e.g. PFM-1, scattered by air or artillery Usually being handled when they explode, therefore injuries are often to the face, chest, hands and thighs.

Pattern D: Fragmentation mines, e.g. M-16 and M-18 Claymore, the Russian OZM series, the MON and POMZ mines. Usually detonated

by a trip-wire This type of mine will typically produce casualties out to a 200m (219yd) radius. Injuries often include penetration injuries of the abdomen, chest or brain. A Pattern D booby trap will kill its intended victim.

Although anti-tank mines are intended to destroy soft-skinned vehicles or disable armoured vehicles, they may be fitted with factory-made or improvised anti-handling devices, which effectively makes them massive anti-personnel weapons.

Booby-Trap Switches

These devices work either electrically or mechanically. Electrical devices work when a circuit is completed; mechanical either by simple

kinetic energy or when a firing pin strikes a percussion cap. They are initiated by one of five principles:

- pressure – from a human foot or vehicle
- pull – on a trip-wire or as something is picked up
- pressure – release as weight is removed from a mechanism
- tension – release of a taut wire
- timed – delay, either chemical, electronic or mechanical.

Booby-traps can sited in locations where the target will trigger them by carrying out a routine act that is second nature, such as switching on a light.

Modern military multi-function switches such as the British and Australian L5A1 Firing

---

THE LETHALITY OF BOOBY TRAPS AND LAND MINES

Type	Mine	Typical Injuries
Pattern A	Small blast mines	Traumatic injury usually below the knee, amputation often required
Pattern B	Larger mines eg PMN	Traumatic amputation of the lower leg and injury to the thighs, genitals and buttocks
Pattern C	"Butterfly" mines eg the PFM-1, scattered by air or to artillery	Usually being handled when they explode, therefore injuries are often the face, chest, hands and eyes
Pattern D	Fragmentation mines such as the M-16 and M-18 Claymore, the Russian OZM series the MON and POMZ mines. Usually detonated by a trip-wire.	Victims within 25m (82ft) of these types of mine are normally killed outright. This type of mine will typically produce casualties out to a 200m (660ft) radius. Injuries often include penetration, injuries of the abdomen, chest or brain. A Pattern D booby trap will kill its intended victim.

▲ *As soldiers take the embrasure of an enemy bunker under fire, their comrades use grenades to clear the trench until they are in a position to 'post' a grenade into the bunker.*

Device Demolition Combination, which in US service is designated the M142, are made from green or tan plastic; however, obsolete metal or brass ones may be encountered around the world. These switches include the:
• British Switch No. 4 Pull, Mark 1, the Switch No. 5 Pressure, Mark 1, and the Switch No. 6 Release, Mark 1. The pull and pressure release switches have been copied by the Yugoslav Army as the UDP-1 and UDOP-1.

• US M1A1 Pressure Firing Device, M3 Pull-Pressure Firing Device and the M1 and M5 Pressure-Release Firing Devices and M1 Delay Firing Device.
• Ex-Soviet MUV, the VPF pull switches, MV-5 pressure switch and VZDKh and EkhZ delay fuses. These can be used to operate explosive devices, including shells and mortar bombs, rigged as booby-traps.

Mines and Improvised Munitions Locations
Booby traps, like any snare or trap, are only effective if their intended victim or quarry is obliged to enter or traverse the area in which they

have been positioned. They may therefore be found at the following locations:

• road bottlenecks and defiles on tracks
• open ground on a track suitable for an ambush, known as a 'killing ground'
• the verges of surfaced roads or in potholes in the road
• around obstacles such as roadblocks and craters
• waiting areas and road exits
• around abandoned stores or equipment
• as part of the field defences of a position
• damaged roads, runways and civilian installations.

• likely helicopter landing zones and parachute drop zones
• on roads into and out of National Governmental Organization (NGO) field locations, e.g. clinics or food distribution centres
• bridges, footpaths and foot-bridges
• paths and roads into or out of refugee camps
• wells and water points
• railways, tracks, bridges and cuttings

• as a part of a larger device, either explosive or incendiary.

Mine or Booby-Trap Indicators

Where booby traps are suspected, it is essential that troops, civilians and aid personnel look for the indicators. These can be:

• disturbed ground – e.g. on roads or crops, loose sand or earth scattered over grass, sawdust or wood shavings in a house
• trampled earth or vegetation, footprints or vehicle tracks in a pattern suggestive of a minefield
• damaged or dead vegetation indicating an attempt at camouflage
• unusual markings, e.g. piled stones, spray painting, metal stakes or pickets driven into the ground to a height of 500mm (19.46in), branches broken to serve as a pointer, knotted grass, marks on tree trunks or walls, or twigs passed through a leaf. Military minefields have fences that are marked with symbols such as a skull and crossed bones
• trip-wires at ankle and neck height, or pegs, nails or electric cable that have no clear function
• partial blocking of a route that forces vehicles or pedestrians onto the soft shoulder
• empty ammunition or mine boxes, wrappings, seals and packing material – boxes may also be booby-trapped
• animals or people killed by no obvious means
• damaged vehicles on or beside the road
• an apparently undamaged and unattended vehicle
• an attractive object in an abandoned building, vehicle or in the open – e.g. weapons, binoculars, cooking utensils, electronic goods, food or drink containers
• subsidence in the ground – particularly after rain
• breaks in the continuity of vegetation, dust, paintwork or timbering

◀ *Trenches are not normally as wide as this, so throwing a grenade from cover can be difficult if long range is required – the nightmare is dropping a grenade in a trench once the pin has been pulled.*

◄ The British L2 grenade is based on the American M26 and has a thin tin body with a notched steel wire inside that shreds into tiny fragments. These may not kill but will incapacitate an enemy long enough for soldiers to kill or capture him.

used as a command-detonated mine in an ambush with an electric detonator inserted into plastic explosive in the fuse well.

In the trip-wire device, a fragmentation grenade such as the British L2, US M26, or Russian M75 is wired onto a stake about 350mm (14in) above the ground. The split pin is flattened out so that it can be withdrawn easily, and a trip-wire is attached to the ring. When a soldier snags his ankle on the trip wire, the pin is pulled out of the grenade and the handle flies off. After an interval of between four and five seconds, the grenade explodes.

The delay may give combatants time to take cover; however, even a prone man stands a 50 per cent chance of being hit within 10m (33ft). The M26 has a 50 per cent lethality within a 15m (49ft) radius, while the L2 is lethal up to 10m. Beyond this range, small fragments can wound. The trip-wire device has a C and D lethality pattern, and it is used in zones IV, VI and VII – South America, Southeast Asia and the former Yugoslavia (or Balkans as the area is known today).

In the tin can device, a fragmentation grenade such as the British L2, US M26 or Russian M75 is inserted into an opened and empty commercial food can. The can is anchored securely, and a trip wire is attached to the

• loose floorboards, signs of digging, recently re-laid brick work, cobblestones or hollow-sounding walls.

USING GRENADES AND IMPROVISED EXPLOSIVES

The hand-grenade, which is widely available in low-level conflicts as well as conventional war, makes a very effective field-expedient booby-trap. Modern grenade designs may use electronic initiation, but the majority consist of a charge weighing about 75g (2.65oz) inside a metal case. The case may, as in the US M26 or British L2, have a notched wire liner to produce small pre-fragmented projectiles, or it may be made from cast iron, as in the Russian F1 or Chinese 'Chicom' stick grenade. Most grenades have a split (cotter)

pin that holds a handle (spoon), which in turn holds back the spring-loaded striker. The user pulls the pin and throws the grenade, the handle flies off, releases the striker, which hits a percussion cap and, after an interval of four to five seconds, the grenade explodes.

Although the standard high-explosive grenade is most widely used as a booby-trap, the white phosphorus (WP), with its shorter delay before the main charge explodes, has a significant advantage as an anti-personnel weapon. A very simple delay device is a high-explosive or white phosphorus grenade with the pin removed and handle secured by an elastic band. The elastic band will eventually stretch or perish, and the handle flies off. Grenades may also be grenade. When the split pin is removed from the grenade, the handle springs away, but is held in place by the side of the can. When a soldier snags his ankle on the trip-wire, the grenade is pulled clear of the can and the handle is released. After an interval of between four and five seconds, the grenade explodes.

The delay may give soldiers time to take cover; however, once again, even a prone man stands a 50 per cent chance of being hit within 10m (33ft). The M26 has a 50 per cent lethality within a 15m (49ft) radius, while the L2 is lethal up to 10m. Beyond this range, small fragments can wound. The tin can device has a C and D lethality pattern, and is used in zones IV, VI and VII – South America, Southeast Asia and the former Yugoslavia (the Balkans).

A pressure-release device can be made by taking a fragmentation grenade such as the British L2, US M26 or Russian M75 and positioning it under a weight heavy enough to keep the handle in place. Ideally, the object should be something that will attract a soldier, either through curiosity or greed. The pin is then removed. When the weight is taken off the grenade, the handle flies off. After an interval of between four and five seconds, the grenade explodes – if the trap has been set in a confined place, the soldier will have little time to escape. The device has a C and D lethality pattern, and is used in zones IV, VI and VII – South America, Southeast Asia and the Balkans.

An anti-helicopter device can be constructed by taking a fragmentation grenade such as the

British L2, US M26 or Russian M75 and wiring it to a stake about 350mm (14in) above the ground on a likely helicopter landing zone. Sufficient string to hold the handle in place is wrapped around the grenade to secure the handle; at the free end of the string, there is a length of cloth about 500mm (20in) long and 100mm (4in) wide.

▲ A British paratrooper in training in North Africa in World War II prepares to throw a No.36 grenade. Widely known as the Mills Bomb, its design dated back to World War I and, with its pin and handle, it would be widely copied in the 20th Century.

The pin is removed. The grenade is positioned in long grass or scrub on a likely helicopter landing

◄ *During demonstrations in Korea a petrol bomb arcs through the air. One of the simplest anti-personnel or anti-vehicle devices, it was first used in World War II, when it was known as a 'Molotov Cocktail'.*

wall with sandbags can be used as a breaching charge against stud walls. The grenades or mine are detonated, and the blast is contained by the sandbags and directed against the internal wall, creating a 'mouse hole' suitable for troops to crawl through into an adjoining house or room.

The M18A1 is a more suitable weapon as an expedient breaching charge. 'Grenade necklaces' are never entirely reliable and, if there is a misfire or blind, the assaulting troops have the problem of what to do with the unexploded but potentially unstable ordnance. The breaching charge for stud walls has a C and D lethality pattern.

Although these devices are intended to be used in place of a demolition charge, if they were used against a defended room, the blast and fragmentation projected through the wall would be fatal to soldiers in the immediate locality on the far side. They are used in conflicts involving military or paramilitary forces in street-fighting operations.

The Eagle Fireball was developed by the US Army as an improvised weapon to be used against Soviet armour in the event of a conflict in Europe. This device consists of a 7.62mm (0.3in) 100-round ammunition box filled with a petrol and oil mixture, with detonating cord wrapped around an M34 WP grenade. A flash detonator (non-electric blasting cap) with

zone. The down draft from a helicopter as it comes in to land catches the cloth and, as it blows around, this unwinds the string. The handle is eventually freed, and the grenade explodes.

Against personnel, the M26 has a 50 per cent lethality within a 15m (49ft) radius, while the L2 is lethal up to 10m (33ft). Exploding grenades on an LZ may not damage a modern helicopter;

however, they can kill or injure soldiers as they exit the helicopters. The anti-helicopter device has a C and D lethality pattern, and it is used in IV zones and Southeast Asia.

Three or four high-explosive hand grenades, such as the L2 or M26, linked by detonating cord plugged into plastic explosive in the fuse wells or an M18A1 Claymore mine tamped against the

750cm (295in) of safety fuse and an M60 fuse igniter or British L1A1 grip switch is clipped or taped to detonating cord where it protrudes from the ammunition box.

The soldier operates the grip switch or igniter, and the burning safety fuse gives him 60 seconds to throw the Eagle Fireball onto a vehicle. The device should be fitted with wire hooks or a grapnel to ensure that it hooks onto the target vehicle. There is a blast effect from the enclosed grenade, and the fuel and oil will ensure that it adheres to the target. The Eagle Fireball has a D lethality pattern for the crew of the vehicle, with fragmentation of the ammunition box causing injuries to troops in the open within 25m (82ft). It is used in street fighting by military or paramilitary forces.

Finally, the Eagle Cocktail was another weapon developed by the US Army as an improvised anti-tank weapon. It consists of a robust waterproof bag with a capacity of about 5 litres (1 gallon) filled with a mixture of petrol and oil. It is securely sealed, and an AN-M14 TH3 incendiary grenade and an AN-M8 HC smoke grenade are wired to the outside. Care must be taken to ensure that the handles can fly off when the pins are pulled. A cord attached to the split pins will ensure that they are pulled simultaneously.

▸ *Improvised anti-tank charges are best used as part of an ambush. An enemy tank may be forced to use a defile where the charge has been positioned or a come on' may tempt the tank along a route where the charge has been positioned.*

The soldier pulls the pins and throws the device at an enemy armoured vehicle, aiming for the flat rear deck. This produces thick smoke and flame that would effectively blind an enemy vehicle, even if it failed to set fire to it. With older tank designs, the burning fuel would be drawn into the engine if the device hit the rear deck. This would immobilize or possibly destroy the vehicle. The Eagle Cocktail has a D lethality pattern for the vehicle crew, with

burn or blast injury to troops with 25m (82ft). It is used in street fighting by military or paramilitary forces.

Booby-traps, whether constructed using standard switches, improvised devices or hand-grenades, are only effective if they have been intelligently sited and camouflaged. They must either attract their target or be positioned so that the target will be obliged to trigger them through some routine action.

CHAPTER THREE

SUPPORT WEAPONS

Support weapons are the tools of heavy firepower used in co-ordination with infantry manoeuvres. They include mortars, anti-tank weapons, anti-aircraft missiles and air strikes. Some support weapons, such as anti-tank rockets and mortars, are often manoeuvred and launched by infantry units themselves. Others, primarily artillery fire and airstrikes, are guided onto the target by specialized controllers and observers. Intelligently used, support fire creates a lethal environment for an enemy, suppressing their tactical movement and fire-response capabilities, and inflicting attrition upon soldiers, vehicles and equipment at long ranges. Almost all modern military campaigns rely on effective pre-emptive usage of support weapons to destroy the enemy's command-and-control structure and means of engagement prior to committing ground troops.

◄ A battery of self-propelled (SP) guns in action. SP guns are able to move rapidly between fire positions after each bombardment. Enemy counter-battery artillery consequently has fewer opportunities for accurate targeting.

Support weapons are divided into three basic types: artillery, mortars and strike aircraft. Whatever their nature, the purpose is the same: to inflict attrition upon the enemy.

Support fire is of two basic varieties: direct and indirect. Direct fire engages an enemy visible to the fire team, shooting or dropping the munitions directly onto the target. Indirect fire is launched against targets which cannot be seen by the fire team, and it either serves as blind area bombardment or is adjusted onto target by an observer who can see the point of impact.

Artillery is by far the most ancient support weapon. The Roman ballista and the medieval trebuchet fired rocks, arrows and various other missiles using a catapult and a counterweight, respectively. By the fourteenth century AD, artillery had been revolutionized by the introduction of gunpowder as a propellant. Within a century, cannons, as they came to

be known, were demolishing castle and fortification walls with stone and iron balls, and scything down infantry with grapeshot and canister rounds. Yet a slow muzzle-loading action, considerable weight and unpredictable accuracy qualified their success for any role other than as crude siege-breaking instruments.

In the mid-nineteenth century, artillery was greatly improved by rifling, better recoil systems and increased understanding of ballistics. At the century's end, new nitro-cellulose propellants working out of unitary cartridges were being used, which in turn enabled fast breech loading. By World War I, artillery was exercising significant tactical impact, even if it was mainly in the role of area bombardment as a prelude to infantry assault. During World War II, a multitude of different artillery pieces, including anti-aircraft and anti-tank weapons, were developed to meet the new airborne and armoured threats

intrinsic to mechanized warfare. Artillery itself therefore became more intrinsic to infantry manoeuvres, with large-calibre artillery in the rear providing heavy indirect shelling, while front-line units were accompanied by various field artillery pieces for direct-fire missions.

Following World War II, missile technology became the major area of artillery development. Today, a modern infantry unit will be supported by anti-tank and anti-aircraft missiles, huge area weapons such as the multiple launch rocket system (MLRS) and batteries of more traditional artillery pieces which now use global positioning systems (GPS) and laser targeting systems to put down fire with pinpoint accuracy. Mobile artillery in the form of tanks and other armed vehicles also accompany the soldier into the battlefield, acting as protective vanguards for manoeuvre and engaging enemy tanks and positions at distances of up to 6km (3.75 miles).

Mortars have an equally venerable history. They were first used in the siege of Constantinople in the mid-1400s, but later found applications as naval weapons in US and British forces in the nineteenth century. These early mortars, however, were weighty and unwieldy items. It was not until World War I that the familiar portable infantry mortars appeared. The first of these, the British 76.2mm (3in) Stokes mortar, established the basic

◄ US troops prepare to fire an 81mm (3.2in) mortar. Mortars such as this have an effective range of over 5000m (15,243ft) while new Global Positioning Satellite System (GPS) targeting systems give high first-round hit probability.

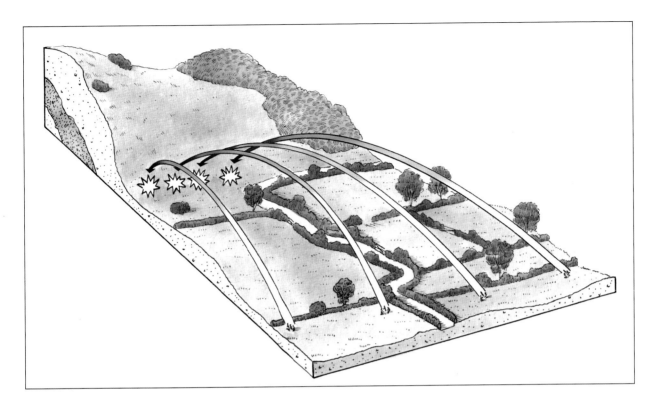

▲ *A mortar battery will enforce a minimum distance of 300m (914ft) between each mortar unit. The distance means that there is less chance of the entire battery being knocked out by enemy counter-mortar fire.*

construction – launch tube, base plate, support frame and adjustment mechanism – which has been seen in mortars ever since. Although mortars are simple in principle, they have become possibly the most important support weapon for immediate use in frontline battle, as they are accurate and powerful within the short–medium range combat area.

Air support for ground troops, as distinct from any other type of air operation, is known as close-air support (CAS). The practice of CAS was refined by the Germans during the blitzkrieg actions of World War II, where Ju-87 Stuka dive-bombers were used in a direct-fire artillery role ahead of ground-troop operations. The principle soon caught on, and postwar operations have become increasingly reliant on air support. In Vietnam, US forces would direct heavy napalm and high-explosive strikes onto suspected or actual enemy positions in preparation for patrol or combat missions. The lessons of the Vietnam War, with its politically embarrassing civilian and military death tolls, mean that air support is now frequently used in preference to the unpredictability of deploying ground forces.

The challenge for a modern infantryman controlling fire-support weaponry is to be conversant with the many technicalities and tactics of its use. Incompetent handling can result in the fratricide, or 'friendly fire' incidents, which commonly occurred in Vietnam and persisted in conflicts such as the 1991 Gulf War. Yet, if support weaponry is mastered, the combat force of the ground unit is tremendously magnified.

MORTARS

Mortars are the most flexible method a unit has of applying indirect fire at close–medium ranges – approximately 100m (328ft) to 3.2km (2 miles) – although modern heavy mortars have ranges up to 25km (15.5 miles). Mortar teams accompany all company- or battalion-strength operations. The tubes and base plates are portable enough to carry at the vanguard of offensive operations and can produce accurate and heavy anti-personnel and anti-materiel fire within less than a minute of set-up.

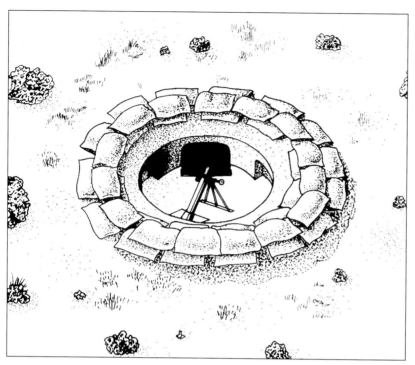

Their very flexibility, however, means that they can be called upon too frequently in action. Strict command relationships must be established to avoid their misuse or the rapid exhaustion of ammunition.

THE APPLICATION OF MORTARS
Mortar fire has limited destructive potential when compared to heavy

◄ *A mortar pit allows 360 degree traversing of the weapon and provides substantial protection against small-arms and direct-fire infantry weapons. Note the grenade sumps set into the side walls of the pit.*

▼ *Two US mortar operators make targeting corrections. Manual adjustment like this is increasingly replaced by automatic Global Positioning Satellite (GPS) adjustment.*

artillery. Its high-arcing trajectory removes the velocity needed for penetration of armoured targets. Only high-explosive 120mm (4.72in) mortar rounds can destroy fortified bunkers and some types of overhead tank armour. Even then, it may take many rounds to accomplish destruction. Mortars are much better employed in anti-personnel, suppressive, obscuration or marking roles.

Personnel are very vulnerable to mortar fire. Mortar rounds' steep angle of drop enables them to fall unimpeded into fighting dug-outs, and a low speed of impact means that less of the explosion is absorbed by the earth. The kill radius of a 60mm (2.44in) mortar can be up to 20m (66ft), depending on shell type. Shell splinters and blast will also damage and destroy soft-skinned vehicles, unprotected equipment and obstacles. British mortars at the Arras/Vimy ridge in 1917, for example, were used effectively to slash through enemy barbed-wire defences prior to infantry assault. In military terminology, if 30 per cent casualties are imposed, the enemy unit is classed as 'destroyed'; if 10 per cent casualties are inflicted, the enemy is temporarily 'neutralized' (ineffective for a period of a few hours). Mortars can impose destruction only on exposed troops caught in a concentrated barrage, but neutralization can be achieved against even dug-in enemy units.

Suppressive mortar fire is used to disrupt an enemy assault, force enemy soldiers into cover and spoil the accuracy and weight of return fire. Suppressive fire can include obscuration. Obscuration involves firing smoke rounds in front of

MORTAR TACTICS – VIETNAM

Mortar rounds are effective in jungle terrain because they drop down through foliage to the jungle floor, rather than approach at a shallow angle and risk deflection by upper tree trunks, as is the case with artillery shells. During the Burma campaign in 1945, for example, British forces found the mortar so effective that most anti-tank guns were changed for 76.2mm (3in) or 190mm (7.5in) mortars. In Vietnam, the mortar was also vital to US tactics. Isolated jungle bases were protected by sections of emplaced mortars at the base centre that could bombard the perimeter treeline when the base was under attack. On 3 January 1963, an entire Vietcong company attacked one such base, a Special

Forces camp at Plei Mrong. The Vietcong easily punched through the perimeter defences, which had been cut by saboteurs in the night, and penetrated into the interior of the camp. The Special Forces response was to open up with their machine guns and one 81mm (3.18in) mortar. The short-range capability of the mortar enabled the Green Berets to pummel the Vietcong soldiers even when they were almost on top of the mortar position. Two Vietcong attacks were defeated in this way, the mortar fire following the enemy as they retreated into the treeline. Although all four men in the mortar pit were wounded by the end of the attack, the single mortar eventually helped repulse the entire assault.

enemy positions during an attack or withdrawal to deny them visual targets or a clear sense of the battlefield. Marking fire consists of the mortar putting down rounds as range-finding or target-locating markers for heavier weaponry such as field artillery or ground-attack aircraft.

During unit operations, mortars will be employed in three tactical roles. First, they will support assault troops by destroying, neutralizing or suppressing enemy positions. This is termed close-support fire. Mortars are ideal in this role because they are quick to deploy and their portability enables close liaison with forward combat troops. In World War II, German forces emplaced their mortars only 550–800m (1800–2625ft) from opposing positions so that they could bombard the enemy from positions too close for the

enemy to reply with heavy artillery fire. Using this method, German mortars accounted for 70 per cent of Allied casualties in the Normandy campaign. Second, mortars can provide counterfire against enemy indirect- and direct-fire weapons, observation posts and command-and-control facilities. Usually the mortar is the first counterfire response before heavier artillery can be brought to bear, and the mortars often act in a marking role. Finally, mortars impose attrition upon enemy forces that have yet to enter an offensive or defensive operation. Targets for this type of mission, known as interdiction fire, include enemy bases, supply routes, rally points and logistic centres.

CONTROLLING MORTAR FIRE

Mortar fire is usually directed by an observer or by the leader of a combat

unit acting as an observer. As mortars are used in close proximity to friendly troops, the boundaries of fire are rigorously defined by the observer or by higher fire control officers. Fire control officers work under restrictive or permissive guidelines. Restrictive guidelines prohibit calls for fire which are not part of the support-fire programme already agreed with the unit commander on the ground. Permissive guidelines allow the observer to bring in any fire that he deems necessary within given locations. The German mortar units mentioned

above were the first to link observers and detecting radar to the mortar teams and so achieve an excellent fast-response in permissive environments.

The boundaries of mortar fire vary with the mission and are set as either fire lines or fire areas. A fire line is a geographical line beyond which mortars are able to fire upon enemy positions or targets. The mortars must not fire in front of the line because of danger to friendly forces. A fire area is a specific geographical area into which the mortars may target and fire. Mortars

▲ An Allied 81mm (3.2in) mortar section during the Gulf War. 81mm (3.2in) mortar rounds weigh about 4.3kg (9.6lb) and are available with high-explosive, obscuration (smoke), incendiary and phosphorous warheads.

fire across fire lines or into fire areas under different degrees of control. Sometimes the observer will pick out opportunistic targets; on other occasions, a pre-determined schedule and a fixed group of targets will control the mortar fire. Targeting must be based upon those positions the destruction of which will enhance mission success or soldier survivability.

When calling in unplanned mortar fire, the observer first identifies himself to the mortar platoon or team, then proceeds to give full target information (or designate the target from a pre-prepared list). The target information will include:

• a description of the target and recommendations for the type of ammunition most suited to destroying, neutralizing or suppressing that target
• its location defined by precise map grid co-ordinates
• the altitude of the target above sea level
• the target's length, width, radius and the angle of its position.

The forward observer (FO) will then radio this information to the fire-co-ordinating officer (if there is a battery of mortars) or the mortar team leader (if there is only one). The mortar will then fire onto the target and either the FO will give adjustment or the mortar team itself will adjust using visual, GPS or laser-targeting methods (see 'Controlling Artillery' below). More often than not, the mortars will fire a restricted number of rounds – usually enough to allow the attacking infantry to close distance or make a withdrawal. Unlike artillery, mortars are rarely used as a self-sufficient means of pounding the enemy.

▸ *An artillery observer's range card. The axis of the semicircles is the observer's position and the circles represent 100m (304ft) intervals. The observer plots salient features of landscape and enemy positions on the range card.*

CONTROLLING ARTILLERY

The process of controlling artillery fire involves three elements: an observer, a fire direction centre (FDC) and a fire unit. The observer is anyone qualified or competent in directing artillery fire. It can be an official forward observer (FO), but all combat officers and many NCOs are trained in indirect-fire control. The FDC is the unit or individual that receives the request for fire and turns it into a tactical and technical directive for the firing unit. The firing unit is the team that works the gun itself or the battery of guns.

The ability to request and control indirect fire amplifies a combat leader's means to suppress, interdict and destroy the enemy at long range. During World War II, almost 70 per cent of combat casualties during the entire war were caused by artillery fire. A massed artillery firing against a specified area can decimate enemy personnel and armour. Soviet forces, for example, utilized more than 45,000 artillery pieces in a pre-offensive barrage of the city of Berlin in 1945. In the Gulf War, a single salvo from a British multiple-launch rocket system (MLRS) left only 70 out of 250 men of an Iraqi company alive. Such artillery fire saps enemy morale and unit strength, and only the toughest underground bunkers are immune from the effects of artillery shells.

CALLING IN FIRE

The first stage of a fire request involves locating the target for the FDC. There are three main ways of designating a target location: polar plot, grid co-ordinates and shift from a known point.

The polar plot method requires that the FDC know the position of the observer (it is agreed in advance or transmitted during the deployment). The observer then describes the target's direction, distance and vertical shift (difference in altitude) from his position. The

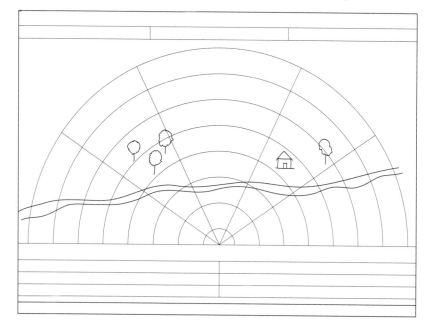

MEASUREMENTS IN MILS

There are 6400 mils in a circle. Military binoculars have horizontal and vertical axes each marked up in 10-mil increments. A cruder method of estimating mils is using the fingers. One finger's width at arm's length is roughly 30 mils, 2 fingers' 70 mils, 3 fingers' 100 mils, four fingers' 125 mils, a bunched fist 180 mils and a spanned hand (measuring from the tip of the little finger to the tip of the thumb) 300 mils. In estimating distance, one mil equals an angular distance of 1m (3.28ft) at 1000m (3281ft), 2m (6.56ft) at 2000m (6562ft) and so on.

grid co-ordinates method is far more typical. Here, the observer gives the FDC six- or eight-figure map co-ordinates for the target. Shift from a known point is somewhere between the other two methods. The observer gives the FDC distance, direction and vertical-shift target data from a known point, usually some prominent and permanent feature on the military maps.

Calculating distance, direction and vertical shift is a mixture of mathematical and estimation processes. Distance is first estimated by using known units of measurement, such as 100m (328ft) lengths. If the target is a vehicle and its actual measurements are known, a range calculation is made using the formula $R = W/m$, where R is range, W is width of object and m is mils. For example, if a tank has a known width of 7m (23ft) and it measures 3 mils above or below the known point (or the point of impact of a shell), the calculation is: $R = 7 \div 3 = 2.3 - 2300m$ (7546ft). More accurate ways of calculating distance are laser range-finders or the flash-to-bang technique. This latter technique works on the principle that sound travels at 350m/sec (1148ft/sec), whereas light arrives at the viewer almost instantaneously. The time elapse between an enemy gun flashing and the observer hearing its bang

▼ *US soldiers open fire with a 105mm (4in) M101A1 howitzer from a Fire Support Base (FSB) in South Vietnam. Almost all infantry manoeuvres in Vietnam were conducted with the on-call support of an FSB.*

▸ *To calculate the height of a feature in metres, the formula a/b x B = A is used (a = visual height on pencil in centimetres; b = distance between pencil and eye; B = distance to feature; A = height of object). To calculate the distance of a feature, move from a start position until the feature is at a 45 degree angle on the compass. A1 or A2 equals the distance to the object (B).*

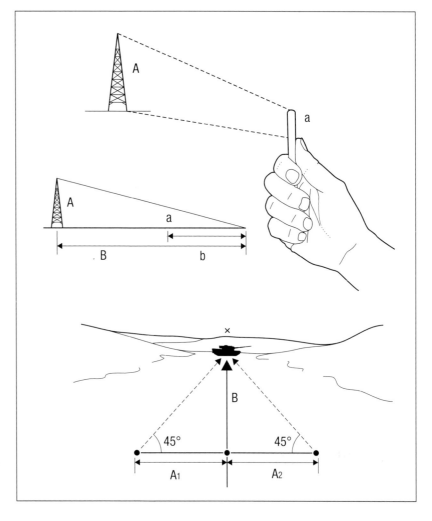

can be multiplied by 350 to obtain its distance from that observer.

Direction and vertical shift are easily quoted to the FDC using the mils measurement on binoculars, range-finding instruments or a clear mils protractor (see box feature). Vertical shift is only calculated if it appears to be a difference (up or down) of more than 30m (99ft) from the observer's position. The vertical shift is rounded up to the nearest 5m (16ft).

CALLING FIRE ONTO THE TARGET

For artillery fire to be effective, the observer must give full details about the target type so that correct ammunition and fire control can be selected. He needs to explain the shape and size of the target and the nature of the target. Shape and size fall into one of four basic categories. A point target is a single target less than 200m (656ft) wide, such as a small military unit or an individual group of vehicles. A linear target is one which is between 200m (656ft) and 600m (1969ft) long. Any longer than 600m (1969ft) and the target will have to be subdivided and allocated to more fire units. A rectangular target has both width and length in excess of 200m (656ft), and a circular target is either round in shape or has no distinct shape. A collection of these various target types can be gathered into one area and is known as a group of targets, or particular types of target, such as anti-aircraft positions, can be treated as a series of targets.

These categories describe the geographical space of a target. The observer must also describe the actual nature of the target, including the strength of forces, what activity the target is engaged in and what protective positions or vehicles are present. Crucially, the observer informs the FDC whether friendly units are close to the proposed impact area. He does this with the call sign 'danger close'. Recommended distances should be kept between forward units and impact areas. At least 600m (1969ft) is advised for mortar and artillery fire, and up to 2000m (6562ft) for the heaviest naval artillery.

Once the FO has all the target information at his fingertips, he is ready to make the request for fire. There are three types of fire mission that the observer can request. The first is 'Adjust fire'. This is the process of methodically adjusting the aim and impact point of the

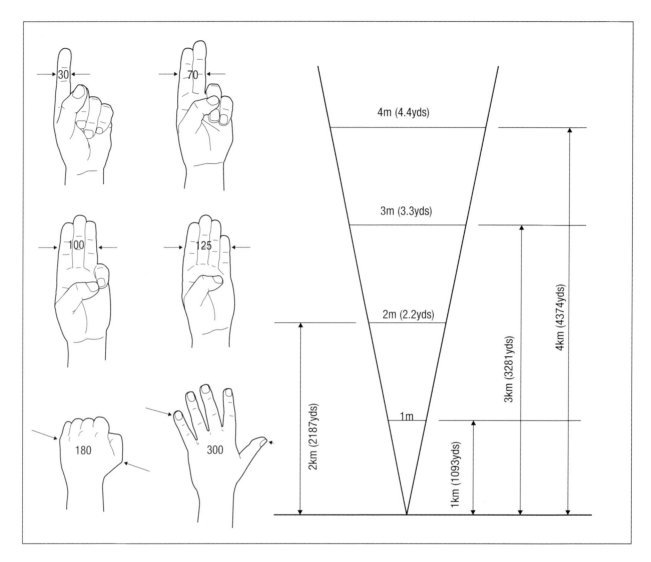

▲ *Using the hand to make mil measurements is sufficiently accurate to allow the observer to adjust observed fire onto a target. One mil equals an angular distance of about 1m (3.28ft) at 1km (0.6 miles), 2m (6ft) at 2km (1.2 miles) and so on.*

artillery to bring it onto target. The second is 'Fire for effect'. Here, the artillery is firing on target, and 'Fire for effect' tells them to open up with the full force of their firepower to destroy the target. Finally, 'Suppression', 'Immediate suppression' and 'Immediate smoke' are all commands to assault inactive enemy units in a pre-emptive role.

The transmission of the fire request to the FDC takes the following sequence:

• identification or authorization code, and the type of fire mission
• the location of the target
• the nature of the target and ammunition advice
• corrections to initial ranging shots.

A typical conversation between an observer and the FDC communications officer might appear as follows:

FO: GH424, this is AW122, adjust fire, over.
FDC: AW122, this is GH424, adjust fire, out.
FO: Grid 191501, over.
FDC: Grid 191501, out.
FO: Infantry platoon in light defensive positions. Two stationary BDRM vehicles.

ICM I/C, over.
FDC: Infantry platoon in light defensive positions. Two stationary BDRM vehicles. ICM I/C, out.
FDC: Bravo, two rounds, over.
FO: Bravo, two rounds, out.

The observer will watch where the initial shells land, then proceed to adjust them onto the target.

There is a range of further requests/commands that the

▾ *Desert environments are extremely hazardous for armoured vehicles that do not have superior air cover. The flat terrain and clear atmospherics makes them easily identifiable by radar, surveillance and vulnerable to strike aircraft.*

SOVIET ARTILLERY TACTICS – WORLD WAR II

The Soviet Union explored the capabilities of heavy artillery more than most other nations in World War II. Following the German invasion of Russia in 1941, Soviet forces found themselves outclassed by the manoeuvrability of German blitzkrieg tactics. However, by 1942–43, Soviet military industry was finally able to increase its output after the displacement of factories following the initial invasion, and thousands of high-quality artillery pieces began to reach the Soviet front line. Whereas the Germans used artillery in localized engagements, the Soviets opted for a mass-attrition strategy of using large numbers of guns centrally controlled. German forces were subjected to truly enormous barrages of heavy artillery shells and the rockets from BM-13 rocket launchers, with Soviet forces generally employing 200–300 artillery pieces to every 1km (0.62 miles) of front line. At Kursk alone, more than 20,000 artillery pieces were used. Although the Germans retained manoeuvring superiority for much of the war, the devastation imposed by such levels of artillery took an unsustainable toll on the German war machine.

observer may issue to control the pattern of fire more closely. (The following commands are those used in US terminology, but other nationalities use similar commands.) 'At my command' signals that the guns are not to fire until the observer gives the command 'Fire'. Prior to this, the fire control officer will have announced that the guns are ready and awaiting the fire order. 'Time on target' is a similar order, but in this case the observer requests a specific time for the barrage to begin. 'Repeat' signals that the observer wants the last action repeated, with either another shell sent over on the last co-ordinates or the last firing pattern repeated. 'Check firing' means halt the barrage. Finally, 'Cannot

observe' indicates that the observer has no visual contact with the target, while 'Correction' indicates that data previously given is incorrect and new data will be sent.

ADJUSTING FIRE

Fire is adjusted onto a target using a method called bracketing. If the first shell is, say, 200m (656ft) long (known as an 'over'), the observer adjusts the range down by double the error – 400m (1312ft), resulting in 200m (656ft) short. These first two shots form the bracket. The bracket distance is then continually subdivided until a 100m (328ft) bracket is split to provide an on-target impact. Once this is achieved, the order 'Fire-for-effect' is given to achieve destruction of the target.

▲ Iraqi vehicles litter the Baghdad road after an Allied air strike during the Gulf War (1990–91). The convoy was destroyed in a matter of hours with over 300 Iraqi troops killed.

Deviation (directional adjustment) begins by measuring the angle of deviation in mils, then estimating the range to the target and dividing it by 1000. If the range is more than 1000m (3281ft), the answer is rounded up or down to the nearest thousand (e.g. 3700 results in four) and if less than 1000m (3281ft), the answer is rounded to the nearest tenth (e.g. 750m results in 0.8). The range divided by 1000 is known as the on target (OT) factor. If the OT factor is multiplied by the deviation in mils,

▸ *A US pilot climbs into the cockpit of his A-10 ground-attack aircraft. In the Gulf War A-10s were responsible for the destruction of more than 1000 Iraqi tanks, 1200 artillery pieces and over 2000 military vehicles.*

the answer provides the deviation in metres. Therefore: 50 mils left x OT factor of 3 = 150m (492ft) left.

The final stage of adjusting fire comes when the fire-for-effect period has ended. The observer now reviews the state of the target and transmits the details back to the FDC. He notes the number of casualties, equipment destroyed, effect of munitions, etc. On the basis of the observer's evaluation, either more fire is called or the mission is terminated.

Modern technology is revolutionizing targeting and fire adjustment. Many observers now use GPS equipment, which provides exact co-ordinates of both the observer and the target. These co-ordinates are transmitted directly to the FDC and the guns themselves, which automatically calculate and make the adjustment to barrel elevation and direction. Using these systems, the first shell is often within 30m (98ft) of the target or closer, and first-round hit probability is high. Increasing the first-round hit ratio in turn raises the possibility of quick destruction of the target through an accurate surprise barrage.

CONTROLLING AN AIR STRIKE

Tactical close air support (CAS) is air power deployed in tactical support of ground forces. CAS can be used to suppress, neutralize or destroy enemy targets, and it usually occurs in close proximity to

friendly forces. Hence it needs rigorous control. There are two forms of request for CAS: planned and immediate.

PLANNED CLOSE AIR SUPPORT

Air strikes involve a complex chain of logistics and intelligence, so are best co-ordinated and planned well in advance of ground operations. Planned CAS is usually applied in the context of a large-scale combined forces operation including attack helicopters, artillery, armour and infantry. The best recent exam-

ple of this type of operation was the UN land offensive, Desert Storm, conducted during the 1991 Gulf War. Once Desert Storm was launched into Iraqi-occupied Kuwait, Allied attack helicopters and fixed-wing aircraft destroyed enemy armour, communications and troop concentrations in the path of the Allied advance (USAF A-10 aircraft, for example, destroyed 23 Iraqi tanks in one day alone). This interdiction severely limited the Iraqi forces' capability to respond to the land campaign.

CLOSE AIR SUPPORT – THE GULF WAR

The Gulf War (1990–91) saw the most extensive use of close air support (CAS) since World War II, 50 years earlier, and proved that air power could be decisive in assisting combined operations. The following are examples of actual CAS incidents:

• Iraqi forces had constructed oil-trench barriers in front of their positions as part of a defensive system in Kuwait. US Marine AV-8B ground-attack aircraft ignited these using 227kg (500lb) napalm bombs to remove the obstacle.

• Two AH-64 Apache and two OH-58 Kiowa helicopters engaged an Iraqi bunker complex on 20 February 1991. The bunkers were laser-designated by the Kiowas while the Apaches fired Hellfire missiles. Such was the violence of the attack that when a loudspeaker-fitted UH-60 helicopter invited survivors to surrender, 400 did so and were airlifted out by a CH-47 Chinook.

• A column of Iraqi tanks was spotted moving into counter-attack positions on 25 February 1991. USAF A-10A Warthogs were given free reign to attack them. Using AGM-65 Maverick anti-tank missiles and the potent GAU-8/A 30mm (1.18in) cannon firing uranium-depleted rounds, the A-10s destroyed eight Iraqi tanks during the first assault alone. Later, the A-10s directly engaged Iraqi tanks that were holding up UN ground troops outside Kuwait City. Fifteen more tanks were destroyed in two sorties, and the ground troops resumed their advance.

◄ *Ground personnel prepare to attach the guidance system to a GBU-24 laser-guided bomb (PGM) for loading on to an F-15 Eagle strike fighter. The Eagle conducted further strike missions over the former Yugoslavia (the Balkans).*

Planned CAS is usually determined up to 72 hours before the operation. The land forces will have a portion of air assets assigned to them, and a target list will be drawn up. Target lists will define the target type, location, the time it will be at that location (or will have moved from that location) and the level of destruction required. Targeting will make allowance for target mobility (such as in the case of mobile Scud missile launchers in the Gulf War) once the operation begins, and the aircraft may be assigned a hunter role over a particular area to track down mobile targets.

Planned CAS is the safest form of air support, as it allows ground forces full awareness of the air

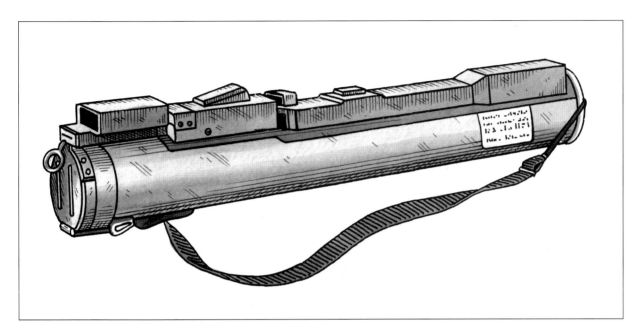

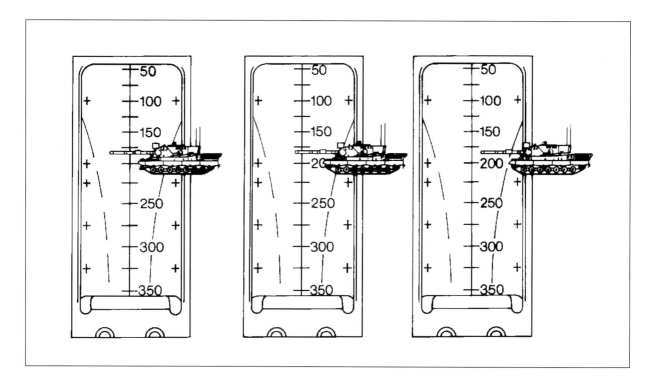

▲ The sight picture of an M72 LAW. The straight vertical line denotes the distance of the target in metres, while the curved vertical lines give the correct lead on the target: (from left to right) 5km/h (3mph), 10km/h (6mph) and 15km/h (9mph).

aim at, and, even if the side armour has been enhanced (as is common on modern tanks), a hit to the tracks will immobilize the vehicle. The rear of the vehicle usually contains the engine compartment. Anti-tank missiles can easily penetrate the light cooling grills over the engine. US doctrine (FM 3-23) states that there are three types of kill an anti-tank team can inflict. The first is a mobility kill, in which the suspension or engine is destroyed. The vehicle cannot move, but it can still return fire from its guns (if its turret remains under power). A firepower kill is when the weapons systems have

been hit, removing the tank's combat potential, but not preventing escape. Finally, there is the catastrophic kill, in which the vehicle's ammunition or fuel stores are hit, resulting in the complete annihilation of structure and crew.

FIRING POSITIONS AND PROCEDURES

When a tank is advancing with hatches shut, the crew will have a 90-degree sweep of vision to the front (the centre of the tank's front takes the 45-degree point). The remaining 270-degree angle that covers the sides and back of the tank offers the best directions for attack. The tank has almost complete visibility in this area when the turret is facing forward. If, however, the anti-tank unit is directly in front of a tank with hatches shut, it can take advantage of the fact that there is about 10m (33ft) of visual dead space in front of the tank.

Within this range, the tank crew will have no vision of the ground immediately before them, and the tank's main gun will not be able to engage targets under 20m (66ft) away – although coaxial machine guns may be able to depress their fire more.

Anti-tank weapons require sound firing positions to preserve the survivability of the crew. An anti-tank position has all the requirements of any other fighting position (see Section 4), such as cover and concealment, protection and open fields of fire; however, there are also some special needs. Firing an anti-tank missile creates a huge backblast of gas. The gas is dangerous to personnel and equipment, so no friendly troops must occupy positions directly behind the anti-tank crew for at least 30m (98ft). The gas also kicks up large amounts of dust and debris, which act as a marker for enemy response fire. There is little the squad can do to stop this marker, but its position should have covered routes of escape through which it can reposition once the weapon has been fired. Special considerations are also required if firing the weapon in an enclosed space such as a room (see Chapter Four, 'Urban Combat',).

The actual holding of the weapon is dictated by the fighting position and the firer's comfort. If standing, the firer needs to keep the weight evenly over both feet with both elbows tucked into the body, and he must make sure his body is behind some cover, such as a wall. The soldier can also fire on a bended knee, although he must swivel the foot of the kneeling leg as far beneath his bottom as possible to protect it from the rocket back blast. A sitting position gives greater stability than the kneeling position, as the legs can be braced out forward. The prone position should usually avoided because of the danger to the back and the legs from the back blast. If the prone position is used, the body should be positioned at a 90-degree angle to the direction of fire.

The firing process varies according to each weapon type, although there are some common procedures. First, the target vehicle's range and speed must be estimated. Range is calculated by either an automated range-finder, by measuring the distance on a map or by using estimation techniques (see 'Controlling Artillery' page 97). If the soldier does not know the range, engagement with an unguided missile should be limited to under 200m (656ft).

ANTI-TANK MISSILES IN THE YOM KIPPUR WAR

The Yom Kippur War was Egypt's attempt to recapture territory lost to Israel during the Six-Day War of 1967. It proved the first major tactical deployment of anti-tank weapons (ATWs) on an open battlefield, and it refined techniques for their future use worldwide. The war began on 6 October 1973, when Egypt launched a major offensive into Israeli-held Sinai, while Syrian forces attacked the Israeli salient of the Golan Heights in western Syria. Egyptian military planners knew that the excellent Israeli armoured units had to be defeated when they counter-attacked. Egypt had amassed more than 2000 tanks – compared with Israel's 1700 – but it had also equipped its infantry units with Soviet ATWs such as the RPG-7 and the AT-3 Sagger anti-tank guided missile (ATGM). The Egyptians crossed the Suez Canal and immediately set up a long and deep screen of ATWs. These helped repel more than 23 Israeli counter-attacks between 6 and 9 October, each containing more than a battalion of armour. The Israelis suffered terrible losses, including the almost total destruction of the 190th Armoured Brigade.

After 9 October, the Israelis made important tactical adjustments. Instead of sending in isolated sections of armour, they deployed entire armoured companies in tandem with copious numbers of infantry armed with machine guns and mortars. The infantry would pour heavy direct and indirect fire on any ATW position or area, and the saturation fire prohibited the Egyptian missile operators from having effective fields of fire and opportunities to aim. From 16 October, the Israelis also started to use US-supplied TOW ATGMs against Egyptian armour, to devastating effect. These combined measures contributed to the hideous defeat finally imposed upon the Arab forces, and they taught the military world much about the possibilities and limits of ATGM usage.

Ranging on the LAW 80 weapon is assisted by an integral 9mm (0.35in) pistol unit built into the rocket frame. This carries a seven-round magazine of tracer ammunition. The flight properties of the bullets are matched with those of the rocket itself, so the firer can shoot off the seven rounds to check his distance and aim before firing the main missile. Speed calculation is particularly crucial when using those weapons which do not have a guided flight. One technique commonly used is to observe the distance a vehicle travels in one second. As soon as the front end of the vehicle passes an object, the soldier counts 'one thousand and one'. If less than half the vehicle has passed the object at the end of the count, the vehicle is classed as slow moving; if more than half, the vehicle is fast moving. The sights on anti-tank weapons are graduated so that the firer can adjust his aiming point to allow for the travel distance of the vehicle during the time the missile is in flight.

Engagement of any enemy tank is usually performed by multiple missile launchers, as it is rare for one missile (particularly the lighter missiles such as the RPG and LAW) to disable totally or destroy a powerful main battle tank, although a

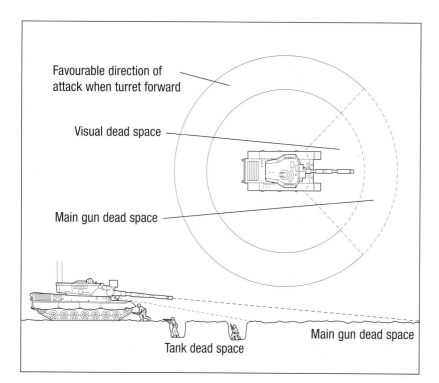

Favourable direction of attack when turret forward

Visual dead space

Main gun dead space

Tank dead space

Main gun dead space

◄ *With hatches closed and turret forward a tank crew cannot see targets closer than 10m (33ft) and cannot fire at targets under 20m (66ft) away. There is also a 270-degree sweep of blind space around the sides and back.*

single weapon can successfully engage an APC or truck. Most anti-tank units consist of several weapons teams who will co-ordinate firing with each other to destroy a single target. The unit has two main firing options: sequential fire or volley fire.

Sequential fire begins when one firer communicates range and speed information to the other firers, then engages the target with his anti-armour weapon. The other firers observe the impact of this first round, then proceed to fire in sequence, adjusting their aim and point of impact in relation to the previous firer. Volley firing differs in that each firer has his own calculation of range and speed, and all firers launch their missiles in a single volley. The volley is usually coordinated by an audible signal such as a whistle or command.

Once the team has either fired

all rounds or destroyed the target vehicle, they should instantly move from their positions. Enemy indirect fire from mortars and artillery is frequently directed against anti-tank teams if an enemy observer sights the back-blast signature.

ANTI-AIRCRAFT WEAPONS AND TACTICS

Attack aircraft are perhaps the single most dangerous weapon systems faced by ground troops. The danger has three main roots: the lethal nature of air-deployed munitions, the speed of attack and the range at which attack can be made.

Air-deployed munitions consist of bombs, missiles and cannon fire. Conventional bombs range from small 113kg (250lb) high-explosive munitions suitable for attacking exposed troops or soft-skinned vehicles, to the enormous BLU-82/D jellied-gasoline explosives

dropped in Vietnam and Afghanistan which incinerate everything within a 600m (1969ft) radius. The most typical bombs employed against ground forces will be free-fall, high-explosive bombs, precision-guided bombs and cluster bombs. Although free-fall weapons have limited accuracy, blast and shrapnel fatalities and injuries will be inflicted many metres from the impact point. Precision-guided bombs have an accuracy down to a few metres, guided onto their targets by either laser designators or television-aiming systems. In the Gulf War, these were used by UN air forces to knock out individual fighting positions, bunkers, armoured vehicles and enemy-occupied buildings while reducing collateral damage (though fewer than one in 10 bombs were precision-guided in the war).

A typical cluster bomb is the US 454kg (1000lb) CBU-87 Combined Effects Munition. This consists of a dispenser which holds 202 BLU-97/B bomblets, each weighing 1.5kg (3.31lb). Once blown from their dispenser over a target, the bomblets will scatter over a wide area, usually in the region of 244 x 122m (800 x 400ft) – the spread can be varied on the CBU-87. These bomblets will detonate on contact with the ground, detonate at a later time using a timer trigger or detonate when trodden on or disturbed. Cluster bombs are thus a powerful area-denial weapon against troop formations, and they have been used extensively in recent military operations in the Gulf, the Balkans and over Afghanistan.

Air-to-surface missiles tend to be used only against key targets such as armoured vehicles, communication installations, roads and bridges, airfields, etc. Anti-tank missiles are particularly sophisticated, and modern attack helicopters armed with these seriously

▾ A Multiple Launch Rocket System (MLRS) fires a salvo. Such rocket launchers are powerful area-denial weapons, especially when using M77 fragmentation-bomblet warheads.

threaten the survivability of main battle tanks. Ground units must operate communications and surveillance equipment sparingly in the presence of attack aircraft, as anti-radiation missiles can track down radar beams or target in on the source of radio transmissions. Missiles are rarely used against personnel only, apart from the 70mm (2.75in) rockets fired in a saturation effect from the rocket pods of attack helicopters. During the Vietnam War, US helicopters used these rockets in both direct- and indirect-fire modes to suppress Vietcong activity around US landing zones. Cannon fire is used primarily from attack-helicopter

platforms, which usually have better cannon-control systems than fixed-wing aircraft. Cannon weapons such as the Hughes Chain Gun will fire 30mm (1.18in) armour-piercing and high-explosive rounds at 754m/sec (2474ft/sec) and 650rpm. The effects against exposed personnel and soft-skinned or lightly armoured vehicles are devastating.

The lethality of air-launched munitions is enhanced by the capabilities of the platform. A modern fixed-wing military jet such as a McDonnell Douglas F-15/E Eagle has a speed at high altitude of Mach 2.5 and an attack speed at sea level of 1481km/h (920mph). It can

▲ During the Vietnam War, North Vietnam developed one of the most sophisticated SAM systems in the world. However, optically aimed heavy machine guns and cannon still accounted for well over 50 per cent of US aircraft downed.

engage ground targets at heights well over 4570m (15,000ft) and at distances of more than 3.2km (2 miles), depending on the munitions used. Helicopters fly much more slowly and at far lower altitudes, but their superior manoeuvrability and quieter noise signature mean that they can achieve great surprise over enemy troop positions. Munitions such as the Hellfire anti-tank missile can even be fired while the helicopter remains behind cover.

COUNTER-AIRCRAFT PROCEDURES

As strike-aircraft capabilities have improved, so have anti-aircraft weapons. The best anti-aircraft system is the fighter aircraft, but modern military units now have advanced surface-to-air missile (SAM) systems for engaging aircraft at any speed and altitude. Here, however, we will look at the short-range air-defence options available to most front-line combat units.

The first line of air defence is air-raid precaution. Troops on the ground should implement full camouflage and concealment measures to prevent them being spotted by enemy reconnaissance aircraft. Fighting positions should have camouflaged overhead cover consisting of logs covered with soil

and foliage. The soil provides some protection against blast, cannon fire and shrapnel, and the foliage obscures the position to aerial reconnaissance. Troops constructing the fighting positions should avoid creating patterns in cut foliage that, although inconspicuous on the ground, may be very visible from the air. Full communications security must be observed at all times (see Chapter Five, 'Unit Tactics'), as enemy ground units can use triangulation systems to locate the source of a transmission and relay the co-ordinates to an attack aircraft via a fire control centre.

If a unit is actually attacked by an aircraft, its members should follow three lines of response. First, the command is given for the unit to disperse as widely as possible to scatter the target available to the strike aircraft. Personnel and vehicles will fan out and widen the distance between themselves and other key targets. Second, each soldier and vehicle must find cover if it has not been pre-prepared. Overhead cover is very desirable, as many aircraft bombs are set to detonate above the ground and spray shrapnel downwards upon the troops below. Vehicles are less likely to find overhead cover. Instead, they should be placed under large trees (foliage degrades many forms of aerial target-acquisition systems), against slopes or steep ground, or in depressions. The final act of air defence is engaging the enemy aircraft with fire.

ENGAGING ENEMY AIRCRAFT

Ground units which are not armed with sophisticated SAM technologies operate under clear guidelines as to when they will engage an enemy aircraft. First, and not to be overlooked, the ground troops must positively identify the aircraft as an enemy aircraft. This is not always easy, as distance, altitude, atmospheric conditions and light levels limit the possibilities for visual identification. An aid to identification is if friendly aircraft or anti-aircraft facilities fire on the aircraft, as they will usually have automatic systems of friend-or-foe identification. If the aircraft is

▸ *A SAM hits a drone target during a night-firing exercise. Modern SAM systems are being redesigned to cope with more unmanned threats such as ballistic missiles, unmanned aerial vehicles (UAVs), cruise missiles and rockets.*

identified as hostile, it may be engaged if it is within range and is approaching in an attack movement such as a rapid dive down onto the unit or a low, fast approach from behind cover. If friendly aircraft are in the area, however, fire may be withheld in case stray rounds hit them.

The three main weapons systems available to regular ground

forces are small arms, heavy cannon and shoulder-launched missile systems. Small arms that are viable for air defence are automatic assault rifles and machine guns. Submachine guns are excluded from this list because their pistol-calibre rounds rarely have the range for engaging even low-flying aircraft. Machine guns such as the Browning .50 M2HB and the

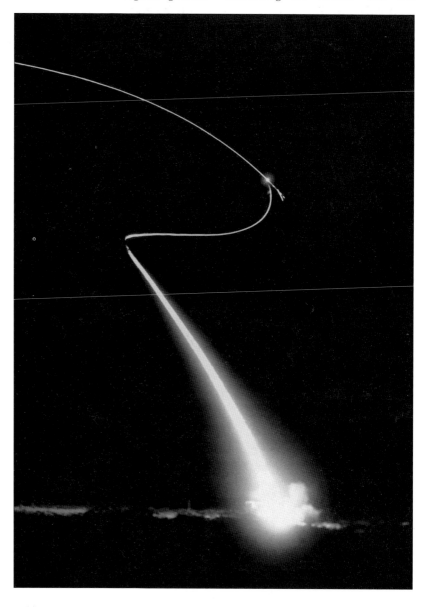

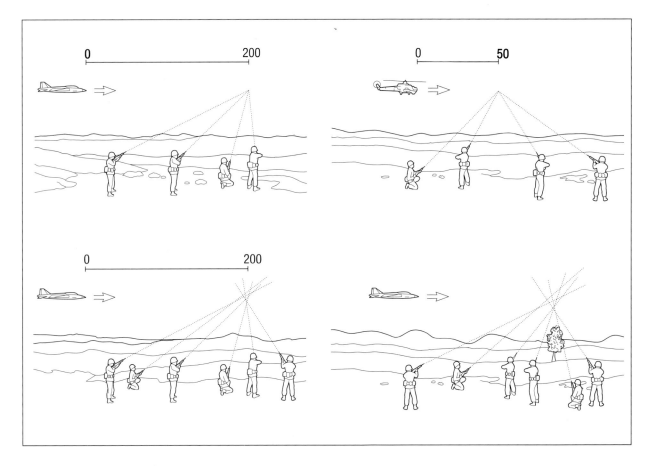

▲ *Shooting down military aircraft with small arms involves creating a 'patch' of fire in the sky through which the aircraft flies. The lead varies with the aircraft's speed – 200m (656ft) for jet aircraft and 50m (152ft) for helicopters. The fire is co-ordinated above a prominent geographical feature to assist aiming.*

▼ *One technique for judging aircraft distance is to align the thumb with the aircraft. In the case of a MiG 21, if the thumb covers the aircraft from the cockpit to the beginning of the tailplane the aircraft is 350m (1148ft) away.*

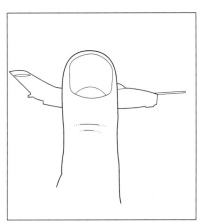

7.62mm (3.0in) GPMG extend engagement range out to 1000m (3281ft), but assault rifles are rarely effective for flying targets more than 500m (1640ft) away. Many modern fighters and helicopters also have heavy armour and will be fairly impervious to 5.56mm (0.22in) rounds. In such cases, heavy machine guns must be the main tool of engagement.

To bring an aircraft down with small-arms fire involves saturating the air space through which the aircraft will fly with hails of bul-

lets. The speed of aircraft means that aiming directly at them will result in a miss – by the time the bullets have flown to the aircraft's initial position, the aircraft has moved. If a fixed-wing jet aircraft is flying across the unit's positions, heavy automatic fire is directed into the airspace about 200m (656ft) in front of it. The unit can co-ordinate its fire more accurately by shooting at a point directly above some recognizable object on the ground. The fire is poured into this space until the aircraft flies right through it, usually resulting in several hits or a kill. When the aircraft is a helicopter, the point of aim will be about 50m (164ft) in front of the nose to allow for its much slower air speed. Should an aircraft be diving directly onto the unit, the point of fire is just above the aircraft's nose, as it will fly into this point as it pulls out of the dive.

It is extremely difficult to bring down a modern fighter or helicopter with small-arms fire alone. Heavy cannon, usually of 20–40mm (0.79–1.57in) calibre, will provide a much greater possibility of destroying the aircraft because of the explosive power of the projectiles. The 40mm (1.57in) Bofors weapon, for example, revolutionized Allied medium-range anti-aircraft capabilities in World War II by firing 40mm (1.57in) shells accurately to an effective ceiling of 7200m (23,622ft) at 120rpm. Batteries of Bofors protected everything from Allied shipping to artillery bases, and they created a very hostile environment for German fighters, ground-attack aircraft and bombers. Range with cannons extends out to 8000m (26,247ft), and they are usually mounted on vehicular or other rigid platforms to give greater stability and accuracy during firing. Targeting ranges from a simple optical sight at its most basic through to fully automated radar systems which feed range, altitude and speed information to a computerized fire control system.

Man-portable air defence systems (MANPADS) forms the cutting edge of short–medium range air defence. MANPADS include

NORTH VIETNAMESE AIR DEFENCES – VIETNAM WAR

One of the most advanced anti-aircraft systems ever employed was that of North Vietnam against US bombing missions during the Vietnam War. Heavy US bombing of North Vietnam began in 1965 with operation Rolling Thunder, and it would continue sporadically until 1975. At first North Vietnam's only anti-aircraft systems were small arms and Soviet-made M38/39 37mm (1.45in) cannons. Although basic, the sheer weight of fire put up from these weapons was highly dangerous to US attack aircraft, particularly during low-level attacks. In fact, of 3000 US aircraft downed in the Vietnam War, 80 per cent were shot down by anti-aircraft artillery. The US response was to raise the operational altitude to 4572m (15,000ft), but from 1967 the North Vietnamese were supplied with Soviet SA-2 Guideline SAMs, which could reach up to 21,031m (69,000ft). The SA-2 was guided to its target by ground-based Fan Song radar. The usual tactic was to fire one SA-2 to bring the aircraft down to a lower altitude through evasive action, then fire a salvo of the missiles to destroy the aircraft.

US countermeasures included silver-foil strips jettisoned into the air to confuse the guidance radar, radar-jamming signals transmitted by Douglas EB-66 Destroyer aircraft and AGM 45A Shrike anti-radar missiles deployed by SA-2–hunting F-4 Wild Weasel aircraft. These countermeasures made the battle more equal, but North Vietnam remained a very dangerous place for US aircraft throughout the war.

the British Blowpipe, the Swedish RBS 70, the Russian SA7 Grail and the US Stinger. In the Gulf War, the venerable SA7 killed US F-16s, A-10s and Harriers, and it is still operated by many countries. The Stinger is one of the most widely used US models, and it is typical of the MANPADS' capability. During the 10-year Soviet occupation of Afghanistan between 1979 and 1989, US-supplied Stingers enabled the Afghan Mujahideen guerrillas to down Soviet assault helicopters and severely restrict the operational freedom of Soviet air traffic.

A Stinger is composed of a guided missile, a fibreglass launcher tube and a gripstock/trigger assembly. Some Stingers are also fitted with Interrogation Friend or Foe (IFF) computers. When the Stinger operator spies what he thinks is an enemy aircraft, he targets it through an optical sight and sends out an IFF signal. If there is no response, the aircraft is classed as hostile. He activates the guidance system and tracks the aircraft until an audible acquisition tone is heard. At this point, he presses the trigger and the missile is launched, guiding itself to the target through tracking the infrared/ultraviolet radiation emitted by the enemy aircraft.

MANPADS extend the range of air defence out to around 5km (3 miles), and they are highly effective in trained hands. As with anti-tank missiles, however, there is a large back blast from MANPADS which requires personnel to give

49m (160ft) of clearance behind the weapon. The MANPADS operator must also move from his position once he has fired, as the dust kicked up from the back blast will act as a locator for enemy ground forces and other attack aircraft.

WORKING WITH ATTACK VEHICLES

Infantry and armour exist in a relationship of mutual support. Infantry assist the safe movement of armour by engaging enemy anti-tank missile units and removing anti-tank obstacles such as mines, and they also help designate enemy targets for the tank's main weapon. Conversely, armoured forces sup-port infantry by destroying enemy tanks, bunkers and weapons at extended ranges, and also by acting as a protective vanguard for soldiers moving into open terrain. Armoured support is divided into two categories: heavy armour (tanks) and light armour.

MAIN BATTLE TANK OPERATIONS

Main battle tanks (MBTs) are the most powerful armoured vehicles. The summit of the worldwide MBT technology is currently the US M1A2 Abrams. It weighs more than 57,900kg (57 tons), is armed with a 120mm (4.72in) Rheinmetall smoothbore gun which can engage targets over 4000m (13,120ft) away, features armour which can defeat all but the most powerful anti-tank rounds, and operates on a gas-turbine engine which produces 1500bhp. Abrams tanks decimated the Soviet-era T-54, T-62 and T-72 tanks of the Iraqi Army during the Gulf War, using their advanced target acquisition systems to engage them at ranges well beyond the opposing tanks' capabilities. (In total, 3847 Iraqi tanks were destroyed in the war by Allied armour and aircraft.) The capabilities of this tank and its like are utilized to:

• outmanoeuvre and destroy enemy armour and vehicles, fortified positions, personnel
• suppress enemy direct and indirect fire
• work as security and protection for infantry manoeuvres
• secure terrain
• act as a visual deterrent to enemy forces/civilian uprisings;
• conduct armed reconnaissance missions
• operate in nuclear, biological or chemical (NBC) environments if properly equipped
• ford obstacles up to 1.2m (4ft) deep.

Although powerful, the MBT has many limitations. Tanks are vulnerable to infantry-deployed anti-tank weapons, particularly in restricted manoeuvre terrain such as streets

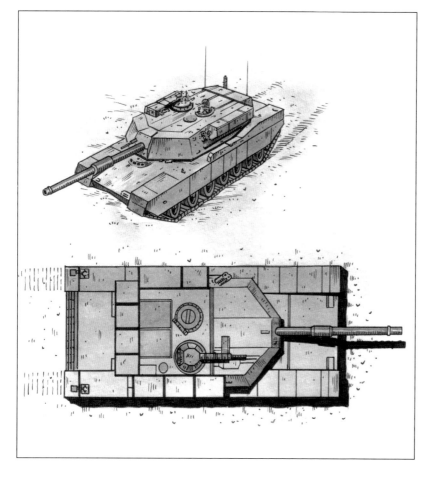

◄ *The US M1 Abrams tank is the current state-of-the-art Main Battle Tank. It is armed with 1 x 105mm (4in) smoothbore gun, 1 x 7.62mm (.3in) coaxial machine-gun, 1 x 12.7mm (.5in) machine-gun (turret) and 2 x 6 smoke-grenade dischargers.*

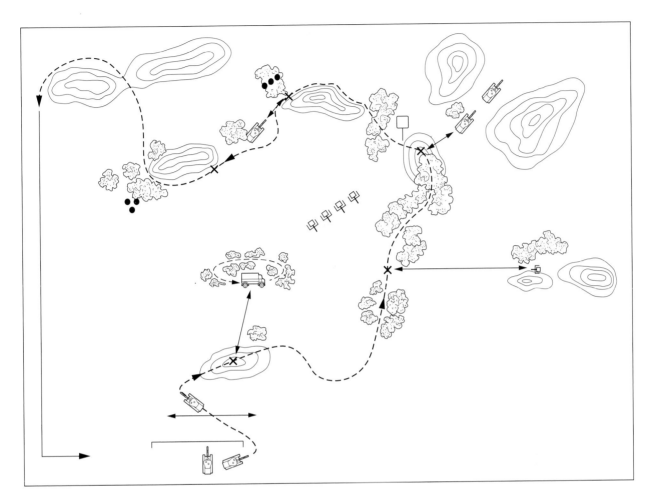

▲ A typical tank commander's test route. Instructors will look for a commander who can switch between offence and defence, while intelligently negotiating the terrain. The arrows off the main route represent engagement points.

or heavily wooded areas. Ground-attack aircraft will easily destroy tanks unless air superiority is secured. The massive weight of an MBT makes them unsuitable for crossing soft or shifting ground, and they are very expensive to transport to the battlefield from a distant location. Tanks are a prodigious drain on logistics, particularly on fuel supplies. As a result of these factors, without infantry support, MBTs have little ability actually to hold ground.

The last point is one of the most important. Infantry in many ways ensure the viability of MBTs as weapons of war. Infantry-to-tank co-operation must therefore be very efficient. Unlike many other support weapons, tanks usually operate with direct radio contact to the infantry units in their immediate vicinity. This enables the infantry to designate targets to the tank without delay. Prior to any operation, infantry and tank communications operators must make sure that they have compatible equipment and agreed protocols for transmission. They will also agree on other forms of battlefield communications such as semaphore and pyrotechnics.

On the battlefield, the infantry units have to appreciate the mode of operation used by MBTs. Like infantry units, tank platoons (usually consisting of four tanks) move in the travelling, travelling overwatch, and bounding overwatch manoeuvres (see Chapter 6, 'Specialist Skills'). They will also adopt wedge, column, file and line formations (also see Chapter Six). Cover and concealment are difficult to find for MBTs, but they

▲ Armour is at its most vulnerable when operating in urban terrain. Light top armour is exposed to explosives and anti-tank missiles, and anti-tank teams are able to deploy their weapons at close ranges while remaining behind cover.

should make maximum use of large overhead terrain features such as hills and of recessed features such as dry river beds as more secure routes of movement.

In combat roles, tanks should be positioned so that they can utilize their main armament. Coaxial machine guns tend to have a range out to around 900m (2953ft), whereas main gun armament can engage at 4000m (13,123ft) – although 2500m (8202ft) is the usual range of firing. If the tanks are armed with tube-launched, optically tracked, wire-guided

(TOW) missiles, they can engage up to 3500m (11,483ft).

Tank units must operate proper fire control if they are to achieve maximum effect from their weaponry and not endanger surrounding infantry. The objective of all tank commanders is to acquire target first and shoot first – in other words, before the enemy. Rather than carrying out a single firing, the unit will attempt to deliver a mass of fire from multiple tanks to maximize the initial destructive effect and limit the enemy's capacity to respond. The target that poses the greatest threat – say, another enemy tank – must be neutralized first. Finally, the tank should adopt a firing position that presents the least visible target for enemy anti-tank forces. Ideally, this should be the hull-down position, with the hull of

the tank being hidden behind earthworks and only the turret visible.

While tanks are in action, surrounding infantry should deploy all available weaponry on enemy troops, tanks and anti-armour teams. Using their own anti-armour weapons creates a multi-dimensional hostility for enemy tanks, while small-arms fire will inhibit enemy troop manoeuvres. By working in co-operation, armour and infantry can achieve battlefield supremacy even over an enemy with a numerical advantage.

LIGHT ARMOUR OPERATIONS
Light armoured vehicles can perform many of the roles of MBTs, with the exception of engaging other MBTs. They can, however, conduct additional duties such as reconnaissance, troop transportation and

anti-aircraft duties. Light armour may be wheeled or tracked, but it all tends to have far greater manoeuvrability and speed than a MBT. Weapon systems fitted to light armoured vehicles include automatic cannon, ATGM pods, SAM pods and even small-calibre guns. A typical light armoured system is the Italian Dardo IFV. This is a tracked vehicle with a maximum speed of 70km/h (43mph), a 520bhp engine and an armament profile of one 25mm (0.98in) cannon, one 7.62mm (3.0in) machine gun, two TOW launchers and two lots of three smoke grenade launchers.

Light armour operates in very close co-operation with infantry units. Its lightness allows it to be transported and deployed very easily. Hence it tends to be found at the front line of rapid-reaction forces or at the head of contingency operations. The capabilities of light armour are to:

• increase the suppressive, neutralizing and destructive firepower available to frontline infantry units
• provide more manoeuvre options in mobile warfare situations
• transport infantry to or around the battlefield in relative safety from small arms and machine gun fire or shrapnel burst (in the case armoured personnel carriers – APCs)

▶ *Fast-Attack Vehicles (FAVs) were first used by Special Forces teams during the Gulf War. The FAVs had powerful on-board weaponry and high mobility, but limited range qualified their success in the desert expanses.*

• destroy enemy positions and forces using ambush or manoeuvre tactics
• assist heavier armour in counter ATGM teams
• provide versatile reconnaissance-in-force platforms.

Most of the limitations of light armour revolve around its relative lack of protection against any weaponry more powerful than machine guns. Cannon fire, anti-tank mines and ATGMs can knock out a light armoured vehicle easily, and even hand grenades can disable them.

To increase survivability, light armoured vehicles are only assigned to operations in which they can maximize their mobility and speed. Restrictive environments such as streets and dense woodland are not suitable, while fairly open terrain with patches of concealment is best.

When in an offensive mode, light armour will resist making the frontal attacks of an MBT, instead preferring to attack from the enemy's rear or the flanks. Infantry units must be deployed around the armour, and ATGM teams can engage enemy MBTs that would seek to destroy the lighter vehicles. Indeed, a traditional role of light armour has been to distract enemy tanks from armoured or ATGM threats and lead them into killing zones.

Light armour is rarely set up in static fire positions as MBTs commonly are. Instead, it is fired while moving or only during brief pauses between movements. As the firepower of light armour is limited, multiple vehicles will usually co-ordinate their weapons together to enhance the effect. Typical targets for light armour are enemy bunkers, soft-skinned vehicles and fighting positions.

CHAPTER FOUR

EXTREME TERRAIN COMBAT

Modern armies have to be able to adapt to all environmental conditions. International deployments have become so regular that a soldier may easily find himself operating within several extreme environments in a single year. Military training programs in professional armies now incorporate advanced instruction in jungle, mountain, desert, arctic and amphibious warfare. Urban areas are also classed as extreme-terrain environments, more for reasons of tactical confusion than problems of climate. All extreme terrains place heavy burdens on logistics, manoeuvring, surveillance, equipment and combat tactics.

◄ *A US Marine patrol searches a jungle trail during operations around Fort Howard, Panama. Note the direction of the weapons – each patrol member takes responsibility for a specific field-of-fire, each field-of-fire adding up to 360 degrees cover.*

The need for soldiers to be adept at fighting in all the world's environments was brought to the fore more than ever during World War II. Before then, crusading and colonial powers such as the United Kingdom, France, Portugal and Spain had indeed been obliged to fight far abroad in difficult landscapes. The British had fought in Africa, India, Afghanistan and the Middle East; the French in French Indochina; the Portuguese in Africa. In World War I, armies battled in the full spectrum of temperate-zone conditions, as well as in the arctic winters of Russia and the tropical heats of the southern Mediterranean and Middle East. These conflicts, however, were often conducted with a psychological disregard for the environment, the product of a widespread belief that simple fortitude was sufficient to defy the elements.

When some troops of the 2nd Welsh Fusiliers were allowed a few days' relief from the appalling mud-locked trenches of the Western Front in October 1917, the medical officer wrote unsympathetically that the action was 'to gratify some mawkish humanitarianism'. Today, it would be seen as necessary R&R. Similarly, the Royal Navy had written truly excellent amphibious-warfare doctrine in the first decades of the twentieth century. In the landings at Gallipoli in 1915, however, officers who celebrated the public school notion of the 'way of the amateur' predictably ignored the doctrine. Consequently, the invasion force became pinned down on the beaches, and the British and Australian forces withdrew nine months after landing with 250,000 casualties.

The change in World War II occurred for several reasons, but principally because adverse terrain could not be avoided. Military campaigns are usually conducted in places where the geography does not hinder tactical movement; indeed, this principle applied to the majority of actions in World War II. The truly global nature of the war, however, meant that many military campaigns were drawn into deeply inhospitable locations. For example, the British Army alone, between 1942 and 1945, operated in the temperate zones of northern Europe, the mountainous regions of Italy and Greece, the deserts of North Africa and the Middle East, and the tropical jungles of Southeast Asia. US forces were engaged in similar environments, as well as in the Pacific Islands. The best example of extreme climatic effects is the German campaign in Russia. Once Operation Taifun had failed to take Moscow during the late summer of 1941, the German Army found itself devastated first by the mud of the autumn (the rasputitsa, or 'roadless period'), then by the Russian winter, losing an estimated 100,000 men to the climate during the first winter alone. Following

◀ *A soldier operating in extreme terrain must have the tools and skills for personal survival, his equipment must be properly adapted for the conditions, and he requires the back-up of efficient logistics to cope with the increased burdens.*

incinerate sections of jungle up to 600m (1969ft) in diameter, killing large numbers of enemy troops and removing cover and concealment. In two major US operations in 1967 (Thayer II and Pershing), more than 140,000 artillery shells and 1,130,000kg (2,500,000lb) of air-dropped explosives were used against Vietcong/NVA positions in Binh Dinh province.

These techniques of fire may seem very crude, but jungle warfare tends to rely on attrition rather than tactical outmanoeuvring and the capture of key terrain. US Army Field Manual 90-5 asserts that jungle warfare means 'orientation...on the enemy rather than on the terrain'. The fact remains that most formations will lose their integrity when passing through the jungle. Military doctrine thus emphasizes innovation and assertiveness on the part of leaders and trains them to respond independently and aggressively to any situation.

During offensive operations, the offensive unit should gather against the enemy positions and build up a heavy concentration of small-arms firepower. This is then bolstered by calling in all indirect-fire support means available. (Note: The use of fire support may require that the unit partially withdraw from the impact zone. This is done by a series of reverse bounding overwatch manoeuvres – one unit covering while another withdraws, then swapping roles.) CS gas also has an application in jungle combat, as it moves efficiently through the foliage and puts the enemy at a physical disadvantage (tear-filled eyes, aggravated breathing, etc.) when the attack begins. Once the enemy position or area has been

VIETCONG/NVA JUNGLE TACTICS – VIETNAM

Between 1965 and 1969, the official US land-war strategy in Vietnam was search and destroy (S&D). This was a tactic of pure attrition. US units were tasked with tracking down and killing as many communist troops and guerrillas as possible, the plan being that the communist cause would not be able to sustain the enormous losses in manpower and equipment. In 1966 alone, it is estimated that 50,000 VC/NVA were killed. The problem for the communists was the awesome display of weaponry used by the United States and ARVN (which was US-supplied). A typical US combat patrol would have M16 rifles, M60 machine guns, M79 grenade launchers, Claymore mines and C4 plastic explosive, plus artillery fire and air strikes as indirect-fire resources.

The communists could not compete with the US firepower and so initiated a tactic of keeping very close to US troops in combat. By staying within a few hundred metres of the enemy, the communists disallowed their use of heavy indirect fire and were able to inflict more casualties during an engagement. (This was actually the same tactic as the Soviet forces used to defeat the Germans at Stalingrad in 1943.) The jungle undergrowth meant that close distances could be maintained while remaining unobserved by the enemy. Search and destroy still inflicted heavy casualties on the communists, but the death toll among US troops became politically unsustainable.

saturated in fire, the unit closes the distance through fire-and-manoeuvre movements using whatever squads have freedom of movement and reasonable fields of fire. In jungle terrain, the advancing unit will not extend itself far from the covering unit, to avoid disappearing ahead into the foliage and losing the value of the covering fire.

If possible, some elements of the unit should try to hook behind the enemy to cut off avenues of escape and launch counter-ambushes. The complete destruction of the enemy is a priority in jungle operations, as any that escape will return to fight at a later

time. Pursuit of the enemy is warranted as long as the unit is not drawn out of the range of indirect fire and if the unit leaders have reconnaissance or intelligence information about the area into which they are heading. Air-mobile forces are best used for pursuit, as they can be airlifted into advance positions ahead of the enemy, where ambushes can be planned.

Once an area is secured, it is thoroughly searched for booby traps, hidden snipers, underground tunnel systems and any valuable documentation. In Vietnam, Vietcong supply dumps would be found close to the combat area, so all searches would be widened beyond apparent positions.

Defensive actions in jungle terrain require the construction of special fighting positions. Any jungle position must have a 360-degree defence capability, as attack can come from any side. Usually, a major defensive base consists of multiple fighting positions surrounded by a booby-trapped perimeter wire. The wire should be beyond hand-grenade throwing distance from the nearest fighting position. The fighting positions should have interlocking fields of fire, and machine guns, grenade launchers and mortars must be able to fire at any point around the perimeter within moments of being engaged. Communications bunkers are set in the middle of the base to protect the unit's ability to call in indirect fire in the case of attack.

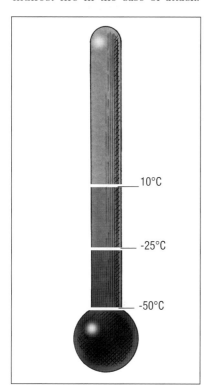

Machine guns and mortars are pre-aimed towards likely routes of enemy attack, such as streambeds, road junctions, jungle clearings and tree lines.

During an attack, an enemy will usually attempt to breach perimeter security and surveillance, and penetrate into the interior of the base. Night-vision scopes are used to give occupying soldiers an advantage at night, the commonest time for infiltration and attempts at sabotage. Defensive fire should be restrained until as many enemy are exposed as possible, as firing too early will allow more of them to escape or plan responses from the security of the surrounding jungle. If the enemy does penetrate the interior of the base, a counter-attack should be launched immediately to repel them.

SUBZERO OPERATIONS

In terms of actual tactical manoeuvres, operations in subzero climates and landscapes are little different from operations in any other climate. The effects that freezing temperatures have on men and equipment, however, mean that subzero operations are some of the most complicated and dangerous.

Any subzero operation must plan for the following range of environmental challenges. Still-air temperatures will be exceptionally cold, pushed even lower by

◄ Operating burdens in arctic conditions increase with every decrease in temperature. Below -12.2°C (10°F) the number of personnel required to complete a task will approximately double, and more than treble below -31.7°C (-25°F).

extreme wind chill factor in exposed locations (a temperature of -14°C/6.8°F, for example, becomes -34°C/ -29.2°F in a 32km/h/20mph wind). Visibility in snowy areas can be very poor because of wind-blown snow, blizzards and fog. The terrain in subarctic and arctic regions is often desolate, unsheltered and largely uninhabited, and the distances which a unit might have to traverse to contact with the enemy can be vast. Deep snow impairs efficient movement of both men and vehicles, and communications are degraded by interference from climatic conditions.

PERSONNEL PROTECTION

A soldier in subzero environments has to combat several threats to health and performance. Frostbite and hypothermia are the most dangerous adversaries to emerge out of the extreme cold. A wind chill temperature of -65°C (-85°F) will flash-freeze unprotected human tissue in 30 seconds alone, and it induces unconsciousness in a poorly dressed person in a couple of hours. Water obstacles litter freezing climates, and immersion in freezing water will result in unconsciousness in seven minutes, and death in about 15 minutes. Subzero temperatures also cloud mental acuity and impair decision-making. Fatigue affects soldiers more acutely when they are working under subzero conditions, as environmental pressures complicate even the most minor tasks, and walking is arduous through deep snow or across ice. For this reason, units operating in subzero climates will dedicate five men to a job that would require only three in a temperate climate.

▲ *US Marines conduct a patrol at the Mountain Warfare Training Center, Bridgeport, California. They wear snow shoes to aid movement and white snow suits for camouflage. The ski sticks serve to relieve pressure off the legs in deep snow.*

The soldier's primary protection against these threats is his uniform. Most modern military combat uniforms follow the layering principle: the soldier wears multiple layers of clothing, each with differing protective properties and each trapping a layer of still air which is then warmed by the body and acts as insulation for the wearer. Layering gives the soldier a flexible approach to temperature control, as he can remove or put on layers according to need. A typical uniform (such as a British Army Combat System 95 uniform) consists of a base layer of thermal underclothes, a cotton T-shirt, a combat jacket, a fleece layer and finally a waterproof and windproof outer layer usually made of Gore-Tex or similar 'breathable' material.

Peripheral items of clothing are a woollen hat and gloves. In arctic conditions, white camouflage overalls will sometimes accompany a uniform.

Unit leaders must enforce strict uniform discipline in subzero conditions. A soldier should never remove warm headgear, as 60 per cent of body heat is lost through the head. Woollen hats and balaclavas also protect the ears, which are especially vulnerable to frostbite. Waterproofs need to be put on whenever there is precipitation,

even if the soldier feels warm – wet clothing combined with wind chill hastens hypothermia. Gloves are requisite to protect the fingers against frostbite and also to stop skin being torn off after sticking to metal equipment. Boots must be dried out at least once a day and wet socks exchanged for dry ones twice a day – these measures help prevent trench foot or frostbitten toes.

EFFECTS ON EQUIPMENT

The strength and resilience of most manufactured materials are degraded by subzero conditions; this in turn has a major impact on military equipment. Metals become brittle and prone to fracture in freezing conditions, and strength is reduced by 50 per cent in temperatures of -29°C (-20°F) or below. Any metal

part that sustains shock impact – such as weapon bolts, shock absorbers and pistons on vehicles, and mortar base plates – can be shattered in action if appropriate measures are not taken.

Rubber is similarly affected. The colder the temperatures, the less flexible rubber becomes; below -29°C (-20°F), rubber will actually become brittle if exposed to these temperatures for long periods. Rubber-covered cables can snap, and tyres suffer from weakened side walls. Tyres are also affected in that cold temperatures lower the PSI pressure by as much as 40 per cent, resulting in tyres slipping off or blowing out. British military doctrine recommends that, in winter operations, tyres should contain 10 PSI more pressure than in the normal range of temperature.

▲ *Vehicles require special maintenance to keep running in subzero conditions. Rubber becomes brittle below -29°C (-20°F) so tyres need to be kept out of the snow as much as possible. Here the truck is parked on platforms of branches.*

Vehicles are among the most severely affected equipment in winter conditions. Some fuels and lubricants are prone to freezing or increased viscosity if not properly treated, and, in severe winter climates, vehicles will have a heavy fuel consumption from increased idling time, which places a further burden on logistics. Vehicle and general-purpose batteries have reduced power output in subzero temperatures. A truck battery at -40°C (-40°F) will have almost no power output whatsoever, and a battery needs to be warmed to 1.7°C

(35°F) before it can be recharged.

A well-trained unit will have measures in place to combat all these problems, although the effort required is a drain on physical and logistical resources. Time allowances for maintenance need to be about five times those of normal conditions. Soldiers have to wear mittens or gloves at all times, which makes engineering projects time-consuming. All machinery must be thawed out and warmed up before maintenance. This can be done in either purpose-built shelters or by using military heaters designed for winter use. Heated shelters are the best option, as without them the hours spent on maintenance can be 200 per cent more than usual. The best maintenance shelter is a properly heated building; however, if this is not available, a heated tent with wood flooring will suffice. Maintenance crews need to ensure that there is proper ventilation to avoid carbon monoxide poisoning when running engines. Engineers also need increased supplies of batteries to support maintenance activities because of the reduced power output from batteries in these temperatures.

Vehicles in subzero conditions should be left idle for a longer time to keep moving parts warm and mobile. Tarpaulins are placed over engine blocks to protect them from frost when the engine is not running, and integral engine heaters are fitted, if possible, to keep the battery permanently warm. Parking vehicles' wheels on platforms of planks or branches protects tyres, as this keeps them out of the freezing snow. All lubricants and anti-freezes must be of arctic specification. Should vehicles need to be towed or winched, the weight capacity stated on the winch should be reduced by 25 per cent to allow for the effect of cold on the metal cable.

A combat soldier needs to pay special attention to the maintenance of weaponry. Small arms are badly affected by cold because the hardened metal used in their manufacture becomes very brittle at extremely low temperatures. Sears, operating rods, firing pins and bolt lugs can shatter upon firing. Plastic handles are vulnerable to cracking. Stoppages are also common, as lubricants thicken in the cold or ice freezes moving parts. The soldier

◀ *A US Marine uses his ski sticks as a bipod for his M16A2 rifle and 40mm (1.6in) M203 grenade launcher. He is issued with special arctic gloves which allow him to operate his weapon without the danger of cold burns from touching freezing metal.*

WINTER DEFEAT – GERMAN OPERATIONS IN RUSSIA 1941–42

The German attempt to conquer Russia in 1941 was effectively halted by the Russian winter of 1941–42. Between 22 June and late November 1941, German forces advanced to within 100km (62 miles) of the gates of Moscow. Although Hitler had made some ill-advised redeployments of Panzer and infantry strength to other sectors of the Eastern Front, it still appeared that the German Army would take the capital by Christmas. Once the political and communications centre of the Soviet Union was taken, it was believed that the rest of the Soviet Union would soon fall. On 4 December 1941, however, the Russian winter began in earnest, with an initial temperature of -34°C (-29°F), dropping lower as winter progressed. The winter devastated the German advance, killing thousands of inappropriately dressed soldiers and totally disabling machinery and vehicles. With the winter climate favouring the conditioned Soviet forces, Moscow was saved from capture, and, many would argue, the war turned against Hitler. Some of the specific effects that stopped the German advance were as follows:

• German uniforms were summer-issue at the start of winter and offered no wind-chill or waterproofing protection. The German leather jackboot cracked open under severe cold, while the hobnails on the sole drew body heat out of the soldiers' feet, resulting in frostbitten and amputated toes.

• German vehicle lubricants were not suitable for arctic conditions. They froze and solidified engines. The only way to keep engines working was to idle them, but this overstretched German fuel supplies and logistics.

• German workhorses suffered from respiratory failure from breathing in ice particles which gathered around their nostrils.

• Fighting positions could not be dug into the frozen ground.

• Spring thaws of snow turned roads into muddy quagmires and further delayed operations.

◀ *Russian troops fight in Rostov-on-Don during the first winter of the German–Soviet war, November 1941. The Soviets generally used crude tactics when compared to German forces, but their handling of the subzero climate was far superior.*

▶ *Mountain troops have to adapt operations to high altitudes. Altitudes above 5000m (15,243ft) can induce altitude sickness unless the soldier has had a period of up to three days of acclimatization.*

should keep his weapon as free from ice and snow as possible, and a cover should protect it when not in use. When firing the weapon, the first few bursts should be kept short to allow the gun to warm up. More spare parts than usual should be carried in case of malfunction, particularly in the case of machine guns. When changing a barrel, the soldier should not lay the hot barrel in the snow, as it will warp as it rapidly cools. It may also be lost in the snow. If the soldier takes the weapon into a warm shelter after being outside, condensation will build up on the metal. This can freeze when the gun is taken back outside. Ideally, the soldier should keep his weapon in a protective cover when entering a shelter and then take the weapon gradually back down to the outside temperature before operations.

Heavier weapons are equally affected by severe cold. Mortars experience problems with their recoil systems and base plates. When a mortar fires, much of the shock is transferred into the ground through the base plate. In winter conditions, frozen ground can be as hard as concrete, so the mortar's base plate and recoil system, already weakened by the cold, take all the impact of firing. Base plates will also slip easily on the icy ground, affecting the weapon's accuracy and even making the weapon collapse (this usually occurs when the elevation is below 900 mils). Secure cushioning placed beneath base plates, such as sandbags (full of sand or snow) or a platform of branches, can protect them. Coating the bottom of the base plate with oil also prevents it sticking to the frozen ground.

Artillery suffers similar problems to mortars. The powerful recoil of an artillery weapon may send it skating across frozen ground if it is not properly secured. US Army doctrine states that 'the choices for firing surfaces should be muskeg, gravel, frozen ground, and ice, in that order' (FM 9-207). The correct lubricants must also be applied, otherwise hand wheels and adjustment mechanisms can freeze up and prohibit rapid-fire response.

With any support weapon, soldiers must take special care not to breathe on optical sights, as the resulting condensation will freeze over the sights. This is particularly critical in the case of anti-tank missiles, some of which rely on line-of-sight guidance through the optical sight.

MOUNTAIN WARFARE

Mountain warfare presents a special range of challenges for tactical planners. Leaders must face these problems by implementing innovative tactics and efficient logistics:

• Visibility is either limited or confusing, particularly when looking upwards at high-altitude ground. Targets appear to be further away than they are when looking up a slope, and nearer than they are when looking down.

• The most convenient routes of travel – ridges, mountain passes and roads, and valleys – are often the most exposed and vulnerable to ambush and fire.

• High altitudes sap the energy of soldiers, make breathing laboured and cloud thought processes. They can even produce fatalities from altitude sickness.

• Weather conditions up mountains can be harsh. A drop in temperature 1.5°C (3–6°F) accompanies every 300m (984ft) increase in elevation. At high altitudes, the climate is often permanently below freezing with extreme wind speeds.

• Undulating terrain makes it difficult to maintain formation integrity.

▼ *Being indigenous to an area of extreme terrain is the best training for combat in that environment. Here, Afghan Mujahedeen warriors adopt craggy firing positions during actions against the Soviets between 1979 and 1989.*

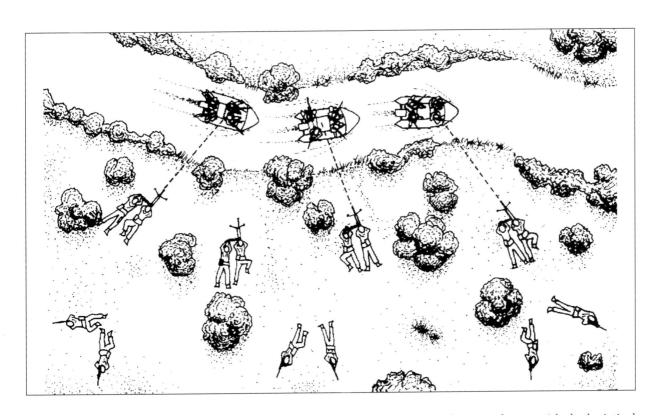

▲ Riverine patrols are most vulnerable to ambushes from the bank. Here a Special Forces team launch an attack on a three-boat patrol, while other troops provide rear and flank security in case of an enemy land-based response.

AMPHIBIOUS OPERATIONS

Amphibious operations range from putting a four-man surveillance team ashore to landing an entire army across a major section of coastline. Whatever the scale, they are some of the most tactically complex operations of all, as they require unusually heavy logistical backup. Most offensive amphibious missions are divided into seven stages:

- planning and preparation
- embarkation
- movement to amphibious objective area
- pre-landing operations
- ship-to-shore movement
- assault
- consolidation.

PLANNING AND PREPARATION

Planning is possibly the most complex stage of an amphibious operation, as it involves co-ordinating multiple arms-of-service into a unitary battle plan. All available reconnaissance of the objective needs to be assimilated. First, a landing site is chosen. This must be conducive to amphibious landings, with open offshore navigation and no adverse sea conditions (such as very strong crosscurrents). There should also be a relatively steep gradient of shoreline (shallower beaches increase the risk of ships grounding themselves before landing), and it must be big enough to deploy all the assault

forces and cope with the logistical follow-up.

Prior reconnaissance should identify all enemy strong points and weapons emplacements at any landing site, especially those weapons that might threaten the offshore shipping and the assault team during the ship-to-shore movement. These positions will usually be suppressed by aerial and naval bombardment prior to landing.

Once the landing area has been chosen and defined, the enormous job of logistical planning begins. Amphibious logistics are co-ordinated between army, navy and air force units. Between them, they ensure that the assault team reaches its destination with a full logistical support that can be maintained in the days and weeks after landing. Once the logistics are finalized, it remains to set the time and

date. Landings are generally timed to coincide with the good weather that facilitates easy movement of shipping and air support, and also with low levels of enemy activity at the landing area. Night landings achieve greater tactical surprise, but also make amphibious actions more unpredictable. Dawn and dusk are the most common landing times.

EMBARKATION

Embarkation consists of gathering the men and equipment for the forthcoming operation and loading them onto the shipping that will take them to the amphibious objective area. This is not simply a matter of putting everything on board before setting sail. In US Marines operations in the Pacific in World War II, it was found that the order in which material is loaded onto shipping dramatically affects the operation at the other end. Ammunition and combat gear are always the last to go on, as they will be the first off. Drinking water occupies a similar place. All equipment must unpack logically on the beachhead without swamping the area and making it uncontrollable for the beachmaster.

▲ *US soldiers row to shore during a riverine training exercise. Once ashore the boat is collapsed and hidden for later exfiltration. Most small-unit amphibious deployments take place under the cover of darkness.*

MOVEMENT TO AMPHIBIOUS OBJECTIVE AREA

The transit period of an amphibious operation is a dangerous stage of the mission. Enemy naval and air forces will usually attempt to interdict the amphibious task force (ATF) before it even reaches its assault position. The chief dangers in modern combat are anti-shipping missiles and sea mines launched by enemy air-craft and shipping, and the under-water threat from submarines (although few nations around the world have highly developed sub-marine fleets). The ATF chooses the least hazardous route. It sticks to open sea as long as possible, stay-ing away from coastlines which will contain enemy reconnaissance and possibly anti-ship weaponry. The open sea also allows the force to disperse in a wide formation with plenty of space between each ship in case of attack.

Most ATFs are very heavily pro-tected during the transit period.

▼ A beach reconnaissance. The soldiers' duties include: measure the gradient of the beach (A); make a record of the surf patterns (B); provide security for the boat and team (C); and survey, plot and photograph the features of the beach (D).

Destroyers protect against enemy shipping and submarines, while accompanying aircraft carriers offer localized air supremacy. Combat ships will be dispersed among the largely unprotected logistics ships. The entire convoy will be protected by long-range surveillance systems such as over-the-horizon radar and circling airborne early warning air-craft (AWAC). Should the ATF be engaged, it will retaliate ferocious-ly while staying on course for its amphibious objective.

As amphibious operations require advanced planning, the weakening of the enemy will begin weeks before the transit period. As a result, most ATFs should have reasonable uncontested transit periods. Far more dangerous is the period of settlement after the land-ings, in which the enemy has more time to plan offensive strikes.

Many of the British ships lost to Argentine aircraft during the Falklands War were lost during this period.

PRE-LANDING OPERATIONS

Before an assault team goes into action, the landing zone is pre-pared to give the assault the best chance of success. The most com-mon type of preparation is a sup-pressive barrage to destroy enemy positions. The run up to the Normandy landings saw Allied bombers drop nearly 80,000 tonnes (79,000 tons) of explosives onto key logistical targets around west-ern France, smashing the road and rail networks that could be used to reinforce a German counter-attack. On the invasion day itself, the Allied naval forces pummelled the enemy coastal positions with heavy barrages of large-calibre shells and

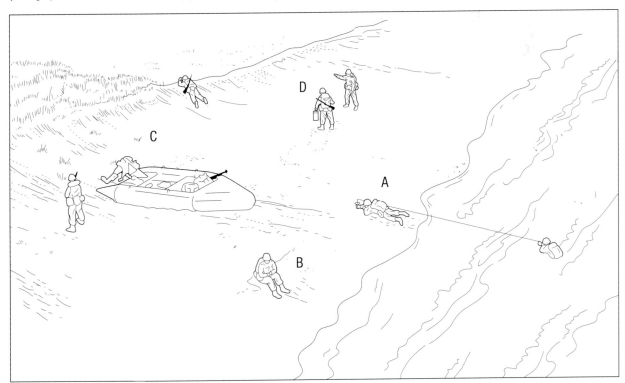

batteries of rocket fire. US Marine operations in the Pacific also used massive firepower to smash the enemy shoreline. On its own, however, firepower direct against coastal targets from the offshore shipping has a limited tactical effect. Japanese forces on the island of Okinawa, for example, moved inland away from the US pre-landing bombardment as a deliberate tactical choice to maintain unit strength, and waited for US forces in the more defendable interior.

Many other types of pre-landing operations are used. Deception

▾ Amphibious warfare is used less for large-scale operations today because of the risks of high casualties to the landing parties from shore resistance, and to civilians from pre-landing bombardments.

is invaluable for distracting the enemy away from the true landing zone. Prior to the Inchon landings in Korea in 1950, US divers deliberately left reconnaissance equipment at a location away from the actual landing zone to deceive enemy forces about UN intentions. Deception may also be achieved through launching an alternative landing or operation elsewhere in the enemy sector. Special forces can be deployed to assault enemy positions away from the landing area, or large-scale parachute drops away from the coastline can draw enemy forces into the interior. Another pre-landing operation is psychological warfare directed against the coastal defenders. By bombarding the defenders with radio or leaflet messages that undermine morale, it is hoped that coastal resistance will be less committed.

Pre-landing operations also include the clearance of obstacles around the landing area. These are usually underwater traps for the assault craft (either mines or metal beams designed to tear open ship hulls) and anti-personnel/anti-tank mines or vehicle traps on the beach itself. Covert teams are deployed prior to the operation either to destroy the obstacles or, more usually, map them so that the assault team can avoid them.

SHIP-TO-SHORE MOVEMENT

During this stage of the operation, the assault team is transported from the main group of shipping to the landing area. It is done by purpose-designed landing craft, including amphibious vehicles, or helicopters despatched from aircraft carriers. The departure will begin from a pre-designated assembly area close to

the shoreline, and the ship-to-shore movement will be covered all the way by supporting fire. It should be noted that, particularly in modern Marine doctrine, the ship-to-shore concept is frequently replaced by a ship-to-objective concept. In this case, the force deployed will aim to move straight from the landing zone to the inland objective area without waiting for a logistical build-up on the beach. Ship-to-objective manoeuvres maintain a fast operational tempo, but require high degrees of self-sufficiency from the assault forces.

ASSAULT

The first objective of the assault team is to gain a lodgement on the beach. Heavy firepower is directed against enemy positions, and the assault units begin fire-and-manoeuvre movements up the landing area. Enemy fortified positions are individually assaulted and destroyed, and onshore obstacles cleared. A section of the landing zone is cleared, sufficient to allow reinforcements and combat logistics to secure a beachhead and support continuing operations. This beachhead is widened and filled as more enemy positions fall. Meanwhile, air power and long-range naval weapons engage enemy positions well behind the landing zone to prevent the build-up of enemy reinforcements.

Once the beach is secured, the assault team either proceeds to its inland objectives or allows others to take over the mission. Casualties are evacuated from the beach to first-aid ships offshore.

CONSOLIDATION

Consolidation is essential to the success of an amphibious opera-

---

THE INCHON LANDINGS

The amphibious landings at the port of Inchon, Korea, in 1950 were a bold operation by UN forces to open an offensive 322km (200 miles) behind enemy lines. The operation was exceptionally difficult. There were actually only four days in the month in which the assault could be made. Outside of these days, the depth of water inside the port – 9m (30ft) – gave insufficient clearance for the draft of the landing craft at 8.8m (29ft). There was no beach – the assault had to go straight into the heart of the city of Inchon. The approach into the port was so narrow that, if one ship were sunk, it would block the passage of all following. The main amphibious force arrived on 14 September. Navy and air-force ground-attack aircraft and heavy naval gunfire pounded enemy positions for nearly two days, destroying most

effective defence. The initial assault went in at 0615 hours on the morning of 15 September. A battalion of the 5th Marines took Wolmi-do, a heavily defended island that dominated the harbour, with the cost of only 17 wounded. The assault against the port itself commenced in the early evening. The Marine unit had only three hours in which to secure the landing zone before the tide dropped and beached its landing craft. Yet the only serious resistance was navigational problems caused by drifting smoke from the bombardment area. Troops quickly landed and entered the city and, by 0130 hours on 16 September, the landing had been consolidated and all objectives completed. Owing to the sheer surprise of the attack, only 20 soldiers were killed out of an attacking force of 70,000 UN troops.

---

tion. A landing is usually followed by a large-scale enemy counter-attack if the enemy has available forces. This will attempt to smash the beachhead, destroy enemy forces and prevent any further logistical build-up. Logistical support and reinforcements are therefore poured onto the beach area as quickly as possible. Vehicular means must also be off-loaded to transport the supplies from the beach area to the forward troop positions. Simultaneously, the offshore shipping must receive logistics from re-supply ships to maintain their tempo of operation.

Effective consolidation manoeuvres result in the beachhead being transformed into a secure

operating base for inland forces and a focal point for expansion into the interior of the country.

DESERT COMBAT

Deserts are high-mobility environments for warfare. Although there are physical obstacles in deserts, such as salt marshes and massive sand dunes, generally the terrain offers excellent prospects for cross-country vehicular movement. Tactical manoeuvres in deserts are not complicated by factors such as the large-scale presence of civilian populations, and surveillance platforms usually enjoy good environmental conditions. Attack aircraft utilize the clear skies to make precision strikes against

enemy positions, and the enemy is often easily spotted because of the lack of natural cover in flat desert areas. Tactical advantage in desert operations is usually held by those armies which can exercise fast mobility, deploy powerful long-range firepower through theatre-wide surveillance and can maintain the logistics necessary to operate across the vast distances of desert terrain. These were the elements which secured the Allied victory over Iraqi forces during Operation Desert Storm in 1991. Iraq suffered an estimated 350,000 dead, while the Allies suffered

only a few hundred because they possessed far superior combat technology. Their target acquisition systems and long-range munitions were ideally suited to the clear desert expanses, while surveillance aircraft and satellites had the unobstructed views to observe every Iraqi tactical manoeuvre well before it reached Allied positions. Compare this operation with the disappointing results of US air strikes against Serbian targets in Kosovo, where inclement weather and dense foliage meant that more than 70 per cent of attacks were unsuccessful or inaccurate.

▲ *The SAS Bravo Two Zero team. During their infamous Gulf War reconnaissance operation into Iraq, three died, four were captured, and one managed to escape to the Syrian border across nearly 300km (186 miles) of desert.*

While open manoeuvre is assisted by the desert climate, there are many environmental and tactical problems that accompany operations in arid regions. Human performance is severely constrained by the extreme desert temperatures. Tactical planners must lengthen operational time frames to make allowance for reduced endurance and performance among personnel through heat-induced fatigue. Heat exhaustion and dehydration afflict many soldiers during operations or periods of manual labour. Water consumption needs to be kept high – about 13.5 litres (3 gallons) per day for a labouring soldier – and this multiplied by battalion or divisional strength places a huge burden on logistics. Soldiers should remain covered at all times to reduce dehydration (clothing soaked in perspiration reduces the rate of fluid evaporation from the skin) and severe sunburn. The head and back of the neck must always be protected to prevent sunstroke. Eyes can become painful because of the reflective glare of the sun off shiny surfaces and sand, and cataracts are a danger to those experiencing long-term

exposure. Sunglasses or other protective eyewear will prevent these conditions, and they also help avoid conjunctivitis caused by the ingress of sand and dust particles into the eyes.

US military theory uses the acronym 'OCOKA' to denote the main considerations behind tactical employment in desert regions. OCOKA stands for:

- observation and fields of fire
- cover and concealment
- obstacles
- key terrain
- avenues of approach.

OBSERVATION AND FIELDS OF FIRE
Unless a sandstorm or heavy rains prevail, observation in the desert is usually clear and unhindered. Long-range visibility is particularly

excellent and permits maximum-range engagement with heavy weaponry. The thinness of desert air also assists the accurate and sustained flight of shells and bullets by offering less air resistance and drag. Long-range visibility can, however, be a problem. Studies show that intuitive range estimation in the desert is often inaccurate; long-range targets are often judged to be closer than they are and close-range targets to be further away. This problem is complicated when heat haze rises from the desert floor. The heat haze distorts

▾ *Desert camouflage is especially reliant upon sand-coloured netting and desert uniforms. Overhead cover is particularly important because reconnaissance aircraft usually have excellent visibility over desert terrain.*

the optical line, a phenomenon known as refraction.

Refraction only occurs in very hot climates when there are clear skies, flat terrain and wind speeds under 16km/h (10mph) during the day and less than 6km/h (4mph) at night. In engagements beyond 1500m (4920ft), refraction causes the target to appear lower than it is during the day and higher than it is during the night. Refraction will even affect laser range-finders and corroborate false range estimations. The best way to avoid refraction is to occupy elevated firing positions at least 10m (33ft) above the ground. Otherwise, adjusting the point of aim up or down (day or night, respectively) by half the height of the target should provide an accurate ranging shot. Further measures to assist accurate long-range firing include keeping the sun behind the firer to reduce glare

and shadowing over optical sights and firing slightly long on the first shot to stop the target being hidden behind clouds of dust created by the first exploding shell.

COVER AND CONCEALMENT

Apart from rocky areas, deserts provide few natural locations for good cover and concealment. Vehicles are very exposed. The dust kicked up by their wheels and tracks creates a visual marker which can be seen for many miles, and glare off metal and glass is perceptible at a distance of 20km (12 miles). Noise carries extremely easily over desert terrain, so both troops and vehicles must operate under strict noise control measures, turning engines off when not needed and keeping conversation to a minimum. Some offensive surprise can be retained if vehicles are operated at night and their paint

schemes changed to match the terrain. Desert-camouflage uniforms and covers are also provided to front-line combat soldiers. A conventional fighting position covered with a sand-coloured and sand-covered sheet will be hard to spot from both ground and aerial observation platforms.

OBSTACLES

The main natural obstacles in a desert are sand dunes, steep terrain, salt marshes and sandstorms. Sand dunes can reach hundreds of metres high and many kilometres long. They consist of nothing more than loose sand and so provide

▼ *A desert fighting position. Cross-beams placed over the hole allow the soldier to build up overhead cover and concealment. A thick layer of sand combined with the wooden boards will be enough to stop shrapnel from air-burst munitions.*

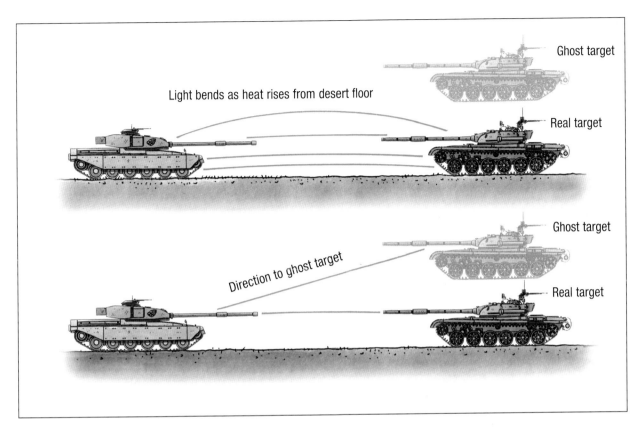

Ghost target

Light bends as heat rises from desert floor

Real target

Ghost target

Direction to ghost target

Real target

▲ At ranges of more than 1500m (4573ft) in the desert, light is bent by heat rising from the desert floor, creating a ghost target. The gunner is consequently likely to aim at the ghost image rather than the real target.

very poor traction to wheels, tracks and human legs. Steep terrain includes mountains, hills, escarpments and dunes. Some slopes are easily surmounted, but those which are littered with loose rock or consist of crumbly soil should be avoided by vehicles and large units of soldiers. Salt marshes are dry lake beds which, during the dry season, have a crusty surface which appears solid, but actually has moist soil beneath. They can be crossed on foot, but vehicles will usually break through the crust

and become stuck in the soil beneath. Sand storms result from storm–hurricane force winds, which whip up vast clouds of sand. The atmospheric sand is so dense it inhibits breathing, chokes vehicle engines and buries materials. Operations must cease in a sandstorm. Soldiers should move into protective environments or at least lay on their sides with their backs to the wind direction. Vehicle engines and air intakes should be covered with tarpaulin.

KEY TERRAIN

Key terrain is any piece of terrain that has tactical significance. In the desert, this usually means high ground, mountain passes, watercourses or places of human occupation. The distances between key ter-

rain in the desert are predictably vast, which in turn makes the key terrain much more important. Military units should make the acquisition, consolidation and protection of key terrain the priority of any offensive or defensive manoeuvre.

AVENUES OF APPROACH

The term avenues of approach (AoA) refers to the routes of manoeuvre in deserts. In rocky or mountainous desert areas, AoA is defined by passes and ridgelines, but in most desert areas the terrain is so open that commanders are faced with endless possibilities for manoeuvre. In World War II, the battles between the Allies and the Axis in the Western Deserts were ones of intense mobility. The biggest problem for both sides was

often maintaining the logistical train to back up the necessary manoeuvres. Indeed, most of the logistical movement was confined to a single coastal road, and this restricted the battlefields to the north of Libya and Egypt. One severe limit of desert manoeuvres is fuel consumption. Motorized units often have to cover vast distances to objectives, so fuel logistics must be a top priority for tactical planners.

Excellent visibility in desert areas enables the enemy to track most offensive manoeuvres against them very easily, especially through radar technology. Multiple lines of attack are the best tactical procedure, throwing the enemy into confusion and dispersing his

forces widely across the terrain. Once dispersed, long-range weaponry can be brought to bear against individual targets, while foot soldiers close the distance. The tactic of Desert Storm was to sweep multiple armoured forces 'deep and long' around the flanks of enemy forces, overwhelming them with multi-point attacks.

URBAN WARFARE

Combat in an urban environment is a complex and stressful tactical scenario. Buildings and other man-made features not only prohibit soldiers having clear fields of fire and surveillance, but also offer a defensive enemy multiple secure firing positions. Fire is as likely to come from above as from ground level.

▲ *Sherman tanks occupy a ruined town square during the push through German-occupied Europe, 1944. In urban areas the lightly armoured Sherman was very exposed to close-range attacks by shoulder-launched Panzerfaust weapons.*

An individual building may have several floors and numerous rooms to clear, and this will impair swift and coherent unit movement through it and around it. Large numbers of civilians may require humanitarian assistance and limit firing positions and options. Smoke and dust create severe obscuration problems, and a soldier's marksmanship is severely tested by having to shoot at oblique angles around corners and at ranges from point-blank to maximum.

▶ *Urban terrain turns most soldiers into snipers. The effective range of a standard issue assault rifle such as the M16A2, about 400m (1219ft), is more than enough to command the close-range spaces of urban combat.*

OFFENSIVE ACTIONS IN URBAN TERRAIN

The most dangerous movement in urban combat is that between positions, when soldiers are exposed to sniper and automatic fire and are clearly framed within streets and against buildings. To reduce the risks, units should make full use of the terrain. Towns and cities offer many protective structures for cover and concealment, including sewers and basements (for underground movement), large buildings, piles of rubble, abandoned vehicles, through the interior of structures and across rooftops. When choosing cover, the soldier should ensure that it is out of the enemy's arc of fire and physically resistant to machine gun rounds and proximate mortar/artillery blasts. While crossing danger areas, one group of soldiers should lay down suppressive fire on enemy positions, while another group crosses the area at speed in rushes of three to five seconds duration between pieces of cover. The roles are then reversed to bring the covering unit across. Moving at night provides a safer option for travelling, although this is counterbalanced by the fact that the enemy itself is more difficult to spot. Night-time engagements also carry a higher risk of fratricide.

A moving soldier should keep himself pressed against the walls of buildings, as this presents a more confusing angle of fire to enemy snipers, although he must be aware

of attacks coming from the windows and doors he passes. He should duck under windows and move quickly past open doors. In very hostile areas, a quick burst of automatic fire around the corner of an open doorway into the interior should precede the crossing.

The urban battlefield's physical structure affects weapons usage. A standard 5.56mm (0.22in) round from an assault rifle such as an M16 will only penetrate light cover such as wooden or plaster walls, but will be arrested by more substantial masonry or brickwork. Automatic rifle fire has a much greater utility at close ranges, such as when clearing buildings, but the soldier needs to exercise fire discipline to avoid quickly depleting his ammunition (the rifle should be set to three-round-burst if it has that option). Sniping duties can be performed with a regular assault rifle because of the shorter ranges involved in urban combat.

Machine guns are mainly used for suppressive fire in urban combat, as they offer advanced penetrative power. A 12.7mm (.50in) Browning M2HB and a 7.62mm (0.3in) general-purpose machine gun, for example, will smash through brickwork and stone structures within the space of a three- to four-second burst. Elevating a machine gun on either a vehicular platform or from a building gives it a much greater range of suppres-

sive options, as at ground level it has less upward angle of fire and more bullets are deflected by low-lying rubble.

Grenades are one of the most useful weapons in urban combat, and they are used for neutralizing enemy forces within enclosed spaces such as rooms and alleyways. They are usually thrown through doorways and windows just prior to entering a building. A modern fragmentation grenade will have a lethal radius of around 15m (49ft), ample for most room clearance operations. Grenade launchers combine the power of hand-grenades with a safer distance of employment. An M203 40mm (1.57in) grenade launcher

can hit a point target (such as a window) at up to 125m (410ft) and an area target at 350m (1148ft). Anti-armour grenades are used to penetrate walls and other substantial structures. Rifle grenades should not be used at ranges of less than 30m (98ft).

Anti-tank weapons have several applications in urban combat. When engaging armour, the basic rule is that the higher the position, the more likelihood of a destructive

▼ *Urban combat requires three levels of terrain awareness: underground, street level and elevated positions. Underground passageways provide the most secure routes for movement, but elevated positions give the best fields of fire.*

hit. Firing from a 45-degree angle doubles the chances of hitting a vehicle compared to shooting at ground level, and the angle also enables the weapon to be used against thinner top armour on tanks and armoured personnel carriers (APCs).

Apart from destroying vehicles, anti-tank weapons can be used against fortified structures. They can penetrate up to 1.2m (4ft) of reinforced concrete (based on data from a tube-launched, optically

▼ In urban combat, armour is only viable with extensive infantry support. While the armour demolishes enemy strongholds, the infantry protect the armour against tank-killing enemy units and weaponry.

tracked, wire-guided, or TOW, weapon). This capability is useful for breaching walls, but often a number of shots are required before an entire wall will come down, and this may not be possible because of ammunition limitations. For this reason alone, wall breaching is generally left to heavier weaponry. Anti-tank weapons can be used, however, to neutralize enemy personnel within confined areas. If enemy troops are positioned in a room, the missile should be fired into a point about 15cm (6in) either side of a firing aperture (such as a window). This target area allows most of the blast to be directed into the interior of the room while propelling mason-

ry fragments as a form of shrapnel.

The biggest problem with anti-tank weapons in urban contexts is back blast. If they are fired in a small, enclosed room, the operator would probably suffer serious injury through the effect of the rearward gas jet expanding inside the room. In addition, the explosive force of the gas may bring down a fragile structure. For a LAW rocket, a minimum masonry structure of 3 x 6m (10 x 20ft) is necessary, with 2m^2 (21.5ft^2) of open ventilation to the rear (an open door will work). At the top end of the scale, a TOW weapon requires a space 6 x 10m (20 x 33ft) and the same ventilation. All ceilings should be 2.1m (7ft) high (data

from US Army FM 90-10). The room should also have all inflammable materials removed (heavy sofas are left to soften the sound of firing), and personnel should wear helmets and earplugs.

CLEARING A BUILDING

Clearing a building held by enemy troops begins with effective fire support. Suppressive fire from all available sources should be poured onto the occupied building and any other occupied buildings adjacent to it. Ideally, a variety of fire support will be available, including, at minimum, grenade launchers, at least one heavy machine gun and a squad of infantry armed with assault rifles and light machine guns.

Every soldier in the support role will be designated a certain area or aperture of the building to cover. These are usually windows, firing holes knocked in the walls, and emplacements. Snipers should be used to intimidate the occupants through precision kills. Anti-tank missiles will demolish light structures (such as locked doors) and clear the way for the entry of the assault team. Mortars and artillery can pour fire down on the roof of the building to create overhead attrition.

Under the cover of the suppressive fire, the assault team moves into positions around the flanks and rear of the building – although, if surrounding buildings are enemy-occupied, a frontal assault may be necessary. Each member or group

within the assault team is designated a particular point of entry. These are typically breached walls, as doors and windows tend to be booby-trapped. Once the assault is under way, the support fire is concentrated on the upper floors and artillery/mortar fire is ceased. Each assault team should throw a grenade through the entry point, allow it to detonate, then enter the building with heavy automatic fire.

Then begins room-by-room clearance. Two-man teams usually

▼ *Cover in urban terrain should provide maximum obscuration of the soldier's body, but maximum fields of fire. Like archer's fire-holes in medieval castles, the cover should not obstruct the wide angling of the weapon.*

carry this out. One soldier shoots open a door and throws in a grenade (this is thrown in hard to bounce off the walls and make it harder to pick up and throw back). Once the grenade goes off, he enters the room with bursts of automatic fire, then takes up an overwatch position inside the room while his comrade enters with more firepower. Together, they clear the room. If possible, the next room along should be cleared by blowing a hole in the connecting wall and entering through that hole in the same manner – the variation of technique confuses the enemy.

Access to the upper floors is treacherous in urban combat. Hand grenades can be dropped from upper floors and stairwells barricaded with obstacles. Modern units are instructed to avoid stairs if the upper floor is not secure. Suppressive fire from outside will attempt to kill the higher defenders. A more direct measure against the defenders is to use explosives against a ceiling to blow out the floor above and kill the occupants – although care should be taken not to blow out a supporting wall and bring down the entire building.

URBAN COMBAT – MOGADISHU 1993

One of the most sobering lessons in urban combat for Western military forces came on 3 October 1993. US forces were stationed in Somalia and engaged in peacekeeping operations. A force of Rangers was given the mission of capturing a Somalian warlord, Mohammed Farah Aided, as he held court with his lieutenants in the Olympic Hotel in the centre of the Somali capital, Mogadishu. As this was a highly trained elite unit, confidence among the Rangers was high. At the hotel, however, the assault team found that Aided had escaped and, during the helicopter deployment, a rocket-propelled grenade had downed a Blackhawk. Rescue units sent to the assistance of the helicopter soon found themselves trapped in an enormous firefight. Hundreds of civilians in Mogadishu have access to AK47s and rocket-propelled grenades –

even children engaged the Rangers – and they knew the terrain of the city intimately.

A rescue convoy heading for the Rangers was beaten back by rocket and small-arms fire, and a second Blackhawk helicopter was shot down. By nightfall, more than 100 Rangers were trapped in the city and taking heavy casualties. After another rescue column had been drive n back, US troops entered the city protected by UN Malaysian and Pakistani armour and, on 4 October, they finally reached the besieged Rangers and initiated a rescue. By this time, 18 Rangers were dead and 84 wounded. More than 350 people died in the engagement. The events in Mogadishu reshaped US foreign policy and showed tacticians how even untrained civilians can have tactical supremacy in familiar urban terrain.

Once the immediate defenders are either neutralized or stunned, the attackers can proceed to the upper floors and clear the rooms as usual.

By using this method of building clearance, a fire team can systematically clear a contested urban area.

CHAPTER FIVE

UNIT TACTICS

With the obvious exception of sniping and covert surveillance (both very much one-person operations), soldiers rarely operate in isolation from one another. A military unit is comprised of individual soldiers, but each will have a specific role to play in helping the unit to fulfil its mission. Essentially, it is a team effort. Whether the soldier acts as a radio operator, gunner, engineer, observer or navigator, the failure to execute his or her role may in turn jeopardize the functioning of the entire unit. Of course, individuals are inevitably killed or wounded in combat. The challenge and purpose of unit tactics is to make the unit resistant to misfortune, disaster and the loss of key personnel, while still retaining its operational functions.

◄ *A combat patrol wades ashore during an exercise. The man at the front, the 'point' man, takes responsibility for navigating the unit during the infiltration, while the troops behind provide flank and rear security.*

The tactical doctrine which dominates modern military thinking is manoeuvre warfare. In essence, manoeuvre warfare describes little more than the movement of armies into tactically advantageous positions from which the enemy can be dominated, annihilated or forced to surrender. Simple envelopment and flanking attacks are both examples of manoeuvre warfare in action. Phrased in this way, manoeuvre warfare is nothing new – Assyrian mounted archers in the ancient Near East sought this style of victory over their adversaries. The modern doctrine, however, puts greater emphasis on outmanoeuvring the enemy at every level, including surveillance, electronic warfare, long-range firepower, air-

borne and amphibious mobility, morale, political negotiations and logistics. The desired effect is that the enemy will utterly collapse without the need for prolonged tactics of attrition with their higher risk of casualties.

Manoeuvre warfare has had many advocates before the twentieth century, including Sun Tzu (c. 400–320 BC), Clausewitz (1780–1831) and Alfred Thayer Mahan (1840–1914). It is in the twentieth century, though, that we see almost all military tacticians accepting the notion (with various slants and amendments). One of the clearest missionaries of the manoeuvre doctrine is General A.M. Gray, 29th Commandant of the US Marine Corps. In 1989, he published the

▲ *Fire teams are dispersed to reduce the risk of single munitions destroying the entire unit. Here, a fire team separates into left flank, central and right flank groupings, with 10–20m (30–61ft) between each group.*

doctrinal manual *Warfighting*, which outlined in detail the principles and tactics of manoeuvre warfare. *Warfighting* has become a seminal text in military academies and training centres the world over.

General Gray defines manoeuvre warfare thus:

Maneuver warfare is a warfighting philosophy that seeks to shatter the enemy's cohesion through a variety of rapid, focused and unexpected actions which create a turbulent and rapidly deteriorating situation with which the enemy cannot cope.

Gray goes on to say that this form of warfare does not seek to engage the enemy's main defences, but attempts to go around them and 'penetrate the enemy system and tear it apart'. There are several operating principles which a unit must apply if it is to impose such a complete breakdown of the enemy's ability to function: surprise, speed, tempo and critical vulnerabilities.

Gray classes surprise as the most important quality in tactical manoeuvre. Surprise is created by deliberate deception, deliberate ambiguity or deliberate stealth in pre-assault manoeuvres. A classic example of a surprise assault was that carried out on the Belgian fortress of Eben Emael in 1940, in which German paras actually landed on top of the fortress in gliders, exploiting the fact that the defenders were expecting a large frontal ground assault.

Gray is at pains to point out that 'speed' and 'tempo' are not the same thing in manoeuvre warfare. Speed is rapidity of movement and firepower, whereas tempo is speed consistently applied over time. If both elements are present in an action, the enemy will not have time to re-form, regroup or take charge of the decision-making process. Effectively, the side which can dictate the

tempo wins. During the Gulf War, the Allies took early charge of the operational tempo by knocking out most of the Iraqi long-range communications and then ceaselessly bombing Iraqi forces day and night to prohibit their movement, manoeuvre or regrouping.

Critical vulnerabilities are those points in the enemy's composition, tactics or positions where it is at its weakest. In World War I, Allied forces were often sent directly into the face of German defences at their strongest points, the result being

hideous attrition. By contrast, manoeuvre warfare dictates that a unit's strongest elements should be pitted against the enemy's weakest links. This is rather like the German blitzkrieg principle of punching through a narrow, weak point in the enemy lines with maximum mechanized strength. The weakest point may not necessarily be a hole in the front line or inadequate weaponry. In the Malayan Emergency of 1948–50, British forces deduced that the critical vulnerability of Malayan communist

▸ *The 'ghillie' suit consists of hundreds of hessian camouflaged strips worn over the uniform. Ghillie suits tend to be worn by snipers and special forces soldiers spending long periods in covert positions.*

insurgents was their food supplies. Cutting off these food supplies with extra security measures over food distribution resulted in the insurgents being reduced to starvation level in many sectors, with a consequent reduction in military activity.

Gray's vision of manoeuvre warfare is recognizable in the tactics outlined in detail below. From utilizing cover and concealment to launching an ambush, the modern soldier has to deceive, outwit and ruthlessly crush an opponent at every level if he is to survive and triumph.

CAMOUFLAGE AND CONCEALMENT

Camouflage, concealment and decoy (CCD) measures are concerned with altering the appearance of soldiers and military positions to achieve tactical advan-tages. Effective CCD has three main operational benefits. First, it limits the authority of enemy surveillance, reconnaissance and decision-making. Secondly, it hides operational intentions from the enemy, restricting or denying it access to offensive and defensive movements against it. Most importantly, CCD enhances soldier survivability by impairing enemy target acquisition. If enemy forces cannot locate or distinguish their opponents, they are naturally less able to bring direct and indirect fire to bear on the force.

In US military terminology, the application of CCD is a customized response to six external forces: mission, enemy, terrain and weather, troops, time and civilian considerations. These are known collectively by the abbreviation METT-TC.

▲ *An Australian sniper takes up position during operations in New Caledonia, May 1942. He has chosen a sound position: deeply recessed into foliage for camouflage but having unrestricted movement of firearm.*

METT-TC

Mission: CCD must improve the chances of mission success and soldier survivability without hindering the operation by being overly complex.

Enemy: CCD must confound the enemy's capabilities, including its weaponry, surveillance technology, number of personnel and intelligence resources.

Terrain and Weather: CCD measures should be in sympathy with the immediate battlefield terrain and the environmental conditions.

Troops: All troops within a force must be trained in CCD to the same standard, and each man or woman must accept responsibility for individual CCD.

Time: CCD must fit within an operational time frame. If it is too elaborate, it can slow the tempo of a mission and impair the achievement of objectives.

CIVILIAN

Considerations: Civilians in an operational area should be used, if possible, to acquire better information about CCD and discover more about enemy positions.

In action, troops must base all their CCD efforts around defeating enemy reconnaissance and surveillance. The means arrayed against them fall into two categories: organizational and sensory/instrumental.

ORGANIZATIONAL SURVEILLANCE

All soldiers are (or should be) trained observers, who will monitor, memorize and report any enemy activity they spot. Professional military units do, however, contain integral surveillance and reconnaissance teams. Among a squad (about four to eight soldiers), there will usually be one dedicated reconnaissance trooper, whose purpose it is to collect intelligence while patrolling. Similarly, a battalion will have one reconnaissance company. As the formations become larger, more specialized reconnaissance units are involved. A motorized rifle and

tank regiment, for example, will have a recon company and a chemical recon platoon. A manoeuvre division usually has an entire recon battalion, as well as an engineer recon platoon, a chemical recon platoon and a target-acquisition battery.

SENSORY/INSTRUMENTAL SURVEILLANCE

Sensory/instrumental surveillance is the physical means of detecting the presence of the enemy. At its most basic, these are the senses of the individual soldier, particularly sight and hearing. Visual surveillance is enhanced by optical tools such as binoculars and telescopic sights, but also image-intensifiers (which boost natural light levels through an optical unit), low-light television (LLTV – a combination of

image-intensification and television technology) and aerial photography. A high percentage of recon information still comes from this level. Increasingly, however, armies rely on more advanced technology to reveal enemy whereabouts. Ultraviolet sensors view the part of the electromagnetic spectrum just above visible light, producing clear images on the blackest of nights and in snowy conditions. Near-infrared and infrared sensors give thermal rather than visual images of a battlefield, with heat sources such as human bodies standing out as bright images on the screen in contrast to colder backgrounds.

Radar is used to pick up metallic objects, and it works even through atmospheric impediments such as smoke and fog. Modern radar technology includes moving-target indi-

▶ *Airman First Class Olivia Latham uses a Wide Angle Surveillance Thermal Imager to scan the control tower at Osan Air Base, Korea, for infiltrators during Exercise Foal Eagle '99 on 27 October, 1999.*

cators (MTIs), which are capable of tracking moving targets (usually of vehicle size) on the ground, and countermortar radar, which is able to plot the origin of a mortar shell

▾ *Jungle CCD is aided by the high density of foliage, which breaks up the soldier's silhouette. On the downside, travel is often very noisy in the jungle and the soldier must make regular stops to listen for an enemy presence.*

by tracking its flight through the air.

The most basic acoustic method of surveillance is the human ear, but used on its own it is one of the least reliable reconnaissance tools. Acoustic technologies are far superior. They include the flash-sound ranger, a tool which deduces the range of enemy artillery via the time-lag between the gun's flash and bang when monitored at distance, and ground-based micro-

phone radars, which record acoustic information and triangulate the position of the noise to provide a location. Enemy troops will also try to intercept any opposing radio communications. Once they detect transmissions, they will either interpret or decode them, jam them or triangulate a position to the person or unit broadcasting.

An advanced enemy recon unit equipped with some of the technologies above presents a severe problem for any unit wishing to move undetected. CCD must therefore defeat multiple surveillance possibilities.

PERSONAL CCD

Soldiers are taught to respect shape, shine, shadow, colour and movement when designing CCD.

Shape: CCD techniques should break up or hide the shape of a soldier against his background. In particular, straight lines should be obscured and made irregular in natural settings.

Shine: A soldier should remove or obscure all areas of shine on his kit or body.

Shadow: A soldier employing CCD should position himself in shadows as further camouflage, but his shadow must not betray him by falling outside his camouflaged position.

Colour: Camouflage is useless if it does not blend its colours with the terrain. CCD techniques should mean that the soldier exposes no distinctive colours.

Movement: Abrupt, exposed or erratic movements are all easily detectable to naked or enhanced eyesight. The soldier should seek to move with stealth along covered routes in the terrain.

The soldier meets these demands through applying CCD kit and field-expedient (improvised) CCD.

The uniform is the most significant element of personal CCD. Most armies of temperate-zone nations use a woodland-pattern camouflage which diffuses the soldier's outline when placed against a foliage background. Advanced uniforms such as the US M81 Woodland pattern and the British Disruptive Pattern Material (DPM) are also printed in near-infrared reflectant dyes which give enhanced CCD against an enemy with night-vision devices. Combat dress must not be starched too often, as this will erode the effectiveness of these dyes, and faded combat uniforms will also have less convincing camouflage.

Some armies are issued with camouflage nets for extra CCD. The more sophisticated of these contain stainless-steel fibres to absorb and deflect radar waves, and so reduce the effectiveness of enemy ground-sweep radar.

Most uniforms require the addition of foliage to complete their camouflage properties in natural environments. Leaves, twigs, grass and branches can be attached to both helmet and uniform. Just enough foliage should be added to break up the soldier's visual signature and make him blend with his environment, but not enough to impair his movement or too give away his position (large quantities of foliage which change position regularly quickly attract attention). When selecting foliage, either to

▲ *A team of infantry move through woodland using textbook cover-and-manoeuvre tactics. The soldier in the foreground provides cover as his comrade advances to a position from which he can take over the covering role.*

wear on the body or to conceal a position, the soldier should pick that which matches the operational area. For example, he should not use coniferous materials in a deciduous location and vice versa. Camouflage foliage will need regular replacement, as, once cut, it fades and browns quite rapidly. The soldier should always aim to present the top side of leaves to the enemy. Leaves have lighter undersides, and these stand out quite clearly in military reconnaissance photography. The white, broken

ROYAL MARINES CCD – FALKLANDS WAR

In May 1982, during the Falklands War, teams from the Special Boat Service (SBS) were put ashore on the Falkland Islands to set up observation posts (OPs) and conduct surveillance on Argentine troops and positions. The SBS troop was airdropped around San Carlos water with the mission of reconnoitring possible landing areas for British troops and spying suitable HQ locations for forthcoming operations. The terrain in the region was especially barren, so the SBS soldiers had to apply innovative CCD. During the night of the deployment, the soldiers hacked out sods of earth which they lay on broad nets of stiff chicken wire. They then dug out positions 500mm (20in) deep. The soldiers lay in the dug-outs and covered the positions over with the platforms of cut sod, thus making the hide blend in with the grassy surroundings. They occupied these hides for more than 10 days, living within a few hundred metres of the Argentine positions. They could not cook or light a fire in the freezing conditions, and movement and talking were prohibited during the day for fear of alerting the enemy to their presence. Bodily functions were performed into plastic bags which were sealed to prevent any scents alerting the enemy. Their CCD measures ensured that the Argentines had no inkling of their presence, and the intelligence they gained assisted a successful British amphibious landing.

ends of branches should be blackened with mud so that they do not stand out. Very fresh undergrowth is receptive to near-infrared (NIR) imaging because of its chlorophyll output, and so it is used to mask soldiers to some extent against near-infrared scanning. This mask will degrade, however, as the foliage wilts (coniferous vegetation provides a more durable chlorophyll response than deciduous vegetation).

Human skin needs special camouflage treatment because its oily content makes it reflective regardless of skin colour. Soldiers should apply camouflage paint sticks to their face, neck, arms and hands. To do this, they should always work in pairs, applying each other's camouflage, as it is easy to miss vital areas such as the backs of the ears if applying camouflage yourself. Prominent areas of the head which exude oils (forehead, nose, cheekbones, ears and chin) require dark colours, while shadowed areas should receive a light-coloured paint. The neck, arms and hands are rendered in irregular, foliage-style patterns. If professional camouflage sticks are not available, field-expedient materials include charcoal, mud, lampblack, clay, soot, burnt cork and an oil-and-earth mix. Canned milk and powdered egg give field-expedient paints better binding properties.

A soldier will also have to camouflage his kit. All shiny objects should be dulled, and any metal objects which might make a noise should either be removed or taped fast. Gun metal should be dulled with camouflage paint or boot polish, and a weapon may be wrapped in pieces of camouflage material or painted in a camouflage colour scheme. Nothing should be added, however, which will impair the operation of the bolt, cocking handle, gas mechanism, sights and selector lever.

The advantages offered by camouflage will be undone if concealment measures are not in place. Noise must be kept to an absolute minimum. Radio transmissions should be limited and brief, and as much inter-unit communication as possible should be conducted using visual signals, rather than speech. Movement should be stealthy, resisting jerky or fast movements, and preferably conducted at night or in low-visibility conditions. Large units are dispersed into small nimble squads which move in stages from one piece of natural cover to the next without silhouetting themselves against a skyline or a contrasting background. All routes taken by the patrol or unit should take full advantage of the terrain, tracking natural features which obscure them from ground and airborne surveillance. These features include woods and forests, valleys, natural depressions in the ground, embankments, rocky outcrops and high ground. An earthen feature such as a hill or rampart will absorb a great deal of infra-red energy, and so it can conceal the soldier against near-infrared and infrared surveillance.

Forests are the best locations for covert movement, as the trees limit the visual range of surveillance at ground level, while the tree canopy above protects against aerial reconnaissance. Conversely, open terrain is the most dangerous. If a unit is obliged to move into open ground, smoke munitions may be required to maintain the CCD. Smoke interferes with the spectral bands of optical and thermal target-acquisition equipment, and so it provides a valuable CCD tool against enemy surveillance technology. It should be laid across a broad front, through which the troops advance at multiple points scattered along the length of the smokescreen. If smoke cannot be used, operating in heavy precipitation or thick fog also degrades enemy thermal and optical surveillance.

DECOY TACTICS

The 'decoy' element of CCD focuses upon misleading the enemy, rather than hiding from it. Decoy positions can force the enemy to make tactical errors, waste its ammunition, expose its positions, reveal its technologies and place them under target acquisition. Decoys must be placed in plausible locations near the target, for, if the enemy soldiers realize that it is a decoy, they will search the area even harder for the real positions. Decoys must also be plausibly constructed and only slightly more visible than the real location. Common decoy tactics include:

• creating false positions
• making slow-burning fires in unoccupied positions so that thermal-imaging systems read signs of human activity
• building decoy vehicles in forest clearings to confuse or draw enemy aerial reconnaissance and fire – this was used to good effect by the Yugoslavian forces in Kosovo

• having supplies airdropped to positions away from the actual route of operations
• deploying metallic strips in the decoy position to produce a reading on enemy ground radar
• firing remotely operated weapons from the decoy positions.

TACTICAL MOVEMENT

Haphazard and indecisive movements on the battlefield usually result in high casualties and operational collapse. Tactical movement differs in that every yard of ground

▼ *When an infantry unit comes under shellfire, it is imperative that they do not split up and become dispersed. Maintaining about 10m (30ft) between each man, the unit should exit the danger area in parallel movements to retain unit integrity.*

covered contributes to mission success. Not only does tactical movement enhance soldier survivability, but it also serves to outwit or outpace the enemy at every level.

PERSONAL TACTICAL MOVEMENT

In combat, a well-trained soldier should move logically around the battlefield, travelling along the safest routes between protected positions and limiting his exposure to enemy fire. The best routes of manoeuvre offer constant cover and concealment: features such as culverts, ditches, trenches, buildings, walls or depressions, anything which obscures the enemy's view of the soldier and provides

adequate protection from small arms and support weapons. Places to avoid include open spaces with clear fields of fire, the tops of hills and ridges, steep slopes (it is harder to attack high ground than it is to defend it) and places strewn with loose dirt or rubble. When moving between positions, the soldier should not be exposed for longer than three to five seconds; any longer and he is likely to attract accurately aimed small-arms fire.

Before leaving a position, the soldier must have a clear idea of his destination, usually another piece of cover which can be reached in the three- to five-second window. He should never move directly

forward from any covered position. Enemy riflemen are likely to have their weapons trained on obvious pieces of cover, especially if they are known to be occupied. Infantry are therefore trained to roll or crawl a short way from their position, then sprint to the next piece of cover from the offside.

In terms of actual physical movement, four basic techniques are taught to most infantry soldiers

▾ *When a unit is surprised by a ground flare, it should move as quickly as possible to available cover and wait for the flare to subside. If caught in the open, troops should drop to the floor and remain as still as possible.*

▸ *Unit movement must take advantage of all available cover and concealment. Here are three suitable routes of travel: a dry river bed (top), behind a piece of raised feature (middle) and around an area of foliage or woodland (bottom).*

throughout the world: the low crawl, the high crawl, the rush and stealth movement.

Low Crawl: The low crawl makes the flattest silhouette and is used for moving behind very low cover. A soldier should execute a low crawl by keeping his body flat to the ground, with his firing hand gripping his rifle just under the front sling-swivel and the front hand-guard resting along the forearm. This grip keeps the muzzle clear of the ground (any dirt intrusion into the barrel may result in a barrel explosion or a stoppage during firing). The soldier moves in this position by putting both hands forward and drawing up one leg to the side. He then pushes with the leg and pulls with both hands. The movement is repeated using alternate legs. During the Vietnam War, the US sniper Carlos Hathcock crawled some 1090m (3576ft) over three days using a similar, modified technique. He managed to put himself within 650m (2130ft) of major enemy positions without being discovered.

High Crawl: The high crawl is essentially a baby crawl. The soldier pulls his body along the ground using the push from a knee and the simultaneous pull from a diagonally opposite elbow. The gun is held differently than in the low crawl: it should be cradled in the elbows across the front of the body.

Rush: The rush is a sudden speed movement ideal for transferring between positions. From a prone position, the soldier should raise his head and select his next position. He then lowers his head (faces are easily visible to opposing troops), pulls his arms into his body and tucks the elbows in close to his sides. One leg is drawn forward.

With a powerful movement, he pushes up with his arms and thrusts himself into a run off the bent leg. To stop running, both feet are planted suddenly in one spot, forcing the soldier to drop to his knees. As this happens, the butt of the rifle is gripped and brought

forwards to break the impact of the torso falling forwards. The soldier should then assume the prone firing position.

Stealth movement: Stealth movement is exhausting and time-consuming. The moving leg is lifted high to avoid snagging on objects at ground level and moved forward with the body weight still retained over the supporting leg. The moving leg should be lowered to the ground toe first, with the soldier using his toe to feel for solid ground and any obstacles. Once the toe is firmly on the ground, the rest of the foot is slowly rolled flat. Only when the

entire foot is on secure ground should the body weight be transferred to the front.

UNIT MOVEMENT
The tactical movement of entire units varies with every mission plan, but there are common procedures used by all infantry. Modern infantry units at their smallest level are usually divided into fire teams of four men, two of these fire teams making a squad. Fire teams will move in wedge, file, column or line formations. The wedge is a V-shaped formation, with the team leader guiding the way at the point of the V. The file formation is a

▲ A group of British Army soldiers stop to make a radio transmission during an urban-combat exercise. The team leader is spotting the team's next position, while the soldiers behind him prepare to adopt covering positions as he moves.

straight single-file line, used mainly for moving through narrow terrain. The column is a staggered line, which gives much better all-around fire protection than a file. Finally, the line formation is simply a line of soldiers walking forwards abreast. In any formation, at least 10m (33ft) between each soldier is mandatory if the terrain allows. This spacing protects the

sandbags 75 per cent full of sand. The frontal cover should be above the soldier's head height when he is standing, and it should be set far enough in front of the hole to give room to rest the elbows on the parapet and allow the positioning of

▼ *A straight trench (top) sits more squarely behind frontal cover, whereas a curved trench (bottom) moves around the front cover, widening fields of fire. The straight trench is preferred when the frontal sector is covered by adjacent positions.*

sector stakes (see page 175). It also needs to be long enough to mask a rifle muzzle flash from front view when the occupant is firing at an oblique angle from the position.

Ideally, a fighting position will also have side, rear and overhead cover of similar strength to the frontal cover. Overhead cover (advisable for protection against anti-personnel air-burst munitions) is usually made from logs, sheet metal or planking, covered with a thick layer of soil and foliage, and

sometimes a plastic sheet for waterproofing. All fighting positions are camouflaged as much as possible using natural, local materials or, even better, constructed behind natural cover which does not require alteration. In all cases, the fighting position must be regularly inspected, particularly after climatic changes. Heavy rain or frost can erode the walls of holes and dugouts, and sudden changes in temperature are likely to strip away foliage cover in deciduous environments.

The construction of fighting position varies with operational requirements and limitations. If time allows, the hole should be dug to an armpit-deep level and several metres in length (US forces recommend a minimum length of two M16 rifles). Two grenade sumps are dug, one at each end of the position. These are narrow holes which go straight down into earth about 0.75–1.5m (2–5ft), or at least the length of an entrenching tool. If a grenade is thrown into the position, the soldier can simply roll or kick the grenade into one of the sumps, where most of the explosive force and fragments will be soaked up by the soil. The floor of the position should slope down from the centre towards each hole. On the lip of the hole, behind the frontal cover, the soldier should dig two elbow rests. Sitting his elbows in these when firing will result in more accurate shooting. If a bipod-mounted weapon is in the position, a narrow trench for the bipod legs serves the same purpose.

In any firing position, the soldier should mark out sectors and fields of fire. These are the areas into which the soldier will target and shoot his weapon, and they are marked out to prevent shooting into friendly positions or the unnecessary duplication of fire with other positions. There are two firing sectors, known as the primary and secondary sectors. The primary sector extends at an oblique angle from each corner of the trench, shooting around the edge of the frontal cover. It might seem strange that the primary firing position is not directly to the front. Firing at an oblique, however, hits the enemy with fire from unexpected directions and also interlocks fire with other fighting positions. During World War II, German machine-gunners found that, by positioning their weapons at opposite flanks of their trench systems, two broad cones of fire would interlock and decimate troops before them in open ground. Their fire could achieve in-depth destruction by playing up the flanks of the attack rather than just the face.

The secondary sector is the zone directly in front of the position. It is targeted by angling the

◄ *The floor of a fighting position is angled downwards from the centre so that enemy grenades are easily kicked into the grenade sumps at either end. The grenade sumps should be 0.75–1.5m (2–5ft) deep to absorb blast and shrapnel.*

▲ A trained observer will make a systematic scan of the terrain and assume nothing. The human mind has a tendency to skip over familiar features without really studying them; the observer must control this tendency and study every detail.

rifle around the frontal cover. To increase his fire discipline, the soldier marks out the primary sectors by knocking two stakes into the ground in front of each firing position. Known as sector stakes, the distance between these two stakes marks the boundaries of rifle movement when shooting and stops the soldier shooting into friendly positions or duplicating fire. Between the sector stakes, some soldiers will also place an aiming stake, a marker

which assists the alignment of the rifle sights on the target.

The nature of a firing position changes according to the speed of construction, the number of people occupying it and the type of weapons deployed.

HASTY FIGHTING POSITION

A hasty fighting position is used when there is little time to construct an advanced structure. It can be any substantial piece of natural cover, such as a fallen tree trunk or rocky outcrop. Hasty positions do not, however, exclude digging. A hole should be dug to 0.5m (20in) deep, and the soil from the hole packed up in front to provide additional frontal cover. Sometimes the nature of the terrain prohibits dig-

ging. US Marines assaulting the Japanese-held island of Iwo Jima in February 1945 found that the beach consisted entirely of a crumbly black volcanic sand. Any hole dug a few metres down into the sand collapsed in on itself. Furthermore, the volcanic activity of the island meant that any foxholes became red hot and full of sulphurous gas and had to be abandoned. By contrast, the Japanese had created resilient fortified positions on the edge of the beach using rocks and logs, and they inflicted a huge death toll on US troops at the waterline.

ONE-PERSON FIGHTING POSITION

A one-person position is large enough for a single soldier in full combat gear. It must allow him to

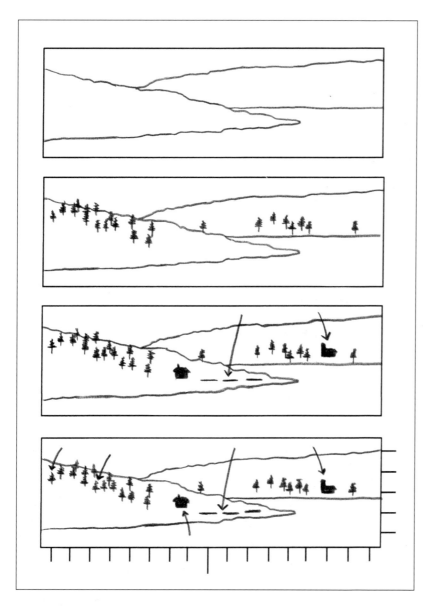

◄ A terrain map begins by sketching the basic geological features of the terrain, then steadily filling in more detail about the landscape, habitations and enemy positions. For artillery control, the map includes scale and bearing information.

enemy activity to the front. A two-man position usually has a single grenade sump in the middle of the hole with the floor sloping down to this point from both ends.

THREE-SOLDIER FIGHTING POSITION

Seen from above, the hole of a three-man position is cut in a T-shape, each soldier occupying an extremity of the T. The grenade sump is in the centre of the T's crossbar. A three-man position gives 360-degree fire coverage, but for this reason the soldiers must be very clear when setting up their sector stakes to avoid fratricide.

These three types of position can be adapted to take various kinds of weaponry. Machine gun positions usually have dedicated platforms of earth on which the machine gun sits inside the hole. Mortar positions are constructed in a circular hole that allows the crew ease of movement around the weapon. Anti-tank missile positions require the ground to be cleared of debris in front and behind the position to reduce the level of dust raised by the firing of the weapon.

RECONNAISSANCE AND OBSERVATION

Intelligent unit tactics depend on information about the enemy's position, strength and movement, and the terrain through which the unit will move. Gathering this information is the job of reconnais-

switch easily between primary sectors of fire while remaining behind the frontal cover. This type of position usually has the hole extended slightly further out from behind the frontal cover than other positions to give the isolated soldier more firing options in the secondary sector.

TWO-PERSON FIGHTING POSITION

A two-man hole needs to be big enough to accept two soldiers with full combat loads. It should also be as small as possible – the smaller the position, the less likely it is to be hit by grenades, mortar rounds and artillery shells, or affected by airburst munitions. The hole may be dug in a straight line or curved around the frontal cover to provide wider primary sectors of fire for each soldier and improve observation of sance teams. Although platoons and companies will usually have dedicated reconnaissance teams, each soldier in a modern army is trained in techniques of observation and reporting. A common method used by soldiers to organize their observation is the SALUTE formula: size, activity, location, unit, time and equipment.

Size: How many soldiers and vehi-

▼ A Boeing E-3A Sentry surveillance aircraft takes off on a patrol. The Sentry's radar has a range of over 375km (250 miles) and also incorporates a friend-or-foe system to classify the status of unidentified aircraft or ground vehicles.

cles are visible? Soldiers are encouraged to provide specific figures rather than general impressions of unit strength (e.g. '40 infantry' rather than 'an infantry platoon').

Activity: What is the enemy doing? What is their main activity? (e.g. building defensive positions, refuelling vehicles)

Location: What is the enemy's position and in which direction is he heading? When giving a position, the soldier should provide a six-figure map reference. If this is not possible, he should relate the enemy's position to surrounding features of the terrain which can be

easily identified by intelligence.

Unit: What enemy units are present? The soldier should note features such as vehicle pennants, special uniform badges and colour schemes, and types of equipment, all of which will help intelligence identify the units.

Time: At what time, or during what period of time, was the enemy seen? The time given should be local time.

Equipment: What type of equipment is being used or carried? This includes weaponry, vehicles, engineering equipment and communications systems. If a piece of equipment cannot be identified, the sol-

◀ A US Army officer adjusts his night-vision goggles on his flight helmet in preparation for a night helicopter mission. Night-vision goggles work through either image-intensification or thermal imaging.

conducts a general area surveillance. This involves scanning the visual sector for any prominent or obvious features which will need reporting. This initial scan should pick up on any unusual colours, shapes or movements which will lead to closer examination. Once this is complete, the soldier should proceed to refine his observation by separating the landscape in front of him into 50m (164ft) wide horizontal strips. Starting with ground nearest to him, he should scan each strip rigorously for relevant features, working to the horizon or the furthest limit of his sector.

At night-time, this process has to be altered because of the limits of human night vision. There are three methods of night observation according to the *US Army's Field Manual FM 21-75, Combat Skills of the Soldier*: dark-adaptation technique, off-centre vision technique and scanning technique.

Dark-Adaptation Technique: The soldier allows his eyes to adjust to the dark by staying in a dark place for 30 minutes or a place lit by red light for 20 minutes, then complete darkness for a further 10 minutes. The red light method is often preferred, as it allows the soldier to make preparations even while undergoing night-vision adjustment.

Off-Centre Vision Technique: At night, objects appear clearer when looked at with peripheral vision rather than direct vision. This technique involves focusing the eyes on a

dier should make a sketch of it to submit to intelligence.

A full SALUTE report might appear as follows:

16 infantry mounted on 2 tanks moving along main route road at grid MW177841. Time spotted: 0830. Tank speed of approx 13km/h (8mph), stopping frequently for observation. Tank personnel wearing blue collar patches; red

pennant suspended from radio aerial. Tanks T-62 type; infantry contain two RPK machine guns.

OBSERVATION TECHNIQUES

Active reconnaissance requires a more rigorous and systematic use of the senses than normal. A reconnaissance trooper uses a systematic method of looking to avoid the omission of vital information.

Observation during the daytime has two stages. First, the soldier position just to the side of the object being viewed.

Scanning Technique: The soldier moves his eyes abruptly and quickly over the observed object in short movements, pausing for a few seconds after each move. The changes in perspective will give increased visual information.

One of the greatest impairments to good reconnaissance is if the soldier assumes he knows what he sees in front of him. Reconnaissance and surveillance personnel are therefore trained to pick up on the full range of visual and auditory signs. After looking for enemy positions in obvious, open places, the soldier should then scan shaded areas looking for unusual shadow patterns that might indicate an enemy vehicle, gun or emplacement. He should also look for incidents of shine or glare in the sector. At night, these might indicate an enemy soldier smoking a cigarette, while in the day they can come from vehicle windscreens or headlights, or even wristwatch faces. Rising dust, smoke and vehicle exhaust are signs of human activity which can be seen at great distances in clear weather. Furthermore, the soldier should listen for any sounds of human activity – voices, twigs breaking underfoot, coughing, etc.

As the soldier scans the sector and notes key features using the SALUTE format, he must record the information for later reporting or transmission. The best way of doing this is by making a terrain sketch. The first stage of a terrain sketch is drawing the geological outlines of the landscape without any detail. Next, prominent or important features are added to the sketched landscape, including significant trees (which can be useful artillery ranging points), buildings, etc. Enemy positions and sites of activity are then drawn and noted. Finally, the soldier adds a scale and compass bearings to each significant feature, plus time, date and name. Once drawn, the terrain sketch is used by the soldier as an *aide-mémoire* or given directly to intelligence forces.

RECONNAISSANCE POSITIONS AND TOOLS

Reconnaissance troops will make most of their observations from a static observation post (OP). During the Falklands War, for example, British Special Boat Service troopers established OPs in the hulls of wrecked ships just off the Falklands coastline to observe Argentine shore movements prior to the British landings. For units operating behind enemy lines, the OP must be constructed using all CCD measures. It must have clear exit and entry points (although the soldiers will rarely leave the OP during the mission) and pre-arranged escape routes should it be discovered. Wooded hillsides are amenable locations for OPs, as the foliage provides cover while the elevation gives good distance viewing. As OPs may be occupied for some time, they should be near

▶ US Army Sgt. Daniel Ledesman works on a AN/TPQ-36 Fire Finder Radar System set up at the International Airport in Sarajevo, Bosnia and Herzegovina, on 20 April 1996. The Fire Finder Radar has the capability to determine where a round was fired from, and where it will land, and will compute co-ordinates for a counter-attack if needed.

sources of water. Special forces generally operate four-man OPs. One man acts as an observer and sentry, another as a communications officer and the third man as another sentry, while the fourth rests until the duties are rotated. Rotation of duties usually occurs every hour to keep the soldiers fresh and responsive.

Observing one sector of terrain hour after hour is physically and mentally exhausting. The endurance and capabilities of a reconnaissance team are, however, enhanced by a powerful array of surveillance equipment. Unless they are part of a large vehicular or stationary unit, recon forces have limited capacity for carrying some of the more sizeable surveillance devices such as ground-based radar and counterbattery systems. Small recon teams rely on the following equipment when in the field: night-vision devices and remote sensors.

Night-Vision Devices: Most infantry night-vision devices (NVDs) work on the principle of image-intensification, magnifying existing light levels (which at night are often beyond the limits of human sight) through a lens and presenting the image to the viewer. NVDs vary in their portability. The US Army currently uses two systems for its infantry: the AN/PVS-4, a weapon-mounted starlight scope which doubles as a hand-held surveillance tool; and the AN/PVS-7, a set of image-intensifying goggles held like binoculars or worn on the head. Tactical surveillance at night is much improved by NVDs. The AN/PVS-4, for example, gives clear vision out to 600m (1968ft) under bright moonlight, and vision up to 300m (984ft) under starlight only.

NVDs are crucial to night-time surveillance operations, but they are not fail-safe. Bright artificial lights (such as searchlights) within the terrain can dazzle or even temporarily blind the NVD operator, as can explosions, pyrotechnics, fires and illumination devices. Recon soldiers train themselves to shut their eyes or redirect the NVD when detonations occur to protect their eyesight. NVDs also suffer from reduced range in fog or rain.

Remote Sensors: Remote sensors (REMS) are devices left by a recon unit in a surveillance area which provide information on enemy movement without an observer being present. There are three basic types: magnetic sensor (MAG); seismic-acoustic sensor (SA); and infrared-passive sensor (IP). Each sensor, when left undisturbed, will transmit information concerning physical disturbances in their vicinity back to a central receiver for about 30 days (depending on battery durability).

The MAG detects the passage of metallic objects – usually vehicles – and deduces the direction of movement. Range is about 15–25m (49–82ft) for vehicles, although only tanks tend to be readable at the further ranges. Recon units tend to place MAG sensors by the side of roads and common routes of travel. IP devices also provide information on direction of travel, but they do so through measuring passing variations in temperature. Their range for tracked vehicles is up to 50m (164ft). The SA reads seismic and acoustic signals in its vicinity, then classifies it according to P – personnel, V – vehicles, W – wheeled vehicles, and T – tracked vehicles. It then transmits

SAS RECONNAISSANCE IN BOSNIA

SAS forces were deployed into Bosnia in 1994 to conduct reconnaissance and targeting duties for NATO forces. One of their first operations was to designate landing zones for US Air Force food drops into the besieged town of Maglai, in March 1994. Having penetrated the Serb positions around the town, the SAS group completed their initial mission before being switched to targeting operations. A British relief convoy was heading into Maglai, and SAS recon teams provided target information about Serbian troop movements to the US fighter aircraft circling overhead as cover for the convoy.

A month later, the SAS were sent into the Moslem town of Gorazde, also under siege from the Serbs. From concealed observation posts, the seven-man SAS team observed Serbian armoured movements, then targeted key vehicles with laser-designators, which NATO F-16 aircraft subsequently destroyed with precision-guided munitions (PGMs). SAS teams continued to operate throughout Bosnia for over a year and, in August 1995, they were deployed to Sarajevo. Their role was similar to that in Gorazde, and with meticulous efficiency they plotted the positions of almost every Serbian tank, artillery piece, fighting position and anti-aircraft battery. This information was used to devastating effect when NATO aircraft bombed the Serbian positions around Sarajevo on 30 August.

▸ *US troops patrol near Khe Sanh, Vietnam, in the hunt for North Vietnamese troops entering South Vietnam. The M60 machine-gunner walks point to give an instant fire-response to an ambush.*

its deductions back to a recon receiver. The range of detection is greater than the MAG: the Seismic-Acoustic Sensor DT-562/GSQ, for example, has a range of 50m (164ft) for personnel, 250m (820ft) for wheeled vehicles and 350m (1148ft) for tracked vehicles.

Recon teams have to spend as much time on CCD measures applied to remote sensors as they do to occupied positions. If discovered by the enemy, a remote sensor's information can be easily manipulated for the purposes of deception. Most remote sensors consist of a small sensing unit connected by a wire to a transmitter. The sensor should be placed inconspicuously among vegetation and away from places where it might be disturbed by civilian or animal activity. The wire which connects it to the transmitter should be covered with earth or buried in grass, and the transmitter sited in undergrowth tall enough to mask its prominent aerial.

By using on-site and remote surveillance techniques, a soldier is able to produce a detailed account of the presence of both humans and vehicles in a particular area.

PATROLLING

Patrols essentially have three functions: reconnaissance, combat and tracking. A reconnaissance patrol serves to gather information about the threats present in an area of operation. A combat patrol seeks out and engages enemy forces either to capture terrain or inflict attrition. A tracking patrol follows an enemy unit with a view to recording its position and movement, possibly for target-acquisition purposes. In practice, the three purposes of patrols usually bleed into one another.

Possibly the most important stage in any patrol manoeuvre is planning. For patrols to be successful, they must have rigorously defined goals and time-lines, and each member of the patrol must be aware of his or her specific function. Patrols vary in size from four-man fire teams to platoon and company proportions, but within each patrol there are usually a common set of elements:

• headquarters element – the leadership of the patrol, usually

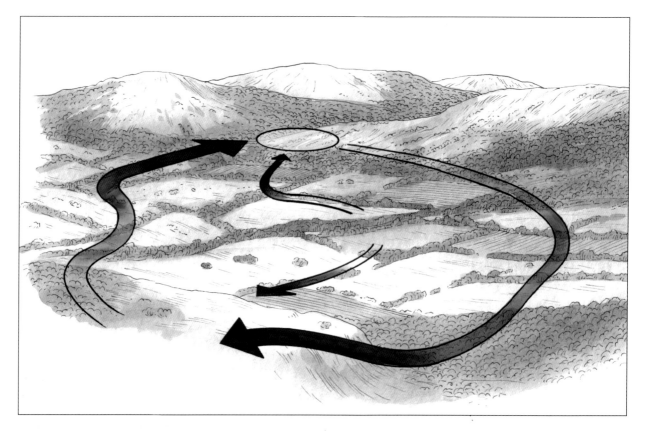

consisting of an officer and senior NCOs

• navigation element – responsible for the accurate navigation of the patrol around all its objectives

• surveillance element – an individual or team who gathers and processes data and intelligence during the operation

• the combat/support element –engages in combat when required or performs a multitude of support roles such as first aid and the evacuation of wounded.

These four elements exist in units from four-man teams to entire companies. Their responsibilities bleed into one another (for example, all patrol members will have to act as combat troops in major hostile encounters), but each role must be fulfilled in some regard.

Patrol planning begins by defining the objectives of the patrol. These objectives need to be communicated clearly throughout all personnel involved in the mission and also among support elements in the rear, such as HQ infantry units and fire-support groups. Key questions which need to be satisfied are:

• How will the terrain and weather affect the accomplishment of the mission?

• What special combat/communications/engineering equipment is required?

• How are deployment and extraction to be performed?

• What enemy forces are in the area?

▲ *All patrols must have primary and secondary routes of manoeuvre in case of mission problems. Here, the large arrows represent the primary routes to an objective, the smaller arrows, the secondary routes.*

• How will the patrol receive intelligence updates when in the field?

• How will the patrol ensure its safety when re-entering friendly lines?

• What fire support is available, and what are the procedures for calling it?

• What is the time frame for accomplishing the mission?

• Are there any other units patrolling in the area?

• Are there any likely ambush points?

▲ The fan method of patrolling. The patrol unit moves to an initial objective and then sends out multiple squads in overlapping circular routes to explore the surrounding area in depth.

Once the team leader has all relevant information, he can then construct a patrol plan. First, he designates specific objectives to each patrol element, including the tasks to be performed, routes to be taken and patrol communication and security procedures. Each element is also given a time-line for completing the tasks. This should take into account the journey to the objective, surveillance of the objective, performance of tasks and extraction. Next, he clarifies the routes to be taken by the patrol. Two routes are typically given. The first of these is the primary route, the route of the outgoing and return journeys, should everything proceed to plan. The return journey always follows a different route to the outgoing journey to foil enemy tracking. The second is an

PATROL FORMATIONS IN VIETNAM

Here, Al Baker, Company Commander, 4/9th Infantry, between 1967 and 1969, reveals the patrol formations he used in Vietnam to counter Vietcong/NVA ambushes:

Most of our operations were in flat jungle. For that terrain, I moved in a modified V formation with Platoons in column. This formation gave me relative ease of movement. We would never operate on a trail or follow a stream bed or other ambushable feature and it gave me flexibility to maneuver. No matter

where the action originated I could quickly get two platoons with a base of fire and one to maneuver to flank the position. If the situation did not permit a maneuver, I had a reserve. I would change lead platoons daily and point men we changed every few hours. I was always with the lead platoon and just behind the point man. It was where 95 per cent of our actions initiated. The point man was always in sight of the platoon. In most terrain, he was 10–20m (30–60ft) ahead. Usually there were two point men.

▸ *Sectors of fire are interlocked to remove safe zones for the enemy. In defensive (top) or patrol (bottom) configurations, each soldier must discipline himself to shoot only into his own sector to avoid unnecessary duplication of fire.*

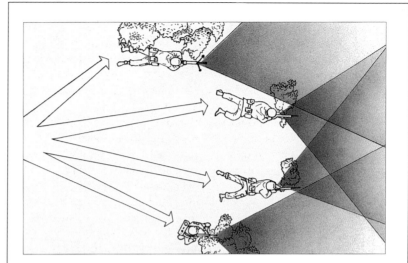

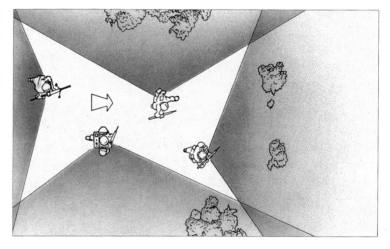

alternate route if unforeseen circumstances prohibit use of the primary route.

Route planning involves defining rally points (RPs). RPs are places at which the patrol regroups and reorganizes. They need to be easily found, but must also provide cover and concealment for defensive purposes. The position of RPs varies with the type of mission, but they can be sited on primary and alternate routes, at the objective itself, at points where the patrol will re-enter friendly lines, at points where airborne extraction of the patrol will take place or on the perimeter of danger points.

Once objectives and routes are established, the patrol leader will also set patrol protocols for communications (including hand signals), passwords, rules of engagement, the location of leaders and, vitally, contingency plans in case the whole operation disintegrates. With every patrol member clear as to his role and route, the patrol can begin.

PATROL FORMATIONS AND MOVEMENT

The structure of a patrol follows the same formats as already discussed in the section on movement: wedge (or spearhead in British terminology), column, file and line. In terms of defensive properties when applied to a four-man fire team, each offers different advantages.

The Wedge: This is an easy formation to navigate, as the team leader is positioned in the centre at the front. It is one of the best formations for crossing open country, as the patrol can suddenly raise heavy frontal and flanking fire if required. Wedge formations of three-platoon size used in the jungles of Vietnam were generally unwieldy, however, having too many scout and lead elements to co-ordinate in response to an attack.

The Column: The column formation also provides concentrated flanking firepower, but its staggered line gives it an excellent 360-degree platform for surveillance and fire discipline – the first and last soldiers in the formation cover the front and rear, while the two soldiers at the side cover the flanks. It is the formation most commonly used by four-man teams. Major combat patrols in Vietnam used a two-column formation. This had the advantage that, if one flank was engaged in ambush, the other flank would be able to move up as a reserve and also prevent the enemy closing around the patrol flanks in encircling manoeuvres.

The File: This is more of an expedient formation, used when the terrain narrows and prohibits the dispersal of personnel out to the sides. When moving into a file formation, each soldier should have an opposite fire sector from the persons in front or behind him (usually the soldiers watch alternate flanks). Once out of narrow terrain, the patrol will move back into its original formation.

The Line: The line formation is useful for a four-man team advancing directly on an enemy position. If engaged, the team members on the flanks of the line (who usually have the squad's heavier firepower) provide suppressive fire against the enemy. In the meantime, the point man (the man at the front of any patrol) and a rifleman will move up to fight the enemy at closer quarters or set up a bounding overwatch manoeuvre with the flank elements.

Whether a patrol is a small fireteam or a company, the most demanding type of patrol it can face is the zone reconnaissance. This is where a patrol investigates an entire sector rather than a single point, scouting the sector for enemy positions, personnel and activity, often with little knowledge of what it might find. The object for the patrol leader is to cover all the sector ground in the

most efficient way. Certain tactical movements are available for him to do this: the fan method, the box method, the converging routes method and stationary teams.

Fan Method: A chain of rally points are set up in a straight line through the zone. From each rally point, multiple surveillance teams set out, each exploring a horseshoe-shaped piece of terrain which leads them out from the rally point and back to it again. The route taken by each team intersects with that of the groups next to it. Visually represented, the whole pattern resembles that of an electric fan, each team charting one of the fan's blades. Once all the teams have returned, the platoon sets out to the next rally point and repeats the process.

Box Method: The sector is divided up into boxes, each box limited by two rally points set on opposing sides of the box. Patrol squads then journey around the edge of the box to explore the perimeter, while another squad goes through the centre of the box to explore the interior. All teams converge on a rally point at an agreed time.

Converging Routes Method: Multiple patrol teams start from different locations on one side of the sector and cross the sector to a common rally point over the other side. At the rally point, they share intelligence before patrolling another sector.

Stationary Teams: Sometimes a patrol is conducted by setting up stationary observation teams and leaving them in position for a set period of

▸ *Soldiers of the Joint Security Area Scout Platoon return from a patrol of the Demilitarized Zone in the Republic of Korea, on 20 October 1998.*

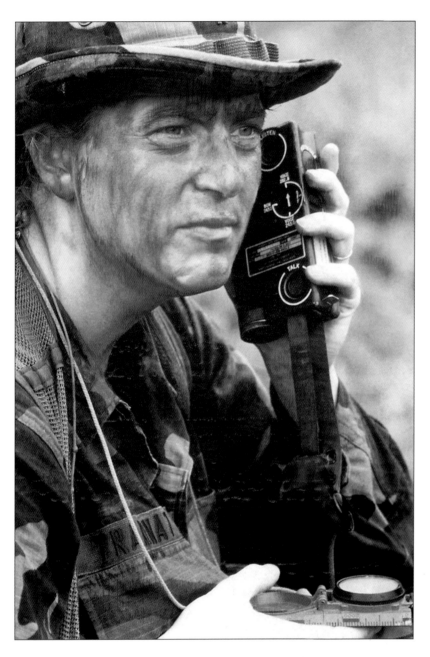

◀ Most important military communications are sent in burst mode. The message is recorded, then transmitted in a data burst of only a few milliseconds, reducing the risk of detection by the enemy.

Areas selected for patrol bases are set away from routes of enemy traffic and situated in places of little tactical value to the enemy. They must provide good CCD opportunities, be near a water source and also have defensive advantages. Conversely, the leader will avoid areas close to enemy or civilian activity, exposed places such as ridgelines or open ground, and sites which limit escape routes (such as narrow valleys or underneath steep rock faces).

When a base is first occupied, two members of the patrol should retrace the route into the base and remove traces of the patrol's entry (checking for litter, removing footprints, etc.). Security is established through machine gun positions and, in some cases, booby-trapped routes. For patrol members, only one exit and one entry point are constructed. Squad leaders will prepare range cards of the surrounding areas in case support fire has to be called. Watches are established for continuous guarding of the base, but it should not be occupied for more than 24 hours unless it is a stationary observation position.

A final problem for any patrol leader to overcome is that of returning to friendly lines without fratricide casualties. If possible, a return-to-lines should be performed in the daylight, as sentries are usually more inclined to open fire at night if approached by an unverified patrol. The patrol leader first halts the patrol at a rally point just out of

time. Stationary teams provide constant updates of enemy activity from a fixed location.

PATROL BASES AND RETURN-TO-LINES

Long-distance patrols often require temporary bases at the rally points. These bases facilitate rest and recuperation, the interchange of information, the cleaning and maintenance of weaponry, reduction in the chances of detection (such as when enemy aerial reconnaissance is attempting to spot moving patrols). They also act as observation posts.

small-arms range of the friendly lines and opposite an agreed re-entry point. From there, he radios his presence to the facing units, giving correct passwords and agreed identifiers. If radio communication is impossible, a small team (including the patrol leader) will approach the lines physically and give the relevant identifiers either verbally or through visual signals. Movement should only be directly towards the lines or laterally if moving across to a re-entry point. Lateral movement, however, should be well beyond small-arms range.

Once the patrol leader has received authorization, he leads the patrol across the lines. He should be the last to cross, as he has to count in the patrol members

to make sure that there are no absences. Once across, he will then proceed to give the information or results of the patrol at a debriefing.

COMBAT COMMUNICATIONS

Despite major advances in military communications technology, most communication among regular infantry forces is still conducted by radio. The electromagnetic activity of radio communications is measured and classified according to the wavelength of the transmission in metres and the frequency with which the wavelength oscillates. The rate of oscillation is measured in Hertz, with one Hertz equalling one cycle per second and so on.

Radio frequencies are sorted into nine bands, ranging from

extra-low frequency to extremely high frequency. Military communications utilize about six of these bands. Extra-low frequency (ELF; 300Hz–3KHz; wavelength 1000–100km/621–62 miles) and very low frequency (VLF; 3–30KHz; wavelength 100–10km/62–6miles) are generally only used for communicating with submerged submarines at sea. Many special forces units use high frequency (HF; 3–30MHz; wavelength 10km–100m/6–0.06 miles). As well as being used as a ground wave, it can also be bounced off the Earth's ionosphere to achieve long-range broadcasts, although HF is more easily intercepted than higher bands. Very high frequency (VHF; 30–300MHz; wavelength 1–10m/3–30ft) is a very common band for short-range military transmissions which do not require high security (thus it tends to be used by lower command levels). The Ultra high frequency (UHF; 300MHz–3GHz; wavelength 10cm–1m/4in–3ft) is a narrower and more secure band than the VHF, and Super high frequency (SHF; 3–30GHz; wavelength 1–10cm/0.3–4in) is very resistant to jamming – although it requires line-of-sight between the transmitter and the receiver. Finally,extremely high frequency (EHF; 30–300GHz; 1mm–1cm/ 0.03–0.4in) is occasionally used for military transmissions, but it tends to be a weak band in adverse weather conditions.

◄ *Large-scale military units will be accompanied into combat by advanced communications vehicles to support inter-unit co-ordination. Here, two US Army soldiers operate in a AN/TSC-85B satellite communications terminal van.*

▲ *More and more 'real-time' imaging is used in military operations. Data from satellites and reconnaissance aircraft is fed back to a central terminal to produce a complete map of allied and enemy positions.*

USING ANTENNAE

Much radio operator training is concerned with the effective use of antennae. Vertical antennae broadcast in all directions, whereas horizontal antennae broadcast bilaterally. The distance of transmission is often directly related to the length of the aerial used. Radio operators are trained in setting up field-expedient antennae made of wire to boost the range of their transmissions. To compute the correct length of aerial, they calculate it as a proportion of the wavelength using the following constants:

- 234 for a 0.25 wavelength antenna
- 468 for a 0.5 wavelength antenna
- 936 for a 1 wavelength antenna.

To deduce the aerial length, the constant is divided by the operating frequency in megahertz to give the length in metres. For example, a 0.5 wavelength antenna for a 50MHz operating frequency would be calculated as 468/50 = 9.36m (30.71ft).

Handling military communications is one of the most essential jobs within any military force and also one of the most complex. Radios are undoubtedly superb tools for battlefield communications, yet enemy forces will also do their utmost to intercept, locate or jam transmissions to gain tactical advantages. The radio operator (RO) must operate within clear guidelines to get the best out of his equipment and maintain security.

EFFECTIVE TRANSMISSIONS

A military radio transmission begins with the radio operator picking the right location. Various man-made objects or natural locations will degrade or prohibit a transmission. Man-made objects include power lines, radio stations (civil and military), television aerials, electrical generators, steel bridges and tall or bulky buildings. Natural locations include deep valleys, densely wooded areas (particularly in wet weather) or behind steep hills or mountains. Ideally, a radio transmission should be made away from power sources or objects that obstruct the easy passage of the transmission through the atmosphere. Line-of-sight between the transmitter and receiver usually produces the best results; however, as some of the more powerful military radios have ranges of more than 644km (400 miles), this is not always possible.

A radio operator must maintain radio security. Enemy tracking systems will monitor all battlefield broadcasts, and some only need a few milliseconds of transmission to triangulate a position to the transmitter and the radio operator's unit. There are many measures the radio operator can use to reduce the security risk of transmitting:

• Transmit data information which is encoded using approved codes instead of voice.
• Use authentication identifiers to precede all broadcasts.
• Turn radios off when not in use.
• Transmit only when absolutely necessary and keep transmissions short.
• Use directional antennae when possible. These are made even more secure by having a large hill or similar object between the enemy and the radio operator.
• Operate the radio on a low-power setting.
• Change frequencies and call signs as often as possible.
• Vary the times and places of transmission.

These measures should help the

▼ A US team establishes a communications post in desert terrain. The correct positioning of the antenna is vital; the surrounding buildings and aircraft will inhibit clear communications if they block the line of transmission.

◄ *A Land Rover lies wrecked after a terrorist explosion in Northern Ireland. Remotely detonated explosives can be so successful that they negate the need for a follow-up ambush by personnel.*

soldier to maintain reasonable security in battlefield conditions. However, jamming is another obstacle. Jamming is created by transmissions which deliberately distort or mask radio transmissions. It can severely hamper tactical efficiency among a unit.

The operator should continue broadcasting even if he is being jammed, because this denies the enemy any certain knowledge that his jamming is proving effective. Other counter-jamming measures include relocating the radio position to put terrain between the transmitter and the enemy, turning the radio's power up to full and turning off the squelch, and fitting a directional antenna to direct the signal away from jamming transmissions.

A final important point in radio security is that the soldier should move once he has completed a transmission. Radio operators are a high priority for enemy target-acquisition units, and triangulation equipment may deduce an artillery range and bearing from the transmission.

MODERN COMMUNICATIONS

Military communications are becoming increasingly sophisticated, and radio operators have many more communication options than they would have had 20 years ago. Digital communications systems are just entering battlefield usage, and some of these (such as the British Army's Bowman system) are supposedly immune to interception. More and

more information today is sent in data bursts. The radio operator keys information into a computer console, which encodes the message using codes known only to the transmission and receiving equipment. Once the message is typed, it is broadcast in a burst of only a few milliseconds. The receiver unravels this burst and decodes it. The advantage of burst communications is that the radio operator has much less exposure to enemy tracking and interception systems than when using real-time voice transmissions.

Another transmission technology is SATCOM – satellite communications. SATCOM technology tends to be used by special forces, although it is working its way into conventional infantry use. Messages are sent and received via orbiting military communications satellites in space. The advantage for the user is that all such transmissions are line-of-sight and thus have excellent clarity. Furthermore, signals transmitted from the satellite to the radio operator are very precisely aimed, and there is little scattered signal to be picked up by interception units.

AMBUSH TACTICS

An ambush is a surprise attack on an enemy unit, position or column, launched with the intention of destroying the target or severely degrading its capabilities. Ambushes are a key part of combat-patrol operations. They can be launched with little preparation or backed by advanced planning. They can be directed against minor units of personnel or launched upon major enemy formations which include armoured elements.

All ambushes are governed by a common series of objectives and operational guidelines. The first, and most important, is that the ambush should be launched from a camouflaged position which provides good fields of fire over the target area. Second, once the ambush is launched, the killing zone must be saturated with efficient and heavy firepower, while allowing the enemy little room or time to escape from the trap. Third, all members of an assault group must initiate the ambush at a common moment, otherwise fire is inefficient and sporadic. Finally, only the assault team should be engaged in the ambush, while security elements serve to defend the assault team, if necessary.

This last point is especially important. Most ambushes consist of two elements: an assault element and security element. The assault element actually springs and conducts the ambush with its heavy firepower. The security element serves to protect the assault team to its rear and along its exposed flanks. When ambushes are triggered, there is usually a rapid reinforcement response from surrounding enemy forces. The security team will prohibit these reinforcements coming to the support the ambushed party. The flanking security elements also set the limits of the ambush area, prohibiting the enemy escaping out of the kill zone and concentrating

them under the fire of the assault team.

An effective ambush must work in sympathy with the terrain. Some of the best locations for ambushes are:

- roads or trails bordered by dense foliage which can hide the ambush team
- narrow passes bordered by steep slopes which limit the enemy's escape options once the ambush has been sprung
- open ground ringed by cover
- enemy rally points or bases which are in a state of low security (usually deep within their own lines, so generally only ambushed by special forces units)
- urban zones which are hemmed in by buildings and offer few escape routes.

Current military doctrine asserts two main types of ambush formation: linear and L-shaped.

Linear: The elements of a linear ambush are positioned parallel to the enemy's route of travel, and so

it is excellent for ambushes against enemy columns travelling on straight road, rail, river or track. A portion of the route is selected for the ambush and booby trapped with a series of Claymore mines, underground mines or explosives. This portion is the kill zone, and the assault team is positioned behind the mantraps across the length of the portion. The security teams are positioned a short distance from each end of the kill zone, while another security team sits behind the assault element. This rear security team occupies the post-ambush rally point. The important point with a linear ambush is that it is not launched until all enemy forces have entered the kill zone. If the ambush is launched too early, and just the head of the column is engaged, the rearward elements of the enemy can fold around the side of the assault team in a flanking manoeuvre, which the security team might not be able to withhold.

L-Shaped: An L-shaped ambush formation is used to launch an

USING CLAYMORE MINES

The Claymore Directional Anti-Personnel Mine has been a key ambush weapon of infantry units since the 1960s. It consists of a curved pack of 680g (1.5lb) of C4 plastic explosive, into which is embedded 700 steel balls. The Claymore is mounted on two steel forks, which are set in the ground, and the firing face is directed towards the target area (the firing face bears the legend 'Front Towards

Enemy'). When the mine is detonated by remote firing handle or trip-wire, the 700 steel balls are blasted outwards in a 60-degree arc at a height of 2m (6.5ft), with a killing range of 50m (164ft). Ambushes often use series of Claymores that have overlapping fields of fire. When detonated simultaneously, few individuals caught unprotected within the rain of steel balls are likely to survive.

▲ Typical positions for an anti-armour ambush team. The high ground provides a better angle of fire down onto the enemy vehicles but allows the team to retreat over the hill if heavy shellfire is returned.

ambush across a route which features a deviation (such as a bend). The assault element and a flanking security team (Team A) are positioned along the long leg which leads up to the bend. These establish the main kill zone. Another security team (Team B) is positioned at right angles to the assault element along the short leg of the route immediately after the deviation. These two positions ensure that the enemy is caught in a boxed kill zone. Once the ambush is launched, Team B will set the limit to which the enemy can retreat from the

assault element by providing heavy cross fire.

Ambushes are further categorized as hasty or deliberate (point and area ambushes are the most typical types of deliberate ambush).

Hasty: A hasty ambush is one set up in response to a sudden proximate sighting of the enemy. As soon as the enemy is spotted, the leader silences verbal communications and the patrol adopts covered positions. From here, the leader surveys the enemy force and makes an assessment of its size, weaponry, direction of travel and ETA at an available ambush point (usually a matter of minutes in the case of a hasty ambush). If the enemy is considered too strong to tackle, the leader will initiate evasion tactics. If an ambush is the chosen option, he uses hand signals to place attack

and security elements and also to mark out the extent of the kill zone.

The soldiers should adopt their positions with a separation of 5–10m (15–30ft) between them if possible, and also set up mines and explosives if there is available time. When the enemy has entered and filled the kill zone, the ambush is initiated. Ambushes tend to last less than 30 seconds – a period of any longer implies that the enemy is mounting some effective resistance. Each soldier shoots down any enemy personnel within his field of fire. The leader will signal when the ambush is complete. An ambush is stopped for one of three reasons: the enemy is destroyed, the enemy is retreating or the ambush has been unsuccessful. If the ambush has been successful, once the firing has stopped, the assault element enters the kill zone and makes a search of

CHAPTER SIX

SPECIALIST SKILLS

Modern military forces have to cope with operational scenarios which would have been alien to soldiers 30 years ago. The rise of Operations Other Than War (OOTW) and the acceleration in military technology has led to increased specialization amongst soldiers. Counter-terrorism, covert infiltration and reconnaissance, humanitarian operations and psychological operations are just some of the roles which the modern combat unit must be able to handle. Many of the most specialized skills, such as hostage-rescue or covert parachuting, are only performed by Special Forces. Other specialisms, like night-fighting, are now the common currency of regular soldiers, and modern armies have never been better trained in the history of men at arms.

◄ *A three-man team prepares to enter a building during hostage-rescue training. The soldier on the right prepares a stun grenade while the soldier on the left is set to enter with automatic fire.*

◄ *An SAS trooper makes a violent building entry. Hostage-rescue teams usually aim to have multiple points of entry into a building to confuse the enemy's defensive response and provide more rapid floor clearance.*

Before World War I, military combat specialization was fairly limited. There were basic unit specialities, such as archer, cavalryman and rifleman. Certain tools of war demanded specially trained units, primarily artillery, which by the sixteenth century had become a sufficiently complicated weapon to necessitate professional associations such as the British Honourable Artillery Company (HAC). Professions in navies also had a high degree of specialization owing to the multitude of on-ship duties.

World War I saw a marginal increase in troop specialization. Tanks and combat aircraft made their first appearance, both requiring skilled personnel to man them, maintain them and fight with them. Teams of soldiers proficient in mining were assigned to dig tunnels under enemy defences,

which were then packed with explosives and detonated. Communications via telegraph or landline became a job in its own right. Two- to four-man teams skilled in sustained fire operated machine guns. The trend of World War I was that technology, rather than tactics, led specialization.

World War II advanced this trend even further with the need for individuals who could operate sophisticated aircraft, armoured units, radar communications and surveillance equipment, combined-arms operations and so on. Yet, during World War II, there also emerged the requirement for tactical specialization. Total war necessitated new styles of covert or behind-the-lines operations which regular troops were not trained to perform. These became the province of special forces.

Special forces are units which are trained to fight types of warfare or enemy outside the remit and skills of ordinary soldiers. The first such unit to emerge was the 800th Special Purpose Training Battalion Brandenburg (better known as the 'Brandenburgers').

The Brandenburgers were ostensibly a Wehrmacht unit, but their directives came from the Abwehr, the German military intelligence and counterintelligence organization headed by Admiral Canaris. The Brandenburgers were employed behind enemy lines to conduct sabotage and demolitions, liaise with German agents and conduct dangerous combat missions in preparation for German offensives. Germany created several more special forces units throughout the duration of the war, including the Freidenthal Special Duties Battalion within the Waffen-SS and the Klein Kampfe Verbände (Small Battle Band) in the navy. Allied forces soon followed suit.

In 1940, Britain created the Special Operations Executive (SOE) to support and establish resistance movements in German-occupied countries (although in essence it was more of an espionage organization than a military unit). In July 1941, the Special Air Service was formed within the British Army, with the initial mission of conducting long-range reconnaissance and attacks behind Axis lines in North Africa. It went on to serve in similar behind-the-lines roles in many other theatres. The United States formed the Office of Strategic Services (OSS), with a Special Operations division conducting raids and covert surveillance across Europe, the Middle East and the Far East. Australia's 'Z' Special Unit teamed up with British special forces to conduct irregular warfare against the Japanese in the Pacific.

With the end of World War II, many special forces units were disbanded, their specialist roles perceived as over. The postwar explosion of insurgency conflicts and the

▾ *Subaqua infiltration is a silent and discreet method of deploying on enemy coastlines. Its main disadvantage is that the divers require another vehicle to place them within convenient swimming distance of the beach.*

onset of the Cold War, however, saw a renewed need for specialist operatives. The 22 SAS was quickly re-formed for service in Malaya, and the Vietnam War saw the creation of many special forces units with the express sanction of President Kennedy, a diligent student of counterinsurgency warfare. Groups created during the Vietnam conflict included the 5th Special Forces group, the Long Range Reconnaissance Patrol (LRRP) and the US Navy SEALs. The Soviet Union also had its own elite body of special forces, the Spetsnaz, although little is known of their precise operations. In Israel, elite Sayeret Matkal commandos have become possibly the most combat-experienced special forces unit of the postwar world, used in Israel's continual fight against Arab military and irregular forces.

The invaluable contribution of special forces to postwar military operations secured their future. An increase of terrorist activity in the 1970s and 1980s led to the formation of many highly trained counterterrorist/hostage rescue units, particularly throughout Europe, while in the United States the US Special Operations Command was established in 1987 to oversee all special forces missions. Today, special forces are often the first deployed into a combat zone. At the time of writing, US and British special forces are conducting intensive combat operations in the mountains of Afghanistan against the Taleban organization implicated in the destruction of the World Trade Center on 11 September 2001.

The skills explored below are not always the province of special

199

◀ The SA80 rifle is one of the most accurate assault rifles in the world. Its SUSAT sight allows sniping out to ranges of 400m (1219ft), though many would argue that the 5.56mm (2in) round has insufficient take-down power.

forces alone – this is particularly the case with airborne assault. Most are, however, the skills which separate the regular run of soldiers from those regarded as part of an elite.

SNIPING

The effect of a capable sniper on the enemy is out of all proportion to the number of troops (one) deployed. The great Russian sniper of Stalingrad, Vasili Zaitsev, killed around 400 German personnel during his period of operation, and the Finnish sniper Simo Häyhä killed more than 500 German and Russian combatants. A sniper can erode enemy decision-making capability by killing officers and radio operators. He can paralyze an entire enemy unit by prohibiting free and open movement between positions. In turn, this results in an

intimidated enemy with lower morale. Snipers can also hit key individuals while leaving surrounding groups, such as a crowd of civilians, unharmed.

THE TOOLS OF SNIPING

Most infantry are armed with an assault rifle which has a competent accuracy up to around 400m (1312ft). A sniper will shoot to ranges in excess of 800m (2625m) and so requires a weapon and ammunition of far greater accuracy. Many snipers have, admittedly, used common weapons. Simo Häyhä used nothing more than a Mosin-Nagant Model 28 fitted with iron sights, and most British Army snipers during World War II and up until the 1960s relied on the standard issue Lee-Enfield rifle. Since the end of World War II, however, sniper rifles have become

increasingly specialized heavy-barrelled weapons firing bullets of 7.62mm (0.3in) calibre and larger. Sighting is almost invariably via an optical telescopic sight or similar magnifying instrument (rarely iron sights), and the rifle's furniture is usually fully adjustable for a customized fit to the shooter. The bolt-action has been traditionally preferred to automatic loading because bolts powered by self-loading actions give less consistent positioning of the bullet in the chamber, which in turn gives a less consistent accuracy over a group of shots. However, weapons such as the Israeli Galil Sniper and the Russian Dragunov SVD are automatic and still retain an effective operational accuracy up to and over 800m (2625ft).

Sniper barrels are heavier and thicker than normal rifle barrels. The extra weight and dimensions make the barrel impervious to heat build-up during firing and fluctuations in environmental temperatures, both of which can fractionally warp a standard rifle barrel. Ammunition is also of better quality than standard ammunition, having first-class aerodynamics, snug seating in the barrel and excellent penetration and accuracy over long range. A typical sniper round used by US forces is the 7.62mm (.3in) Special Ball Bullet. This has a gliding metal jacket over a lead antimony slug and a weight of 173 grains. It is boat-tailed, the base of the bul-

▲ *Two snipers man their 7.62mm (.2in) Mauser 86 rifles. The Mauser 86 is a bolt-action weapon with a nine-round magazine, though more military snipers are moving to semi-automatic weapons with larger magazine capacities.*

let tapered to reduce aerodynamic drag when it dips to subsonic speeds. Fired from a fixed rest to a range of 550m (1804ft), 10 rounds of M118 bullets had a grouping of less than 30cm (12in) (data from US Army FM 23-10).

Sniper rifles are usually fitted with telescopic sights. Some of these have image-intensification properties. Larger night-vision sights can be fitted, but they are often so large that the balance of the weapon is affected. The sights will be zeroed by the operator to the capabilities of the weapon, although

600m (1968ft) is a standard distance at which a first-round kill can be expected. Heavier-calibre weapons such as the .50 (12.7mm) Barrett M82A1 has sights calibrated out to 2000m (6562ft). This distance is rarely attempted by any sniper; however, during the Gulf War, a US sniper killed a Iraqi captain at a distance of 1800m (5906ft) with a Barrett. Barrett fire also accounted for the deaths of British soldiers in Northern Ireland in the border zone of County Armagh in the 1980s. Evidence suggested the sniper was firing from a long-range position actually over the border in the Irish Republic. Most good sniper sights are fully adjustable according to range, image clarity, windage and elevation. The sight fittings must be of as good quality as the sight itself. The M3A Scope Mount fitted to the

M24 sniper rifle (the US Army's standard weapon) allows the sniper to remove and replace the sight with less than half a minute of angle change in the zero.

A sniper must develop a close relationship with his rifle, training with it constantly and to the exclusion of other weapons. The rifle has to be well maintained: sights zeroed and ready for deployment, with the optical glass kept free from scratches and debris; bore and chamber regularly cleaned to prevent the build-up of corrosive propellant deposits; bolt cleaned and very lightly oiled; stored at room temperature and kept free of moisture and condensation; ammunition kept clean and dry; and magazine springs protected by emptying cartridges when not in use.

▲ *Advanced camouflage and concealment skills are required to be a successful sniper. This soldier has camouflaged his gun to avoid glare off the metal and also taped down parts of the gun which might rattle during movement.*

SNIPING TECHNIQUE

Sniper marksmanship is a very advanced skill which requires physical control teamed with a solid working knowledge of ballistics. The first stage of making an accurate long-range shot is adopting the correct firing position. The fore-end of the rifle is almost always supported on a solid rest – a log, table, tree bough, etc. Most snipers carry a small sandbag around with them, which is ideal for this purpose. The firing hand should grip the small of the stock with the index finger on the trigger, but not touching any other part of the stock. If it does touch the stock, it could disturb the balance of the weapon when the trigger is pulled. The non-firing hand is usually placed beneath the stock, and cups the inside of the firing-arm's elbow. This forms a platform on which the stock can rest. The stock itself is nestled firmly into the shoulder, usually on a pad which reduces slight movements from the pulse or breathing being transferred into the rifle. The elbows are placed as most comfortable, usually resting on a soft but firm platform (such as a patch of soft earth). The cheek is rested on the stock. The position of the cheek should not be changed whatever the firing position, as the change will affect the sight alignment. The soldier should find a position in which there is no tension throughout his entire body. Tension produces muscle shake and tense breathing, which in turn will cause the muzzle to circle and wobble during aiming. The soldier should concentrate on making sure his bones are supported, and not just pads of flesh. Finally, the aiming eye should look through the sight in a position close enough to obtain a good sight picture, but far enough away to avoid being injured by the sight rim during recoil.

Once in a comfortable and correct posture, the sniper will put the cross-hairs on his target. For a human being, the target area is generally the torso, as this offers the greatest possibilities for hitting a vital organ. The head is a valid aiming point, but should not be attempted at ranges over about 300–400m (984–1312ft). Head shots are more typical for the close ranges of urban combat.

To take the shot, the sniper should first take two long, deep breaths to oxygenate the blood fully. Without full oxygenation, the muscles will be tense and transfer wobble to the gun. The aim should be made with the whole body, not just the arms. Aligning the body with the target will bear the gun on the target more naturally. The soldier should then take in a deep breath and release it very slowly. At the end of the out-breath, he should hold his breath gently for up to 8–10 seconds. For the moment that the breath is held, his body will be absolutely still. It is in this moment that the sniper should make the final adjustment to targeting and

EXPERT SNIPER – CARLOS HATHCOCK

USMC Gunnery Sergeant Carlos Hathcock was one of the most successful snipers of the Vietnam War, with 93 confirmed kills. Hathcock was a passionate exponent of the art of sniping and did much to change the low opinion of snipers previously held in the military establishment. One of his actions involved the killing of an NVA general after three days of stalking. The distance of the stalk was 1090m (3576ft). Almost all of this stalk was performed using a belly or side crawl (the side crawl was preferred because it left less of a trail in the grass). Such was the need for stealth that Hathcock performed all bodily functions inside his uniform. His arms, legs and hips were horribly blistered from

rubbing over the ground. Ants covered his body.

His tactical priority was to avoid response fire from four NVA .51-calibre machine guns – two on his left flank, two on his right. His shot position was a small rise of earth which gave him a clear view of the positions and quick escape back into a nearby tree line. He had sighted his rifle in advance to 635m (2084ft) and placed himself at that distance using his map and range estimation. He then calculated the effects of humidity, wind and temperature, and fired his shot, killing the NVA general outright. His escape to the tree line was made in a gully which allowed him to stand in a crouch and run unseen.

take the trigger pressure to firing point. When the sight reticule stabilizes on the target, the trigger is squeezed right back and the shot taken. If the sniper holds the breath for too long, the oxygen in his blood will deplete and wobble will come back. The sniper can adopt one of several body positions when taking a shot, although the terrain usually

constrains which is used. He can lie prone, stand, kneel or adopt any other position as long as weapon and body are fully and stably sup-

▼ *The prone sniping position is the most popular for field sniping. The important principle behind a sniping position is that the bones must be supported, not just the muscles, if the position is to be stable.*

ported. If standing and leaning against a tree, a rope can be twisted around the trunk until it is tight and then the barrel inserted between the rope and the tree for a firm grip-hold.

ENVIRONMENTAL CONSIDERATIONS
The flight of a sniper's bullet is affected by several environmental factors: temperature, barometric pressure, humidity and wind.
Temperature: As temperature climbs, air density lessens and subsequently reduces drag on a bullet as it passes through the air. Less drag means more muzzle velocity, a longer period of flat travel and consequently a higher point of impact. The sniper should zero his weapon to the conditions he is likely to experience during combat.

Barometric Pressure: Increased altitude brings a decrease in barometric pressure, which in turn reduces air density. Sniping at high altitudes, therefore, has similar considerations to sniping in high temperatures, the impact point of the bullet being higher than at sea level because of increased muzzle velocity. This equation can be altered by the weather conditions present at high altitude, such as fog.

Humidity: Increased humidity means increased air resistance against the bullet and a lowered impact point, and vice versa.

Wind: Of all the environmental considerations, wind has the most serious effect on the flight of a bullet. Wind deviation increases with range as the bullet slows and has less forward force to resist wind influence. Winds that are at a right angle to the

▲ *An urban sniper takes aim around a street corner. He is leaning his weight against a wall using his left hand, the hand forming a secure support for the front of the gun.*

flight of the bullet will have more influence than winds coming in from 45 degrees. First, the sniper must assign a value to the wind direction using the clock method. The sniper is classed as the centre of the clock and the target as 12 o'clock. Full-value wind blows from three or nine o'clock (at a right angle to the line of shot), and half-value wind from one, two, four, five, seven, eight, 10 and 11 o'clock (it has half the influence over the bullet from full-value wind). The direction of wind can be determined by dropping a handful of grass from shoulder height and observing the direction of fall.

After wind direction comes wind velocity. Suspending a strip of light material from a twig can indicate wind speed using a simple equation. The estimated angle between the blowing piece of the material and the vertical line of the twig, divided by the constant of four, gives approximate wind velocity in km/miles per hour (for example, 60-degree angle divided by four equals 24km/h/15mph). If the 'flag' method cannot be used, the sniper drops some grass or material from shoulder height, observes the point of landing, then calculates the angle between the vertical point of drop and the landing place.

Once the sniper has determined all wind factors, he must translate the data into adjustments of his sniper sight. Sniper sights are adjusted in minutes of angle (a minute is one-sixtieth of a degree).

▾ *The angle at which the sniper looks through his scope affects the placement of the shot. The diagram shows how shot relates to angle of viewing with both post and cross-hairs sights.*

Wind effect is calculated by the following formula:

Range (in 100s of metres) / 100 x wind speed (mph) / Constant = adjustment in minutes for full-value wind

(For half-value wind, the minutes total is divided by two)

The constants are: 100–500m: 15; 600m: 14; 700–800m: 13; 900m: 12; 1000m: 13

For example:

800m / 100 = 8
8 x 15mph wind speed = 120
120/13 = 9.2 minutes of adjustment for full-value wind

TACTICAL CONSIDERATIONS

A sniper's main tactical considerations are insertion and movement to target, establishing a firing position, escape and evasion, and extraction.

Insertion is the means by which the sniper is deployed to the area of operation. This can be anything from walking in on foot to being deployed by helicopter or even parachute. The priority during insertion is stealth: the enemy must have no prior awareness that a sniper is in the area or they will increase anti-sniper surveillance measures (increased patrols, aerial reconnaissance, etc.). Once deployed, the sniper will move to the target area. As seen in the example of Hathcock, moving to shot position can be laborious. Full camouflage, concealment and decoy (CCD) measures must be in place (see 'Camouflage and Concealment', Chapter Five), and the route of travel should not cut through large enemy concentrations. If the sniper is part of a team, communication is by hand signals only, so visual contact must be maintained at all times.

The firing position must be well concealed and with entry and exit routes which allow unobserved movement. During the infamous duel between Vasili Zaitsev and his German counterpart Major Konings of the Berlin sniper school, Konings chose to lay a flat sheet of iron propped up on rubble as his

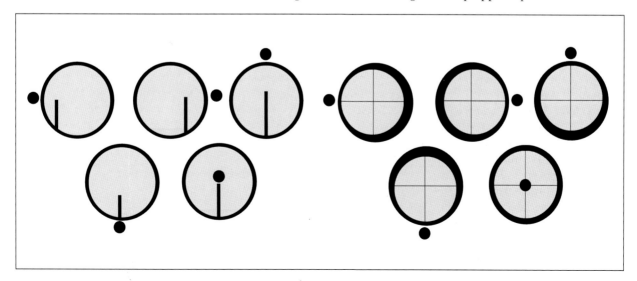

firing position for the final encounter. Only Zaitsev's vast experience in sniping alerted him to this position in Stalingrad's ocean of rubble, and he was able to despatch Konings, but a lesser man would have had little idea of Konings' presence (more basic cover, such as an abandoned tank and a pillbox, were rejected by Konings as too obvious). A sniper position must also have good visual command of the target area, hence high ground is often selected (although never occupying summits or ridgelines). The position should be downwind of enemy positions to avoid guard dogs picking up the sniper's scent. If the position is to be held for a long

time, a water source should be nearby. The position must have as many obstacles as possible, both visual and practical, between it and the enemy to spoil response fire or pursuit operations once the sniper has fired.

Once the shot has be taken, the sniper must either escape or immediately deploy to another firing position. If escaping, he must apply all escape and evasion measures in two phases. First, he must withdraw from the fighting position to a covered rally point (RP). Next, he must move from the rally point to a place from which he can be extracted if necessary. Extraction can be by any of the measures used for infiltration, but with added securi-

▲ Urban sniping. Note how the sniper positions himself back into the room to avoid framing himself in the window. The sandbags against the wall provide some measure of protection against enemy grenades, missiles and shells.

ty measures because the enemy will be aware of the sniper's need to escape from an area. An enemy must not have air superiority if helicopter extraction is used.

HOSTAGE RESCUE IN BUILDINGS

Most hostage-rescue (HR) missions take place in buildings purely because urban centres have the greatest concentration of domestic and terrorist incidents. As soon as a hostage situation is reported, the

▸ A diagram showing the movement of an HR unit through a building. Note how the team mixes the method of entry into each room, sometimes via the door sometimes via an adjoining wall, to confuse the enemy.

hostage rescue unit (HRU) must quickly locate the building in question and deploy rapidly to the site, usually in fast-response vehicles or police cars, but sometimes in undercover vehicles if the operation has a covert element. SAS troops deploying to the Prince's Gate siege in 1980 arrived not in military vehicles, but in civilian cars and wearing civilian clothes. They changed into combat gear on site. At the scene of the incident, the first priority is to set up a tight perimeter around the building. This prohibits the hostage-taker escaping with hostages and stops anyone else from interfering with the situation (such as journalists, family and friends of any parties inside, mailmen, etc.) Around the initial perimeter, another perimeter is established by conventional police units. This takes over the responsibility of handling crowds and other intrusions and leaves the inner HRU to deal with rescue and negotiation.

The HRU straight away sets up covered routes of movement around the building and fields of fire for all its officers. A rapid-response plan is immediately drawn up in case the HRU has to enter the building within minutes of arrival. Snipers occupy salient positions with good views of the hostage building. A command post is set up just behind the inner perimeter. This co-ordinates all aspects of the operation, everything from logistics to negotiations.

Once the area is secured, negotiation and intelligence gathering begins. A negotiator is an integral part of a HRU. The first 15 minutes of a hostage-rescue situation are the most dangerous, as the hostage-taker is usually very excitable or scared, so the negotiator will attempt to talk the hostage-taker through this period. The longer the siege continues, the more likelihood of a peaceful resolution. The negotiator will usually communicate with the hostage-taker via a phone line, which must be isolated very quickly to stop the hostage-taker communicating with other parties outside the HRU.

The negotiator fulfils several roles. First, he has to calm the hostage-taker and thus reduce the

◂ The movements taken by the SAS hostage-rescue team through the first floor of the Iranian Embassy, London, 1980. Entry teams burst through the windows before systematically clearing each room, using stun grenades and automatic fire.

Counsellor's office

Accounts

Telex room

Stairwell

Lift

Ambassador's office

General office

First floor

SAS entry points

Second floor

▲ *The entry procedure for room clearance involves two combatants entering the room and clearing opposite sides of the space, the room being divided in two by an imaginary line between diagonally opposite corners (for rooms with offset doors).*

level of threat to the hostages. Second, he must listen to the hostage-taker's demands and begin to discuss possible resolutions to the siege. Finally, he must make a psychiatric assessment of the hostage-taker to let the HRU know of any mental disorders which may preclude a peaceful resolution.

RESCUE IN LIMA

One of the most interesting and longest hostage-rescue operations took place on 22 April 1997 in the Japanese Ambassador's residence in Lima, Peru. The ambassador and 600 guests at a party in the residence were taken hostage by 14 Marxist Tupac Amaru terrorists (the action was stated as a protest against Japanese involvement in Peruvian politics) on 18 December 1996. Within two weeks, the terrorists had released all but 74 hostages; however, the siege dragged on for another four months after this. During the long stand-off, HRU specialists planted listening devices and cameras all over the building, gaining so much intelligence that they even built a full mock-up of the interior in which to train themselves. They also dug a 220m (722ft) tunnel under the residence to be used as an entry point for an assault team. When the rescue attempt was finally launched, the HRU's intelligence paid off, as all 41 terrorists were killed in less than 41 seconds for the loss of two HRU members and one hostage.

The ideal goal of the negotiator is to make the hostage-taker submit himself to custody without violence. US SWAT negotiators are so experienced and well trained that more than 75 per cent of hostage incidents are usually resolved without violence.

While negotiations are proceeding, the HRU will perform intelligence gathering. Relevant intelligence is anything which will help the HRU perform a successful rescue operation should the negotiations fail or which gives the negotiator extra leverage. Intelligence about the interior of the building is especially vital for planning a possible assault. The construction of walls, floors and doors (including lock types) must be known, as must entry points, flammable materials, burglar alarms or motion-activated lighting systems. The terrain around the building is analyzed for covered routes of approach. Most crucially, the location of the hostage-taker and hostages needs to be pinpointed. This can be achieved by covertly inserting endoscopes through walls or vents to provide pictures of the interior situation or using remote or planted listening devices to monitor auditory signals.

All intelligence is distributed to the members of the HRU, and photographs of the suspects and hostages are viewed and memorized. A comprehensive entry operation is planned out in full.

HOSTAGE RESCUE BY FORCE

A HRU will attempt a rescue by force if a) a hostage has been killed or wounded; b) it looks likely that a hostage will be killed or wounded; or c) security forces surrounding

the building have been attacked by the hostage-taker. The chief officer at the scene will give the signal for the HRU to move in. At the last moment before entry, distraction tactics may be used to confuse or relocate the hostage-taker. The

▲ *A hostage-rescue trooper throws a stun grenade during a training exercise. Stun grenades produce an extremely loud and violent bang and flash, but do not send out lethal fragments like conventional grenades.*

◄ *Fast-roping enables a hostage-rescue team to make surprise entries through upper-floor windows and balconies. Windows are usually demolished using special frame charges or through small-arms fire.*

point man closely into rooms. The team leader backs up the point and clearing men and makes tactical decisions throughout the operation. The fourth man is another clearing man. He is usually employed to blow open doors with a shotgun loaded with Shok Loc rounds, but he also will engage hostage-takers with a handgun if required. Finally, the rear guard protects the back of the team and provides assistance during the operation.

Two forms of entry to the building are available: stealth or dynamic. Stealth involves getting as close as possible to the hostage-taker and hostages without being detected. A dynamic entry is violent; the team enters by shooting doors off their hinges, smashing through windows or blowing entry holes in walls with demolitions.

Once inside, the team must systematically perform room clearance. Each room is cleared according to an established procedure. The point man opens the door into a room, quickly throws a stun grenade inside and allows it to detonate. Stun grenades explode with an excruciatingly loud bang and bright flash, enough to disable a person for several seconds. (Although stun grenades do not kill or wound, the point man may forego their use if there are crowded hostages inside or very old hostages). The point man then enters the room and takes up a position to the left of the door,

negotiator may distract the hostage-taker with another phone call and so bring the hostage-taker to a specific location. Snipers may shoot out a light. Power to the building might be cut, plunging it into darkness.

An entry team will usually consist of five men (or groups of five).

The point man will lead the team and be the first man through the doors. He is usually armed with a pistol so that he has a free hand to open doors and manipulate entry and surveillance equipment. The clearing man is armed with a sub-machine gun and will follow the while the clearing man enters behind him and positions himself on the opposite side of the room. Both men will attempt to neutralize the hostage-taker with accurate fire as soon as they enter the room, each having a fire sector of 50 per cent of the room divided from the left corner behind the door to the diagonally opposite corner. The hostage-taker is shot and secured by the point man and first clearing man, while the team leader and second clearing man enter the room to assist and remove the hostages or make their own assault into any connecting rooms. The rear guard remains in the hallway outside and watches for movement from any other rooms. Once the room is cleared of visible hostage-takers, it is thoroughly searched for any in hiding.

If the locations of the hostage-taker and hostages are not known, the process is repeated from room to room.

HOSTAGE RESCUE WITH AIR-PLANES, TRAINS AND VEHICLES

HR operations against vehicles are more complicated than those of buildings because the hostage-taker has mobility. Mobility in turn denies the establishment of the security perimeters useful to effective negotiation and assault planning. In the case of planes and trains, the hostage-taking situation usually arises during transit. Buses and cars are generally taken when

static or are provided by the HRU itself in response to the demand of a hostage-taker.

The HRU should use all methods to prevent a hostage situation going mobile or mitigate the effects of mobility. If the hostage-taker has requested a vehicle, the HRU negotiator can possibly achieve the release of some hostages if the

vehicle will not take them all. With fewer hostages, the hostage-taker will be more exposed to a well-aimed sniper shot when he crosses from a building to the vehicle. If there is no option but to provide a vehicle, then the vehicle should be fitted with a remote engine cut-off device and have its mirrors and door locks removed.

▸ *The typical SAS hostage-rescue kit: an S6 respirator, flame-resistant overall, kevlar body armour, a Heckler & Koch MP5A3 submachine gun (magazines strapped to left leg) and 9mm (.4in) Browning Hi-Power pistol on the right thigh.*

Once a hostage-situation is mobile, the HRU must: 1) stop the vehicle safely; 2) assault the vehicle and eliminate the hostage-taker; and 3) remove the hostages safely from the vehicle.

AUTOMOBILE HOSTAGE RESCUE

If a remote cut-off has not been fitted, the best way to stop a car is to burst its tyres or block the road. Tyres can be burst by special strips of metallic spikes dragged across the road in front of the car (known as 'stop strips' in the United States and 'Stingers' in the United Kingdom). Shooting a tyre out is not advisable, as a single burst tyre may cause the vehicle to flip at speed. Blocking the road is probably the best option. The blockage

can be any obstruction which stretches across the entire road, including the verges. Usually it is other vehicles, such as a truck. The blockage is positioned around a corner or over the brow of a hill, anywhere as long as the driver is not aware of its presence until the last moment. HRU forces should be positioned in front and to the sides of the blockage so that they can pull out and stop the hostage vehicle reversing away from the trap.

Once a car has been brought to a stop, the first task is to eliminate the hostage-taker before harm can be done to the hostage. This can be done by snipers (who will be positioned at the ambush site) or by an assault team if the snipers cannot achieve a clear shot. In February

▲ *Sniping into vehicles needs to take account of the deflection of the bullet as it passes through the windshield. Bullets tend to curve inward slightly into the angle at which they strike the glass.*

1976, in Djibouti, Somalia, French GIGN snipers shot five terrorists on board a hijacked bus full of school-children. They achieved their clear shots by providing the bus with drugged food which made all the children fall asleep. (Unfortunately, one remaining terrorist managed to run back to the bus to shoot a girl dead before he was himself killed.)

The assault team will consist of six to eight men – four to conduct the assault and the rest to break into the vehicle or conduct further assault duties. The team will approach from both sides of the vehicle to give all-round shot options. A frontal assault will give a clearer sight picture through the windscreen, but a rear assault is better for the quick extraction of hostages because of the direction in which the doors open (the team leader must assess the priority). As the team approaches at speed, the support elements distract the attention of the hostage-taker and smash open the windows with a crowbar-type device or spring-loaded punches. The team then kills the hostage-taker with a short, concentrated burst of sub-machine-gun or handgun fire, or a

▼ *A scene from the aftermath of the GSG 9 rescue at Mogadishu, Somalia. In only a few minutes GSG 9 troopers rescued 89 hostages unharmed from a hijacked Boeing 707 and killed or neutralized all the hijackers.*

shotgun slug. The hostages are then pulled quickly from the vehicle while some team members stay behind to secure the vehicle and hostage-taker.

HOSTAGE RESCUE AND BUSES

Stopping a hijacked bus can be accomplished in the same way as a car, although the bus's greater weight means that it can smash through all but the heaviest blockages. Buses have several mechanical features which facilitate forced stopping. They often feature engine cut-off buttons at the rear over the engine cowling, and if brake lines are cut rear brakes will lock on automatically. Both these measures can be applied if the vehicle comes to a stop at a red light or similar urban stop point.

Once the bus is stopped, access is gained by using a ram against the front doors, by simply opening the

rear door if it has an external handle or by smashing through into the driver's compartment and operating the door controls. As entry is taking place, distraction devices, such as stun grenades, will be thrown against the side of the bus to draw the hostage-taker's attention. Snipers may also choose this moment (if not earlier) to fire on the hostage-taker. Indeed, this can be the best option because of the all-round visibility which a hostage-taker has from a bus.

An assault team moves on the bus and splits into three groups. One group (about four men) enters the bus itself, two covering the aisle and passengers, and two moving down the aisle in search of the hostage-taker. Another group of two covers the rear exit of the bus outside, while the remaining men cover other doors, windows and the driver's compartment. If the

hostage-taker is instantly identified, he will be shot unless he surrenders. If, however, he is mixed in with the passengers, each passenger will be cuffed, searched for weapons and removed from the bus one at a time until the suspect is found.

HOSTAGE RESCUE AND TRAINS
Stopping a hijacked train is reasonably straightforward, as its route is confined to a specific track. The train can be redirected into a railway yard (never a station, which is full of civilians) or a siding, where an HRU ambush waits.

Clearing a train of hostage-takers is similar to clearing a bus, but each carriage may require a full assault team. Again, snipers will attempt to eliminate the hostage-takers at a distance, although some high-speed trains have super-reinforced glass which will deflect the path of even a heavy sniper bullet.

One option used in HRU training is to blow a hole in the roof of the train with a shaped charge, with the hole acting as a fire port into the train interior.

Once inside the train, the assault team should adopt the same assault formation as that used in bus hostage rescue. One of the most spectacular train hostage-rescue operations was that accomplished by Dutch Marines when six South Moluccan terrorists seized the Depunt train and 94 passengers on 23 May 1977 (the terrorists wanted the Netherlands to compel Indonesia to grant independence for the island of South Molucca). After a three-week siege, the Marines arranged a low-level fly-past by Royal Dutch Air Force jets to distract the terrorists, before boarding the train and killing all terrorists (one hostage died).

HOSTAGE RESCUE ABOARD AIRCRAFT
Stopping a hijacked aircraft is rarely a problem. Refuelling requirements will demand that the aircraft touch down at an airport. As flight routes are plotted by traffic control, the HRU is usually waiting at the appropriate airport in advance.

Entry and manoeuvre into a hijacked aircraft is the biggest problem. Sniping is rarely an option because of the narrow width and toughness of the glass apertures. Door entry procedures vary with

◂ *When disembarking from a helicopter, soldiers immediately deploy themselves in an all-round defence. Machine-gunners exit first and the team leader and second-in-command separate to reduce the risk of both being killed by enemy fire.*

▸ *A re-supply aircraft requires ground units to establish two points for an accurate drop: a prominent terrain feature (A) which acts as a line-up point for the actual drop zone (B).*

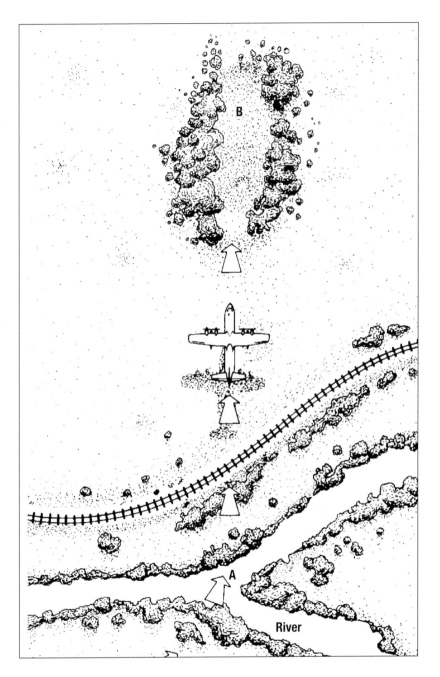

each major aircraft type because of different door opening mechanisms (a 747, for example, has a manual side-hinged door; a 767, an electric upward-opening door; and a 727, a door-and-stair system). The air-hijack HRU will have trained within most standard commercial airliners prior to the event, so should know the entry procedure for most aircraft. However, the hijackers are likely to have the main doors well covered or booby-trapped, so most HRUs will gain entry through emergency exits at wing and cockpit locations or inspection hatches, or through the cargo hold. French GIGN troops assaulting a hijacked Air France flight in Marseilles in 1994 used a mobile aircraft stairway to board, which they had moved into position while pretending to be aircraft engineers.

The HRU will plan a sequence of multiple entries. An aircraft interior is long, fairly narrow and packed with passengers, and it is far too complex for a single assault team. Several simultaneous entries insert as large a number of hostage-rescue operatives as manageable. Care must be taken, however, that one team is not occupying the fire sector of another.

Entry is frequently carried out at night. Distance between perimeter and aircraft is crossed using all available cover and concealment. Normal airport vehicles such as baggage carts can be used, and sound baffles provide good concealment around the edges of open airfields. Once the aircraft is reached, the ascent to wing or door level is usually via purpose-designed assault ladders. The HRU will advance silently across the wings or penetrate through underbelly hatches, often in coordination with a visual or auditory distraction on the opposite side of the place from the assault. Once they enter the aircraft, the HRU will tend to deploy stun grenades, despite their close proximity to the hostages. Fire control elements

◄ A US Navy SEAL practises an amphibious incursion during a riverine exercise. SEALs were created for assassination, reconnaissance and ambush missions for the watery lanes of the Mekong Delta in Vietnam.

types of means: airborne, waterborne and land-based.

PRE-INFILTRATION INTELLIGENCE

The quality of enemy forces and defences in the area to be penetrated dictate the means of infiltration. For airborne and waterborne insertions, the most important intelligence concerns the enemy's technological means of detection. This includes systems such as marine and aviation over-the-horizon (OTH) radar, surveillance aircraft and ships patrolling possible infiltration routes, and underwater sensors deployed off coastal districts and along key rivers. For landbased infiltration, possibly the most viable form of insertion, concerns are more focused on the positions of enemy forces and reconnaissance units. If the land-based insertion must move through a border zone or protected enemy line, however, the unit must have intelligence on features such as enemy night-vision or thermal imaging equipment; the emplacement of defensive devices such as mines, barbed wire, trip-wire-activated flares or guard dogs; and the nature, frequency and remit of border patrols.

Only when all intelligence is gathered can a proper infiltration plan begin. This will usually select the least defended portion of enemy territory as the infiltration point, but not always. Sometimes apparently well-defended areas are ideal

of the HRU must be on immediate standby in case any flammable materials on the aircraft catch light. Immediate incapacitation of the hostage-taker is vital because of the death-toll he could inflict in the close quarters of the plane and also because passengers are likely to panic after the first few seconds and make the HRU's job more difficult.

Clearing the interior of the aircraft consists of two-man teams moving down the aircraft under cover of troopers positioned either

side of the fuselage. Emergency evacuation slides will often be activated to effect a speedy removal of the hostages.

INFILTRATION AND EXFILTRATION

Infiltration is the term used for the covert deployment of forces into enemy territory. Exfiltration is its opposite – the extraction of forces – although in the post-mission environment this may not be a covert process. Both infiltration and exfiltration are separated into three

footprint or on disturbed vegetation helps the tracker match the time of displacement with the time of rainfall.

SPECIFIC SIGN

Although sign is theoretically infinite in nature, in reality there are a few key aspects of sign which are used in military tracking.

Footprints: Footprints yield information such as the number of people who passed, their direction and speed of travel, whether the people were carrying heavy loads and

▼ *British Army Special Forces utilize Nova image-intensification goggles to improve their night vision during an exercise on Dartmoor, England. The SUSAT sights fitted to British SA80 rifles also have some image-intensification properties.*

RHODESIAN TRACKER COMBAT UNIT

During Rhodesia's war against communist insurgents in the 1960s and 1970s, a special forces unit called the Rhodesian Tracker Combat Unit was formed to hunt down and eliminate guerrilla cells. The troops were hand-picked and had excellent bush knowledge. They could track enemy personnel over any type of terrain for days on end. Tracking was performed by four-man teams, each consisting of a controller, a lead tracker and two other trackers on the flanks. The skills of the trackers had a major impact on guerrilla operations. During one mission, the Tracker Combat Unit had to track down 22 guerrillas who had attacked Victoria Falls airport. Most of the sign had been washed away by heavy rain, and the guerrillas were deliberately covering their tracks because of fear of the Tracker Combat Unit. However, a slender trail was picked up and eventually the Tracker Combat Unit found 22 empty sleeping spaces in woodland, hastily abandoned by the guerrillas who sensed the unit closing in. The Tracker Combat Unit eventually tracked down and killed three of the guerrillas in an abandoned quarry, before hunting all the other members down and killing them over the next few days.

even the sex of the tracked group.

Direction is naturally indicated by the direction in which the prints point. If the footprints are heavily impacted into the ground but combined with long strides, fast movement is suggested. A heavy imprint with short steps, frequently slurred and uneven, suggests people moving at walking pace, but carrying heavy loads. Men leave footprints which are slightly turned outwards, whereas women's toes tend to turn inwards during walking.

When a footprint is freshly made, it has a clear, sharp imprint unless in very dry and unstable earth. As the fresh print dries out, after about an hour small particles of earth from the edge crumble and drop into the print, leaving the edge of the footprint appearing more rounded and looser. As discussed above, debris blown by the wind will also gather in the print over time.

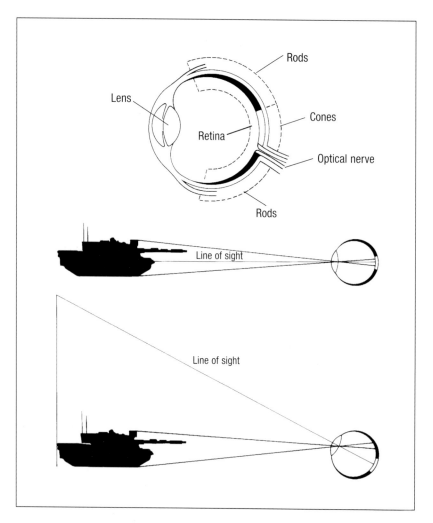

marks will be evident on moss-covered rocks when feet have passed, and areas of flattened grass indicate a resting stop. Sometimes equipment rested on the ground – such as a machine gun tripod – will leave a distinctive mark of its own.

Litter: Few professional military units will drop litter, but not all soldiers are professional or careful. Litter can be any simple sign of human activity, such as a packet of cigarettes, but some litter can provide useful intelligence. Time-dated pages from reading matter or product packaging can narrow the dating possibilities of the sign. Tags from mortars and other such equipment can fall off to inform the tracker of enemy weaponry. Still-smoking cigarette butts indicate recent passage, and, if the ashes of a fire are still warm, the fire will be less than 12 hours old.

Blood: Blood is a sign peculiar to military tracking. A wounded enemy will usually be tracked down by his blood trail. Bleeding will tend to be profuse at the place of wounding, but then be spotted or smeared along the route the enemy takes to escape. The type of blood indicates the wound, which in turn suggests how far the enemy will travel before going to ground. Thick, slimy, shiny, gelatinous blood is produced by head wounds, and pink, frothy blood comes from lung wounds. Torso injuries produce steady drips of bloods, and

To determine the number of people from a mass of footprints, the soldier should first select the set of clearest prints, usually made by the last person in the group. The print is separated from the others by its distinctive tread pattern – even if everyone is wearing the same issue boots, the patterns of wear will differ from person to person. The tracker should then find two consecutive steps made by the key print (a left foot and a right foot) and draw a line across the heel of the first print and through the instep of the second print,

forming a box. The tracker then counts every footprint inside the box and divides by two to find the number of persons. If a key print is not available, an imposed box 76–91cm (30–36in) long can be used for the same purpose.

Disturbed Foliage: Most patrols will displace foliage and branches when moving through natural areas. Twigs are broken, leaves dragged off branches, bushes bent back and so on. The broken ends of twigs stand out particularly well, even in low-light conditions, because of the exposed white inner wood. Scuff blood from abdominal wounds is malodorous because it contains digestive juices.

NIGHT FIGHTING

Night operations complicate military actions because they impair the visual capabilities of soldiers. Human beings adapt to night conditions in several different ways. In daylight, the lens of the human eye focuses light onto a section of light-receptive cones at the back of the central portion of the retina. In this mode, the eye sees an object best by looking at it directly. At night or in conditions of darkness, however, special cells called 'rods'

▼ *Special Forces teams moving at night will tend to make right-angled or 45-degree deviations along the route. The regularity of the deviations makes it easier for lost members of the team to retrace their steps in the darkness.*

around the periphery of the retina are activated to provide some degree of night vision (the rods are adapted to work in conditions of low illumination). This night vision usually activates itself after about 30 minutes of darkness, although it can take up to 36 hours if the soldier has been exposed to very bright sunshine during the preceding day.

As the rods are on the peripheries of the eye, looking directly at an object at night will actually cause it visually to disappear into blackness as the light falls on the inactive daytime cones. Soldiers on night operations, therefore, must develop special ways of looking to utilize their night vision. They are trained to look slightly to the side of an object, rather than directly at it, and use their peripheral vision to decipher shape and position. Another way to do this is

to move the eyes in a skipping motion quickly over the object in many different directions, pausing at the end of each movement for about two or three seconds. Soldiers who are to embark on night operations should spend the daytime wearing dark sunglasses and the period several hours before the operation in a dark room or a room lit by a red light (red light affects night vision the least of any colour in the spectrum).

Soldiers must also adjust their distance estimations at night. Small objects appear further away than they are and larger objects closer as the brain attempts to make size relations between the two with inadequate references. Untrained soldiers also tend to focus on the horizon at night in an attempt to see silhouettes (this is known as the 'moth' effect) and consequently miss information closer to hand.

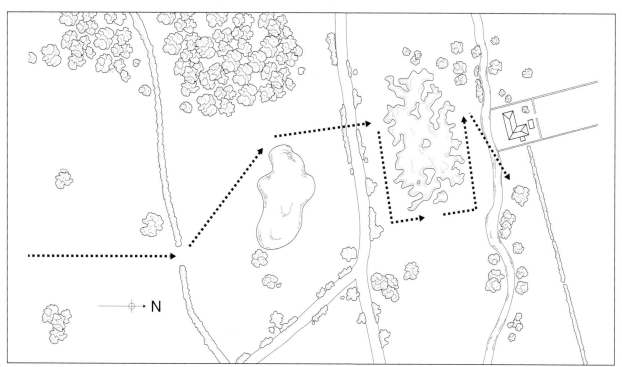

Some adjustments, however, have operational benefits. Hearing becomes more acute to compensate for the reduction in vision, and this takes advantage of the fact that sound carries better on cold, moist night air.

Military planners must evaluate three main operational factors for night operations:

• The tempo of the operation will be dramatically reduced over daytime operations.
• Accurate targeting of direct and indirect fire is difficult.
• Units will require closer formations.

OPERATIONAL TEMPO

Three factors hinder rapid manoeuvres at night: difficulty in navigation, slowness of movement, and fatigue. Navigation suffers because the usual visual land references are either invisible in the darkness or poorly visible. Note, however, that the actual methods of navigation remain the same as in daytime (map-and-compass, GPS, dead reckoning, etc.), but progress is in the region of 50 per cent slower than daytime travel. Navigators must rely more on very prominent silhouetted landmarks, rather than recessed features of the terrain, and they should use their hearing to pick up the sound of water or road traffic as further guides to where they are on the map. Operational tempo is retarded further by longer periods spent in decision-making, as the leaders attempt to decipher navigational and reconnaissance information in the low-light conditions.

Physical movement is slowed by having to walk tentatively to avoid unseen ground-based obstacles. The action of walking at night is the same as the stealth movement described in Section 3 – a high step and body weight not transferred to the stepping foot until the foot is flat on a piece of ground free of obstacles.

Tempo can be sped up by using night-vision equipment and also by attaching luminous or reflective marks on key points around the terrain to aid easy retracing of steps and to guide navigation.

TARGETING

Soldiers firing small arms in night-time conditions have a tendency to shoot high because of the peculiar optics of night vision. Night-trained soldiers remedy this by focusing on the base of the target and slightly lowering the point of aim of the rifle (this is aided by moving the front hand further along the fore-end of the rifle). Training for night fighting involves the soldier looking at his target, then closing his eyes and pointing at it with his finger and then his rifle. He then opens his eyes to judge his point of aim. This activity trains the soldier to overcome visual judgement in favour of a broader spatial awareness, leading

◄ *Night walking. The front foot is lifted high and placed down toe-first without transferring any weight on to the foot. The toe feels for any obstacles, and if all is clear the weight is transferred to the front foot.*

ILLUMINATION

Illumination is used when soldiers need to acquire a clear visual picture of the terrain ahead. The best kind of illumination throws its light down at an angle onto the forward terrain. The angle creates more shadow and contrast than overhead lighting achieves and so makes it easier to spot targets, cover and terrain features. Searchlights can be used in this role, but they are easily targeted by enemy fire. Flares are the most popular battlefield illumination. They can be extremely powerful – a 155mm (6.10in) howitzer fires an illumination round which will illuminate a 2000m (6562ft) diameter circle. Smaller mortar rounds illuminate to a diameter of 1100m (3609ft). During illumination, ground commanders should extract as much information about the enemy positions as possible, but be careful of moving friendly troops forwards while they are exposed by the light. Illumination is also used to support direct- and indirect-fire strategies.

to more accurate targeting. The process needs to be sped up until the soldier can respond to a night target instantly. Keeping both eyes open during firing can also assist aiming, as binocular vision has about two and half times the light receptivity as viewing through only one eye.

For more specialist units (particularly special forces and machine gun teams), weaponry may be fitted with either image-intensification or thermal-imaging sights. These can be fitted direct to the gun as a sight or worn by the operator as goggles. Image-intensifiers are excellent tools for night combat; however, if the action involves heavy use of pyrotechnics or artillery, the user may have to remove the goggles to avoid blinding blasts of light. Spoiling night-vision devices can be a tactic within itself. During the Falklands War in 1982, paras assaulting Mount Longdon on the night of 11–12 June fired illumination rounds over Argentine positions, temporarily blinding the effectiveness of Argentine night-vision devices and senses. Once the light had died down, British snipers turned their own night-vision devices on and started to pick off the vulnerable enemy soldiers.

Targeting indirect fire is complicated by the confusion over ranges at night. GPS tools overcome this problem by plotting the unit and target location with surety. The range of initial adjustment fire should be overestimated to allow a safe drop over the observing unit, the fire then being walked back in to achieve the target. Again, night-vision devices tend to be applied now by observers.

FORMATIONS

Formations are less easily con- trolled in night conditions, but they are essential if night-combat fratricide is to be avoided. The lead elements set a pace which all others in the unit can match to avoid an accordion effect in the movement. Soldiers should stay within visual range of their immediate companion to maintain a close grouping. On occasions, a unit may attach luminous markers to the backs of their helmets so that each soldier can keep track of the man in front. These markers will be removed during operations where contact is very likely, otherwise they will act as target points for enemy snipers.

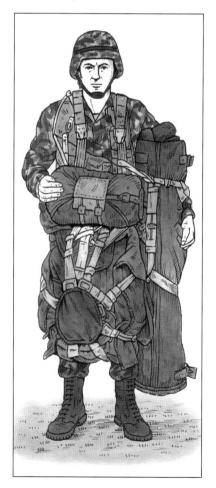

▶ *Standard equipment for a US paratrooper is a T-10C or MC1-1B/C main parachute with a T-10 reserve chute, a PASGT helmet with foam parachutist's impact liner (PIL) and an equipment container on a lowering rig.*

◄ *Static-line parachuting is the standard parachute technique taught to regular airborne forces. Static-line jumps ensure fairly tight patterns of landing at the drop zone and a rapid exit from the aircraft of large numbers of soldiers.*

parachute units such as Pathfinders, whereas static line has been the standard parachute technique of airborne units since the 1930s.

STATIC-LINE JUMPS

Static line refers to the physical mechanism of parachute deployment. The para attaches his parachute ripcord to a cable running along the inside of the jump aircraft via a length of line. When he jumps, the line unravels to its full length (usually about 30m/100ft) before pulling taut and drawing the parachute from the pack. Free-fall time is limited to about two or three seconds, and static-line jumps are usually performed at about 152–244m (500–800ft), the low altitude reducing the time the para is exposed to enemy surface-to-air fire to about 30 seconds. Using special low-altitude, low-opening parachutes can reduce jump altitude to 76m (250ft).

Static-line jumps are almost always restricted to large-unit deployments in which the friendly forces have complete dominance of airspace. Units such as the US 82nd Airborne Division and the British Parachute Regiment can deploy their entire strength by parachute. Typically each man will carry up to 45kg (100lb) of equipment dangling below his legs in a container (the container hits the ground before the soldier does), while support weapons and vehicles are dropped

Most importantly, soldiers must set their sectors of fire rigidly in a patrol situation or from a fighting position. Once combat starts, they must adhere to these sectors unless the situation changes or they are instructed otherwise. Soldiers should make their movements and intentions clear to companions if

they wish to cross through sectors of fire, using the proper passwords or call signals for identification.

COMBAT PARACHUTING

Combat parachuting has three forms: static line, HALO and HAHO. The last two are only taught to special forces and specialist on protective platforms. Further equipment loads are dropped by high-velocity (a small drogue chute stabilizes the load, but does not slow it down), free fall or full-parachute means, depending on the durability of the contents and the container. The deployment aircraft will try to deliver paras and equipment in a single pass over the drop zone, the paras leaving the aircraft at only two-second intervals to produce a tight landing pattern.

Landing patterns have traditionally proved the biggest problem for static-line operations. Static-line parachutes have limited manoeuvrability (high manoeuvrability would run the risk of paras crashing into one another in the air) and are susceptible to wind-drift. Dispersion over and beyond the drop zone (DZ) is common, diffusing the unit's strength and leaving isolated groups exposed to enemy counter-attack. The German airborne assault over Crete in World War II saw entire platoons drowning in the waters off the Cretan coast after overflying the drop zone. During the pre-emptive airborne operations on D-Day, 6 June 1944, parachutists were scattered many miles from their drop zones. The result was hundreds of small units wandering behind enemy lines and forming larger ad hoc units upon meeting. Ironically, although the insertion was chaotic, the wide dispersion confused the German tactical

response and actually assisted the Allied landings. To counter the effects of dispersion, each soldier must have clearly designated rally points along the length of the drop zone and contingency rally points if the dispersion is too wide to be quickly remedied.

Large-scale static-line jumps are seldom used by military planners today because of dispersion, dam-age to equipment and men on landing (impact is at around 25km/h/16mph for a static-line para), and the dangers of sustaining heavy casualties mid-air. Although Germany's airborne invasion of Crete was an eventual success, the losses of paras led Hitler to decree that paras would never again be used in large-scale operations. Many of the 7000 paras killed or

▸ *A para disembarks from an aircraft during a High-Altitude Low-Opening jump at over 8200m (25,000ft). Moving through the cloud cover is a disorientating moment and the para will have to rely entirely on his altimeter to gauge his height.*

▸ *A parachutist making a HALO parachute jump must make allowance for the wind direction to place himself accurately over the drop zone. The drop aircraft will usually face into the wind direction for the actual jump.*

wounded during the operation were shot in their parachutes as they drifted down or killed as they tried to extricate themselves from parachute lines on the ground. One of the last major static-line jumps took place during the US invasion of Panama in 1989 (Operation Just Cause). Dispersion put many soldiers into fields of elephant grass bordering the drop zone, where they were lost for several hours, and equipment and vehicles (including tanks) were lost when they were dropped into a nearby bog.

HALO AND HAHO PARACHUTING

High-altitude, low-opening (HALO) and high-altitude high-opening (HAHO) parachute techniques are used by special forces or similar small-unit operations which require methods of convert insertion. HALO and HAHO deployment begins at altitudes in excess of 8200m (26,000ft), well above the visual and auditory range of enemy ground troops. The HALO parachutist disembarks the aircraft and free falls for about 95 per cent of the drop distance. This free fall will take around two minutes before he deploys his parachute at between 304m and 610m (1000ft and 2000ft). The advantage of this method is that the insertion is silent, there being no aircraft noise on the ground, and the parachutist is visible in the air for only a short space of time. This visibility is further reduced by performing the jump in night conditions.

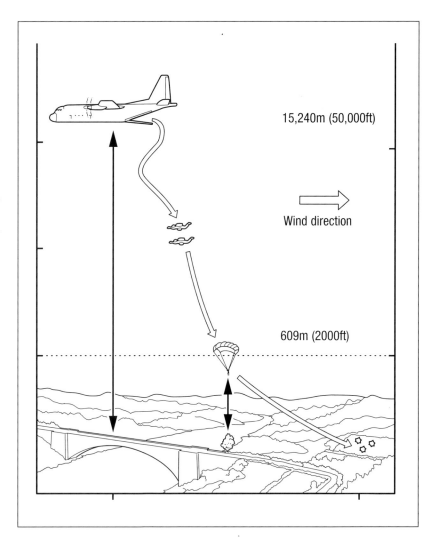

15,240m (50,000ft)

Wind direction

609m (2000ft)

In HAHO jumps, the parachutist opens his parachute after only a few seconds of free fall and adopts parachute-retarded descent from the high altitude. Using a specialized wing-canopied parachute which is fully steerable, the parachutist 'flies' himself to a distant drop zone. The properties of the parachute allow the para up to 120 per cent more airborne time than if a static-line parachute were used, and a well-trained HAHO para can travel for up to 80 minutes and cover a distance of 80km (50 miles).

Navigation to the distant drop zone is assisted by GPS systems attached to the chest which give distance, direction and altitude readings. The advantage of HAHO is that the para is invisible to enemy tracking radar and allows the deploying aircraft to remain outside of enemy air-surveillance range.

The disadvantages with both HAHO and HALO are the environmental pressures. The initial jump altitude will have subzero temperatures around -46°C (-50°F), extreme wind speeds and limited oxygen.

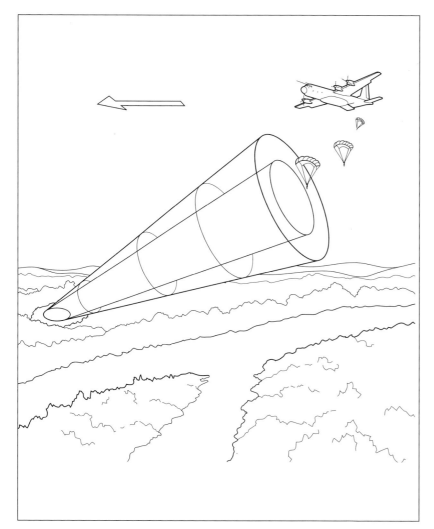

◄ *HAHO parachute jumps are inherently risky. Flying up to 80km (50 miles) on an open-wing parachute makes attaining the landing zone unpredictable. The parachutist aims to keep himself within a specific air corridor which will lead to the Drop Zone (DZ).*

cles. They must be accessible to the drop aircraft, the avenues of approach being as free as possible from enemy ground fire and the drop zone itself being clearly visible to the pilot. The approach should not conflict with any other air operations present in the vicinity; if a low-altitude drop is used, there should be no tall obstructions such as television masts or tall buildings.

The location of the drop zone depends on the mission directive. On rare occasions, troops will be dropped straight into the combat zone, although this is unlikely unless the area has been sup-

To combat these, the para must wear bulky protective clothing and carry oxygen cylinders to sustain them to below 3050m (10,000ft), these in turn limiting the amount of military equipment which can be carried. HAHO paras need more oxygen, but suffer from less extreme temperatures, whereas HALO paras need less oxygen, but the wind-chill factor of free fall can lower temperatures to -62°C (-80°F) – free fall speeds from high altitudes are as high as 290km/h (180mph). In both cases, the para

must check his equipment thoroughly after landing to remove any ice build-up.

DROP-ZONE PROCEDURES

Drop zones (DZs) are selected according to their accessibility, location and freedom from obsta-

▶ *The German Fallschirmjäger paras were the first troops to master combat parachuting. The were used heavily in the opening campaigns of World War II until heavy losses on Crete forces them into a ground role.*

pressed with heavy support fire in advance. More commonly, a drop zone will be positioned within a convenient range of the battle front, in a location which is as unexposed as possible to enemy indirect fire. The drop zone is the main rally point, so any surrounding natural features should not impede access to it for dispersed soldiers, and it should have roads or trails leading into it for convenient re-supply after the drop.

A suitable drop zone is free from all obstacles which may injure or restrict the paras during their landing. Water over 1.2m (4ft) deep should not be within 1000m (3280ft) of the drop zone, and the

area should be as free as possible of trees more than 11m (36ft) tall (the taller the tree, the less easy it is to recover equipment from it). Electrical overhead power lines must be disconnected from power or demolished by advance air strikes or sabotage. The ground itself should be flat and with few or no depressions, ditches, gullies or rocky areas.

Parachute operations usually involve dropping security elements first. These will be combat troops whose purpose is to neutralize enemy forces at the drop zone and quickly secure the drop zone perimeter. Once this is accomplished, units will organize themselves at the drop

▲ *A helicopter door gunner opens up with twin .30 calibre Browning machine guns during a strafing run in Vietnam. Strafing and rocketing remain standard practice for preparing hostile landing zones.*

zone, analyse the implications of any damage sustained during the drop, clarify objectives and proceed on the ground mission.

AIRBORNE ASSAULT

An airborne assault is the operational deployment of troops using rotary-wing or fixed-wing aircraft. Airborne assault offers a military commander unique advantages over other forms of deployment. It can traverse distances at great speed to surprise the enemy. It is able to bypass enemy positions or obstacles, and engage the enemy in the rear. It can be created very quickly in response to battlefield developments and large quantities of troops deployed to a single point of concentration. Finally, it is ideal for assaulting or capturing key terrain features or positions which are inaccessible for units using ground-based movement (such as in mountainous terrain).

▼ *A typical attack pattern from an attack helicopter involves an dive of 10–30-degree angle with the rockets fired on the dive (rockets perform better in fast windspeeds). The helicopter avoids overflying the target to stay clear of air defences.*

PLANNING THE MISSION

The tactical considerations in planning an airborne assault are: objective intelligence; the loading plan; the transit routes between embarkation point and landing zone; support fire delivered at the landing zone prior to landing; the landing itself; and coordination of forces to complete the mission once on the ground.

Intelligence concerns prior to the mission are focused mainly upon the capabilities and positions of hostile forces in the mission area. Airborne assaults are especially vulnerable to ground fire during landing at the landing zone, when aircraft airspeed is low or static, and the combat personnel are unable to deploy their weapons from the interior of the helicopter.

Intelligence officers must analyse all military threats in the area and select routes of travel to the landing zone that avoid enemy surface-to-air capabilities or electronic warfare measures. Travel to the landing zone will utilize terrain to the best advantage. Flying down valleys and similar geological corridors can provide a helicopter with protection from line-of-sight surface-to-air missile systems, but also limits the manoeuvrability of the aircraft (which may need to take evasive action). Most airborne assault routes follow the cover and concealment of large terrain features (such as mountains) while maintaining open air space and not 'canalizing' themselves into narrow terrain.

A landing zone is selected according to strict criteria. It must

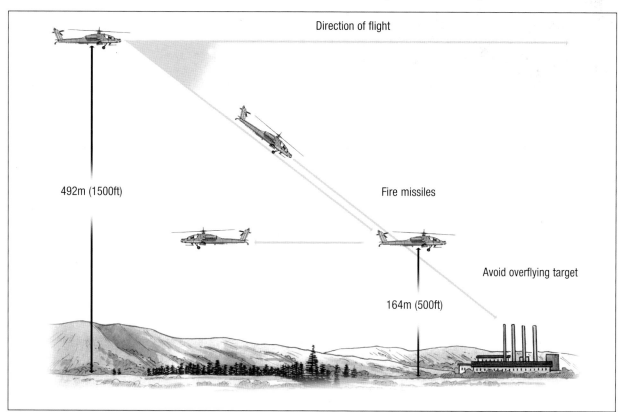

Direction of flight

492m (1500ft)

Fire missiles

164m (500ft)

Avoid overflying target

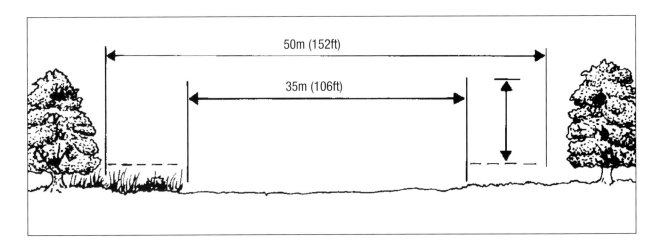

50m (152ft)

35m (106ft)

▲ A helicopter landing zone must accommodate two dimensions. About 35m (106ft) is required for the body of the helicopter and 50m (152ft) is needed to for main rotor clearance.

be able to handle the landing force of helicopters, being of flat, clear terrain. It should also have perimeter cover so that disembarking troops can set up security positions, and it should be large enough for the logistical and consolidation activities of the landing forces. It should be located away from the enemy's main concentrations of firepower and units, particularly heavy anti-aircraft weaponry, and be free from booby traps (the Vietcong used to string heavy cables across open expanses of ground to deny US and ARVN troops landing zones). Finally, a landing zone must be easily identified from the air.

The size of the landing zone will restrict whether the assault can be deployed in one go or whether it will require several landings. For large-scale operations, multiple landing zones may be used. A single landing zone has the advantage that it is easy to concentrate forces, making the communications and logistics of an operation less problematic. It also creates a strong combat vanguard in a single location for narrow offensive operations. Multiple landing zones are more complicated to use, but they allow the prosecution of several mutually supportive operations at once and also serve to confuse the enemy about the direction of attack. Whether single or multiple

◄ A US Army AH-64A Apache attack helicopter from Task Force Hawk comes in for a landing at Rinas Airport in Tirana, Albania, on 21 April 1999.

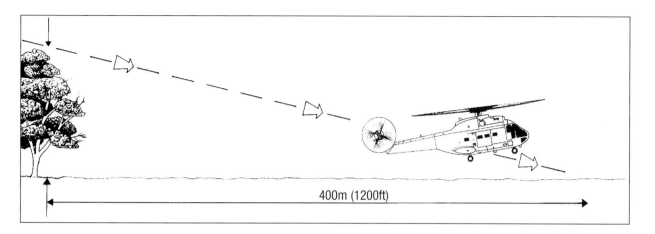

400m (1200ft)

landing zones are used will be dictated by the nature of the mission.

The loading plan is the logistical phase of the operation and must be designed to make the units deployed on the ground as combat effective as possible. Squads and fire teams should never be split between aircraft, and each should board the helicopter with the weapons and equipment that will be required for immediate use. However, officers should be distributed among the helicopters to prevent the mission leadership being destroyed in one helicopter en route to the objective. After the loading plan, the flight sequence is calculated. The most essential personnel and equipment will be deployed in the lead flight so that

▲ *Though helicopters are quite capable of vertical landing, they still require a landing strip of several hundred metres to allow them to make a proper approach and landing, particularly in high winds.*

they arrive first and can secure the landing zone. Any personnel or equipment which is not required straight away at the landing zone is consigned to later flights or even

OPERATION CEDAR FALLS – VIETNAM 1966

Operation Cedar Falls is a cautionary lesson of the airborne assault applied as part of a combined-arms operation. Its objective was to clear an area of Vietcong infiltration and build-up known as the 'Iron Triangle', 64km (40 miles) north of Saigon. The Iron Triangle name came from triangular shape of the region between the Saigon and Thi Tinh rivers and the Than Dien forest reserve. Airborne elements were to play a vital role in the operation. While the borders of the triangle would be secured by US army and artillery units, soldiers of the 1st Infantry Division, 11th Armoured Cavalry Regiment and 173rd Airborne Brigade would be transported in by helicopter to sweep the area. As they progressed through the Triangle, it was intended that they would crush the enemy against units from the US 25th Infantry Division and 196th Infantry Division who were in static positions south of the Saigon River (a classic 'hammer and anvil' manoeuvre).

Early assessments showed the operation to be a success. It was launched on 5 January 1967, and the airborne units hammered Vietcong positions from the air before establishing their landing zones and disembarking thousands of troops. The village of Ben Suc, a Vietcong strongpoint, was entirely destroyed by the helicopter force in a shock landing, and airborne troops swept through the area. By mid-January, more than 750 Vietcong were dead for only 72 US dead and two helicopters damaged. In hindsight, however, the mission was not a success. The noise of the helicopter landing warned the Vietcong in advance, who fled into underground tunnel networks to sit out the US assault. Furthermore, the devastating effects of indiscriminate air-delivered rockets and cannon shells alienated the local population and drove more people to join the Vietcong. The Iron Triangle remained a Vietcong stronghold until the end of the war in 1975, illustrating that sheer weight of assault is often inappropriate for sophisticated anti-guerrilla actions.

different landing zones to meet up with ground units at later locations. If there are significant logistical requirements in the operation, a timed arrival sequence is planned to allow the efficient offloading of supplies and to avoid swamping the landing zone with too many arrivals.

THE LANDING

Once transportation to the landing zone begins, the lead elements of the flight will communicate infor-mation about the condition and/or hostility of the landing zone as they go in. Contingency plans will have been established for the assault to deal with hostile landing zones. During the Vietnam conflict, a landing zone was pronounced as 'hot' when the landing was opposed by enemy fire. The lead flight would have to decide whether to abandon the landing, saturate the area with direct and indirect fire to force a landing, or switch to an alternative landing zone.

Most assault helicopters are either heavily armed or are accompanied by attack helicopters to provide support fire at or around the landing zone. A Hughes AH-64 Apache, for example, is armed with a 30mm (1.18in) Chain Gun, up to 16 Hellfire laser-guided anti-armour missiles and four 18-round pods of 70mm (2.75in) rockets. The Chain Gun and the rocket pods are ideal for area denial and strikes against exposed enemy personnel and unarmoured vehicles. The Hellfires will be used to knock out enemy armour which may around the landing zone, with an engagement distance of many miles. Helicopters will fire from either stationary or moving positions. The best attack flight profile for a helicopter is during diving, as the increased airspeed improves the flight properties and accuracy of rockets.

Support fire for a landing can also be delivered by artillery and mortar units. Prior planning of this support is essential, as the helicopters must avoid flying through the flight path of the projectiles. Support fire for airborne assaults is usually directed at the area around the landing zone. Support fire into the landing zone itself can neutralize enemy resistance at the point of landing, but it can also destroy the integrity of the terrain and prohibit the helicopters making a stable landing. The fire must

◄ *A US pilot receives some medical treatment from his captors after being shot down over North Vietnam. The photograph seems destined for propaganda, as most US pilots captured in Vietnam usually received appalling physical treatment.*

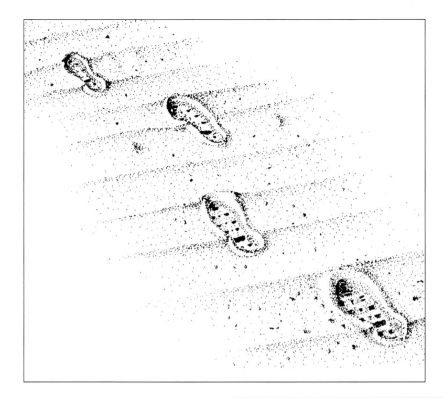

◀ *Footprints in sand are easily read by an enemy tracking team. If it is essential to cross sand, the evading soldier should drag a leafy tree limb behind him to obscure the tracks, though this is an imperfect method.*

in prone positions on the floor with weapons at the ready. The soldiers will often remain in this position until the helicopter has lifted off. During night-time or covert operations, troops will remain silent and motionless for up to five minutes after the helicopter has left. This enables their senses to adjust from the noise and motion of the helicopter interior to the new operational environment.

If hostile fire is encountered, the lead units will immediately open up with suppressive fire and try to move out of the landing zone

be lifted on the command of the flight leader to allow the safe deployment of troops.

The landing phase is the most dangerous part of the airborne assault. Units aboard the helicopters must be prepared to fight in any direction once they leave the helicopter. Most assault helicopters have doors on both sides of the fuselage. When the helicopter lands, the unit on board will disembark from the two doors and immediately create a perimeter defence surrounding the helicopter. This will consist of a ring of men just outside of the circumference of the travelling rotor blades,

▶ *Footprints left in mud are one of the most durable forms of sign. Mud has a predictable rate of drying, so a competent tracker can deduce the time at which the footprints were made.*

◄ *A Special Forces soldier evades an enemy watchtower. Evasion training teaches soldiers to take advantage of established patterns of behaviour. Sentries, for instance, will often unconsciously set up regular patterns of movement around their post.*

must prevent the unit from being severed from that landing zone by enemy troop manoeuvres. The ground commanders will often operate within restrictive boundaries which ensures that they do not travel too far from a convenient landing zone. If the mission extends over many days, re-supply landing zones must be secured at key stages along the line of advance to avoid the units being starved of operational equipment and rations.

When an airborne extraction is planned, it may take place from a designated landing zone at a designated time, or it can be controlled entirely by the ground-force commanders. If the latter, it is their responsibility to ensure that the landing zone is of the correct terrain, is as secure as possible from enemy fire and that the troops are arranged into an intelligent embarkation schedule. Medical emergencies are the first to board and security elements are the last.

and attack enemy positions. By doing this, they create a defensive perimeter around the landing zone to provide subsequent landings with a compliant landing. Support fire will usually be on standby for any further requests for fire from the ground units, so communications must be secured at the earliest possible moment after touch down. Once the landing zone is secured and all troops and equipment

deployed, the ground operation can then begin.

Airborne assaults often terminate with airborne extractions of the ground units, and this places special demands on the mission. From the moment of landing, security elements must establish tight defensive borders or perimeters around the operation. If the unit is to be extracted from a particular landing zone, the security troops

ESCAPE AND EVASION

Escape and evasion (E&E) tactics are employed by a soldier who finds himself either separated from friendly forces behind enemy lines or who has managed to escape enemy captivity. The former is far more likely, as it is very rare for soldiers to actually escape from captivity because of the counter-E&E measures employed by captors (particularly military captors).

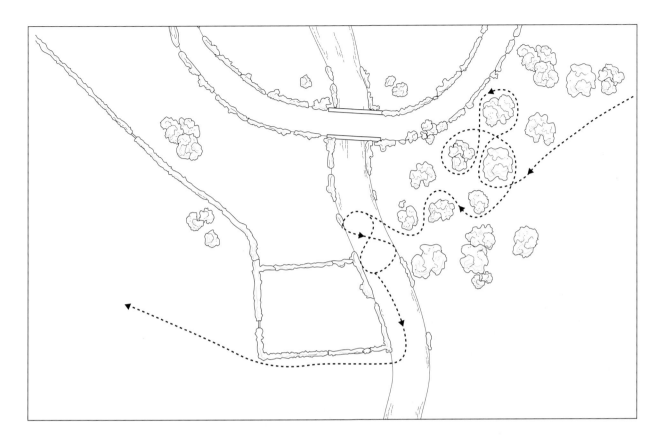

Escapes are, however, possible. As soon as a soldier is captured, he must concentrate hard to pick up any information which may aid his escape. When first entering a prison camp, he should memorize as much of the security arrangements as possible, including positions of watchtowers, perimeter security, signs indicating the presence of perimeter mines, number of personnel on guard duty and number of guard dogs. SAS men captured during the Gulf War feigned unconsciousness from the beatings they had earlier received, all the while using their hearing to garner valuable information about where they were and what was about to happen to them.

A soldier should attempt to make his escape as soon as possible.

The first enemy soldiers who hold him are likely to have less experience of handling prisoners than those further back in a prison camp. Indeed, escape prior to the arrival at a formal – and usually highly secure – camp is a priority. Once in a camp, the soldier may suffer ill treatment which, over time, will deprive him of the physical and mental strength to conduct an escape. Early escapes also have the advantage that the soldier knows something about his location in relation to friendly forces.

Taking advantage of distractions is the key to early escape. Friendly indirect fire or air strikes creates confusion in enemy ranks and may well provide an opening for escape. Walking wounded soldiers are often used to guard pris-

▲ *An example of an evasion pattern intended to confuse tracker dogs. The pattern is deliberately convoluted to set the dog turning back on itself or following blind trails.*

oners, and moments in which they are distracted by their injuries may create opportunities for escape. When the moment is right, the soldier should strike fast for a position of cover away from the prisoner-holding area. Once he attains this cover, he should observe the enemy's response to his escape and begin a series of bounding rushes from one covered position to the next, putting as much distance between him and his captors as possible. The soldier should avoid killing any enemy guards or even guard dogs

◄ *The German Shepherd Dog (GSD) is the most common type of military tracker dog. It has excellent powers of smell and vision and is capable of bursts of speed of 40–48km/h (25–30mph).*

cross into a friendly or neutral country. Crossing friendly lines is possibly the best option, as there are often prearranged re-entry points for escaping soldiers to use to cross safely back into friendly positions. The option of signalling friendly forces and summoning a search-and-rescue operation is applied when the soldier has been separated, rather than captured, and retains communications equipment such as a locator beacon (more common in the case of airmen) or a radio. Crossing into friendly or neutral territory is a medium-risk option. Soldiers taking this course of action need to be sure that the country they are crossing into will not return them as prisoners of war because of pre-existing political agreements. They must also ensure that they have really crossed the border before they reveal themselves (some borders follow more erratic contours than are shown on maps).

EVASIVE MOVEMENT

From the moment an enemy discovers that a prisoner has escaped, he will usually send out a dedicated pursuit team which specializes in tracking human quarry. The escaped soldier employs evasive movement and countertracking practices.

The soldier's first priority is to establish the goal of his movement, i.e. a certain direction or destination which will result in his eventual rescue. He must then plan a

in case he is later recaptured and executed in revenge.

The more time it takes for the enemy to discover the escape, the better, as it increases the area of search which they have to manage. For example, if a soldier flees for one hour in one direction at a pace of 8km/h (5mph), he creates a circle of 8km (5 miles) in radius which has an area of 201 km² (78 miles²). If the time is two hours at the same pace, the radius of 16km (10 miles) equates to a search area of 812km² (314miles²). Naturally, the enemy will narrow this search area to likely avenues of escape (usually towards friendly lines).

Once the soldier has escaped, he must cross friendly lines, signal friendly forces and summon a search-and-rescue operation, or route of travel which will provide the greatest security. This means avoiding: military and civilian personnel, silhouetted terrain, any sort of blockade, key terrain used by the enemy, roads, watercourses, bridges and buildings (especially farms, as they will usually contain guard dogs). Instead, the soldier should utilize the principles of cover and concealment outlined in Chapter Four. He should avoid open ground and choose to move between concealed positions. Patches of undergrowth or low-lying plants are excellent positions for cover, especially if they are mixed into a wooded landscape.

The soldier should attempt to travel mainly at night for greater security, finding or making shelter at first light and resting up for the rest of the day. The shelter should be heavily camouflaged. Although survival shelters must be built in arctic or desert conditions, in temperate climates the shelter should be left as natural as possible – thick undergrowth is ideal. Once inside the shelter, the soldier should limit his activities to the bare essentials. Staying as still as possible and breathing shallowly in a face-down position reduce the scent signature issuing from the hide shelter and make it harder for enemy tracker dogs to discover.

The enemy tracker team will be using all available technologies and talents to track down the escaped soldier. During SAS escape and evasion training, the pursuing forces are a local infantry unit with night-vision and thermal-imaging devices, helicopters, tracker dogs and cross-country vehicles to assist them in the pursuit, and they are promised an extra week's leave if they discover the SAS soldiers. To evade such forces, the SAS soldiers employ countertracking procedures.

Countertracking movement involves leaving tracks which are confusing and contradictory to the pursuers' technology and interpretation. The primary goal of evasive movement is to leave a trail that is as irregular as possible. There are several techniques to achieve this:

- At regular points, the soldier should make convoluted patterns

▼ Footprints are the clearest indicators of human presence. Here, an escaping soldier stealing food avoids leaving footprints in the perimeter mud of a field by lying flat on his stomach and leaving his feet in the undergrowth.

SAS EVASION – GULF WAR

Some of the most famous evasion exploits of recent years are those of SAS soldiers deployed into Iraq during the Gulf War as reconnaissance and attack units. Three SAS units (known as Road-Watch South, Central and North) were tasked with the destruction of Scud missile carriers travelling down three roads which ran from central Iraq to airfields near the Syrian border. All three teams suffered from navigational errors in insertion, and although Road-Watch South aborted, North and Central were deployed in the middle of very hostile terrain.

Road-Watch North suffered from a string of bad luck and was compromised by an Iraqi boy who managed to get away and alert a local anti-aircraft battery. A heavy firefight ensured, and the SAS men only just managed to escape with basic survival equipment and a little ammunition. Freakish weather conditions attacked the soldiers with a blizzard and subzero temperatures. The group became split up and eventually all but one of the unit was either killed, died of hypothermia or captured. Corporal Chris Ryan, however, escaped into the Euphrates valley (which offered more cover), and he moved by night, tracking the Euphrates river as navigational guidance (the river ran into Syria, a friendly nation). He used the reeds which grow by the sides of the river as cover for when filling his water bottle and was constantly evading Iraqi patrols. Eventually, he made it to Syria having walked nearly 190km (120 miles) in seven days, one of the greatest acts of evasion in the SAS Regiment's history.

team (including dogs) into the open area, which is then harder to probe.
• The soldier should move across hard rocky surfaces as much as possible to limit sign and restrict the amount of clear tracks available to the pursuers.

By following these measures, and avoiding making any other conspicuous sign (such as making a fire), the soldier should be able to avoid the pursuers' best efforts until he reaches a position of safety.

BORDERS AND FRIENDLY LINES

Ironically, crossing into a friendly or neutral country, or into friendly lines, can be the most dangerous part of an evasion. Borders and military lines are very sensitive to intruders and will use deadly force readily if security troops believe the line is being crossed by an aggressive third party. Tragedies have occurred when escaped soldiers have been shot dead by their own forces. Soldiers should never just walk up to the lines or border in jubilation and expect the soldiers there to make an open welcome.

Prior to the crossing, the soldier should set up an observation post and identify all security features of the friendly lines. This surveillance should last for a period of 24 hours if possible, so that night and day security can be observed. If a gap can be found in the line, the line should be crossed and another observation post set up behind the line. From here, the soldier should identify friendly units with certainty. He then advances to a position close to the friendly units and identifies himself verbally and using a white

of movement around as many obstacles as possible, looping around trees several times, crossing walls and streams, walking backwards for several hundred metres. Even if this measure does not throw the enemy off the scent, it will at least delay them while they attempt to decipher the tracks.
• When crossing a road or stream, the soldier should approach it at a right angle until about 100m (328ft) from it and then deviate, approaching the road or stream at a 45-degree angle. When the stream is reached, the soldier should leave a obvious mark of his entry on the bank or verge (such as a footprint). He should then move about 20–30m (65–98ft) downstream before doubling back to the point at which he entered the stream and cross the stream at that point, leaving no marker of his presence on the other side.
• Another technique for throwing off trackers is to walk along the centre of a stream for as long as possible, then walk out backwards when necessary to create the impression that this was the point where the stream was entered.
• When moving towards an open area, the soldier should approach it on one side of a large tree, pass the tree, then walk into the open area for about 2–3m (6–9ft). He should then stop, retrace his steps and take a 90-degree detour around the tree and set off in a different direction away from the open area. The effect of this is to draw the enemy tracker

cloth if available, but still remaining under cover in case the troops open fire. He should also use any pre-agreed passwords if they are in use. The friendly troops will then give him instructions as to how he should reveal himself, and the soldier should follow these to the letter. Identity papers or dog tags should be kept easily accessible and no weapons should be carried during the final contacts. If the soldier has just entered a neutral country, he can expect to be incarcerated as an

illegal entrant to the country, and his embassy will initiate release proceedings.

A more dangerous situation is if the soldier is attempting to cross into friendly lines during combat, as the high emotions of combat troops makes them more likely to shoot on sight. If friendly forces are advancing, the soldier should find a concealed position and let the lines pass over him before revealing himself once he is behind friendly lines. If the enemy is advancing, moving deeper into the enemy rear before

▲ *A rule of interrogation is that each prisoner must be isolated from his comrades. Isolation inclines the prisoner to make bonds with his captors to compensate for his loss of social place, achieving this by divulging information.*

attempting to reach a safer sector of the front may be a safer option.

COUNTERINSURGENCY OPERATIONS

Counterinsurgency operations are those designed to defeat or limit guerrilla, terrorist and insurgent

◀ *An interrogator observes the prisoner for signals that the may be lying or concealing the truth. Nervousness is often belied by inadvertent face rubbing, the prisoner in effect trying physically to hide his deceit.*

openly on the battlefield, and they utilize the conventional tools and tactics of war. An insurgency army, by contrast, fights an 'irregular' war. Among the characteristics of this irregular war are:

• Terror tactics: Insurgent forces impose small but regular casualties upon opposing regular forces and civilian political opponents through tactics such as assassinations, ambushes, bombings, torture and booby traps.
• Invisibility: The insurgents are most commonly local people who mingle with the populace and do not define themselves openly with any form of military dress or presence.
• Extended time scale: Most insurgency campaigns are designed not to defeat enemy forces on the battlefield, but rely on the collapse of public support for counterinsurgency campaigns over prolonged periods.
• Political motivation: Insurgency campaigns almost always have a clear political ideology informing them or at least a clear socio-political grievance.
• Public involvement: All insurgency campaigns require public support on some level if they are to have sustainable finance, logistics, recruits and intelligence.

This list is not exhaustive, and the tactics and nature of insurgency conflict differ with each situation. New forms of insurgency are being

added all the time, including computer terrorism (the sending of electronic 'viruses') and biological terrorism.

One of the most influential exponents of guerrilla war was the Chinese revolutionary leader Mao Tse Tung. Mao defined three stages of evolution in an insurgency campaign. Stage one consists of the revolutionary group establishing support for itself amongst the local populace. This stage is intended to swell the ranks of the guerrilla army and create the logistical and intelligence infrastructure to begin military action. It can include minor acts of terrorism and subversion, but nothing to expose the fledgling guerrilla army to excessive danger. The second phase is full guerrilla warfare. Here the insurgents use all available means to impose localized military defeats upon opposing forces and political disruption to the establishment. Finally, stage three occurs when the guerrilla forces are strong enough to launch themselves into open warfare and achieve an outright victory. This usually occurs when the government is militarily and politically weakened and in no position to sustain a large-scale defence. Note that in the course of an actual guerrilla campaign, these stages might not be sequential. Note also that guerrilla forces may be working in support of a regular army engaged in a conventional war. In the Vietnam War, Vietcong were indigenous communist South Vietnamese acting in concert with the regular North Vietnamese Army, both dedicated to the overthrow of the South Vietnamese regime.

actions. Special forces or dedicated counterinsurgency troops usually perform these operations, and they require a range of skills not often possessed by most regular units. Furthermore, regular army tactics, disciplines and formations are often the very elements of which insurgent forces take advantage.

THE NATURE OF INSURGENCY

During regular conflicts, armies are pitted against one another with a desire to confront opposing forces

▸ *In civilian areas an escaped soldier is less likely be stopped if he carries something, usually an item of work or shopping bags. These give the impression that he has a real place in the society.*

The challenge for counterinsurgency is to cut off the system of support enjoyed by the insurgents, defeat them militarily in the field and establish a social order resistant to the insurgent's ideology. To do this, they require two strands of operations: counterinsurgency and counterguerrilla. Insurgency refers to the entire system of irregular warfare, including its political, logistical and social manifestations. Guerrillas are the military element of the insurgency, those who actually conduct the combat operations.

COUNTERGUERRILLA OPERATIONS

Guerrilla fighters have many roles within an insurgency campaign. They weaken the military, psychological and moral strength of enemy forces through constant small-scale actions. They conduct intimidation, propaganda and recruitment campaigns among the local population. They place a heavy burden on government resources and conduct operations which result in unpopular government actions (such as heavy-handed retaliations).

The tactical advantages a guerrilla force possesses are as follows:

• They will be very familiar with the local terrain and will often reside in their homes between operations.
• They will understand their society very well and are perfectly placed to foster resentments and

hostilities against the government.
• They will tend to be part of an advanced intelligence network which will feed them politically and militarily advantageous information about their opponents.
• They will be very motivated by their cause and exercise high self-discipline.
• They have very small logistical needs and consequently have high mobility.

A further advantage is that most counterguerrilla operations are conducted under severe restrictions to avoid civilian casualties.

The general rule for counterinsurgency forces is that the level of force used must equal the guerrilla's campaign and that nothing is done which will alienate the population further and create more recruits for the insurgents.

Counterguerrilla actions always begin with intelligence. A unit commander must have a full profile of guerrilla personalities, operating methods, ideology, future plans and weaponry. This intelligence comes from local police forces, compliant sectors of the population, enemy prisoners and the full range of reconnaissance technologies and personnel available to the unit. Operating patterns are a useful indicator of future guerrilla operations, and full reports should be made by friendly forces after each encounter. These reports taken together may provide commanders with a detailed insight into the guerrilla combat methods, the geographical focus of their efforts, their common objectives and the equipment available to them.

Counterguerrilla units (CGUs) will be organized according to the level of threat and the nature of the

operation. In general, CGUs will be the same size or one unit size larger than the enemy they expect to meet. Heavily outnumbering the guerrillas has limited advantage, as very large units do not have the surprise capability of small, flexible units. Mobility is vital. CGUs should be able to deploy with great speed to the site of any guerrilla activity. The helicopter is the primary vehicle because of its speed and manoeuvrability. Military helicopters also have the advantage of on-board firepower which can be used to suppress enemy activity around a landing zone before deployment.

Counterguerrilla operations have four basic forms: search, patrol, raid and ambush. The search is a useful tool to disrupt guerrilla logistics. Searches are

conducted against people, buildings, vehicles and natural areas which might contain supplies or intelligence regarding guerrilla activity. A search must be conducted lawfully and with sensitivity. Aggressive and even violent house searches by US forces were an important catalyst for Vietcong recruitment during the Vietnam War and alienated many people from the government cause. Female personnel should be on hand to conduct body searches of female civilians, and everything taken during the search must be properly inventoried. When searching individuals, soldiers will usually work in pairs – one to search the person, the other to act as security. Road checkpoints are important to stop enemy vehicular movement. The checkpoint should be positioned

▼ *VIP protection formations.*
The bodyguards (shaded dark) must adopt formations which protect the VIP with their own bodies but also allow them clear view of the surroundings and good fields of fire.

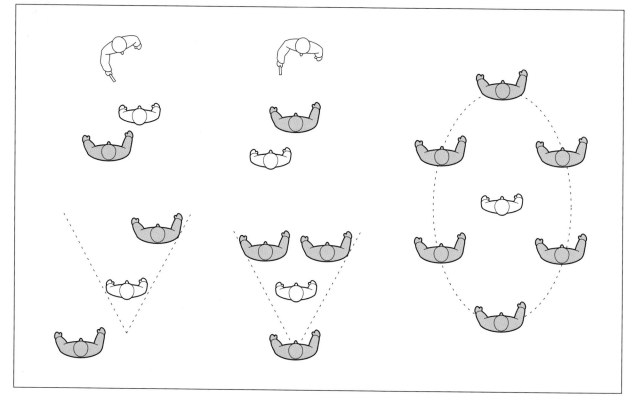

on a stretch of road which is difficult for a vehicle to turn in and set around a bend if possible to delay sight of the checkpoint until the last moment. Urban searches are conducted by multiple units, each assigned a designated area which is part of a full-scale reconnaissance. These units will operate in two elements: a search element to enter a dwelling and a security element to establish a perimeter around the building to stop anyone escaping or stop guerrilla reinforcements coming into the area.

Counterguerrilla patrols are used when there is little or no intelligence about guerrilla activity in a particular area. The purposes of the patrol are to gather intelligence,

deny the guerrillas free movement around an area, conduct combat actions against any guerrilla forces discovered and track guerrilla movements. Counterguerrilla patrols obey most conventional rules of patrolling (see Chapter Four), but there are some specialist techniques. One is saturation patrolling. Here, an area is patrolled by multiple small units on a 24-hour, seven-day-a-week basis. The routes of the patrols are changed frequently to inhibit enemy ambush planning and to disrupt enemy movement. The objective is to keep an area so rigorously patrolled that it effectively becomes unsuitable for guerrilla operations.

▲ US troops practise urban warfare operations. Smoke is one of the biggest problems in urban combat, as it inhibits breathing and impairs vision. Respirators and thermal-imaging equipment can overcome both these problems.

The raid and ambush are the aggressive end of counterguerrilla actions. Raids are conducted against enemy base camps, usually located in isolated rural areas. Intelligence about the base must be first-rate, including number of personnel likely to be present, layout of the base and enemy weaponry. The raid is conducted like any other offensive operation; however, surprise is of the utmost importance and special forces soldiers are usually used for their greater ability in stealth and fieldcraft. The raid should be conducted as violently as possible, and all guerrillas fleeing the assault zone should be ruthlessly hunted down. Snipers are often position on the peripheries of the operation to monitor and kill any escaping guerrillas.

The ambush (see Chapter Five) is used to destroy enemy forces and equipment, and inflict psychological intimidation upon the enemy. Ambushes fight the guerrilla with his own tactics, and the fear of ambush will limit his movements and operational confidence. As guerrillas often wear civilian dress, great care must be taken not to ambush innocent civilian parties, particularly when operating near populated areas.

COUNTERINSURGENCY OPERATIONS

Counterinsurgency operations are the full spectrum of measures taken against the insurgency forces, not just the military element. All the counterguerrilla tactics described above have their use in this context, but there are many more specialist tasks. Most of these are the sole responsibility of the government and local police forces, but special forces soldiers may find themselves in the following roles:

• Hearts and minds operations: operations which aim to bolster support for anti-guerrilla activities and the incumbent government. In the Malayan Emergency in the 1950s and 1960s, British SAS troops conducted extensive hearts and mind operations by delivering services such as medical treatment and vaccination programmes, veterinary care of livestock and assis-

tance with construction projects.
• Protective programmes: guerrilla forces frequently use intimidation, violence or propaganda to sustain their cause. Counterinsurgency troops are used to establish protective areas for civilian populations free from guerrilla interference, often becoming near-permanent residents of the area and instructing the locals in self-defence measures.
• Police support: local police,

▲ A US Special Forces soldier assists a Vietnamese boy during 'hearts and minds' operations in Vietnam. The 'hearts and minds' concept of counterinsurgency warfare was first introduced by the British Army operating in Malaya in the 1960s.

who usually have the best intelligence available, perform most counterinsurgency duties. The military may liaise with the police in

COUNTERINSURGENCY TACTICS IN MALAYA – 1948–60

The Malayan 'Emergency' lasted from 1948–60, a period in which communist Malayan Races Liberation Army (MRLA) guerrillas attempted to overthrow British colonial rule. Malaya did eventually achieve its independence from the United Kingdom in 1960, but not under the communists, who had been savaged by intelligent British counterinsurgency tactics which laid the foundation for much later counterinsurgency theory.

The MRLA had a strength of about 8000 men, but enjoyed massive support from the 500,000 ethnic Chinese in Malaya, who lived mainly in remote jungle areas outside government control. Among Malayans themselves, the MRLA found little support. The first two years of counterinsurgency operations against the MRLA had limited success. British military activity was vigorous and consisted of combat patrols, aerial and artillery bombardments and ambushes. Eight- or 10-man ambushes were found to be particularly useful, inflicting attrition upon the MRLA and often capturing valuable documentation. By 1950, however, a British assessment found the MRLA still in a position of strength, and their numbers or activities had not been significantly reduced.

In 1951, the appointment of Lieutenant General Sir Gerald Templer as head of operations changed the nature of British counterinsurgency tactics. Templer viewed MRLA military actions as 'only 25 per cent of the trouble' and placed more emphasis on political and social counterinsurgency operations. SAS and other British units initiated 'hearts and minds' campaigns among the ethnic Chinese, removing much hostility to government forces. Special forces also conducted deep-penetration missions into the heart of the jungle to assassinate key MRLA personnel. Most importantly, the British designed a food-denial programme. This concentrated food supplies for the ethnic Chinese population into specially designated areas surrounded by police and military security. The consequence was that MRLA soldiers (often on the brink of starvation) were forced to move through dense security zones to reach food and support. Many were killed or captured doing so. Combined with better intelligence from the Malayan police, the British were able to break up the MRLA into fragmented and inefficient units cut off from their logistical base.

The MRLA eventually collapsed with 7000 dead, although in their favour it has to be said that they had no external source of weaponry or supplies outside what they could manufacture themselves or capture.

roles such as the appropriation of suspects, interrogation, security for police operations, controlling civil disturbances (a typical feature of countries with insurgency problems) and providing reconnaissance information.

The key lesson to emerge from the twentieth century about counterinsurgency operations is that the military option is only a part of the solution. Military means must be backed with political and social measures if the counterinsurgency operation is to be successful.

Glossary

Air Support Operations Centre (ASOC) – A command-and-control centre for air-support activities.

Amphibious Objective Area (AOE) – This is the area designated for the launch of an amphibious-assault landing.

Anti-handling devices – Devices which detonate anti-tank and anti-personnel mines when they are lifted by enemy engineers.

AP – Armour-piercing.

APC – Armoured Personnel Carrier.

Area ambush – An ambush designed to destroy an enemy unit within a particular sector, as opposed to a single location.

Assault rifle – An automatic, magazine-fed rifle firing medium-range ammunition.

ATGM – Anti-tank Guided Missile.

AWAC – Airborne Early Warning Aircraft.

Beaten Zone – The area on the ground on which fire falls.

Booby trap – An apparently harmless object which causes injury or death when touched.

Bounding Overwatch – A manoeuvre in which one unit provides covering fire from static positions while another unit advances. The two units swap roles at regular intervals.

Bracketing – A method of artillery fire adjustment involving placing shells in front of and behind the target, then subdividing the distance continually until the shells are on target.

Burst transmission – A communication transmitted in a burst of data only a few milliseconds long.

CCD – Camouflage, Concealment and Decoy.

CGU – Counter-Guerrilla Units.

CQB – Close-Quarter Battle.

Claymore – A very destructive type of anti-personnel mine which fires out a hail of steel balls when detonated.

Clearing Man – A member of a Hostage-Rescue unit who is submachine-gun armed and follows the Point Man closely into rooms.

Close Air Support (CAS) – The use of ground-attack aircraft to support an infantry unit which has encountered an enemy position.

COIN – Counter Insurgency.

Column – A simple unit formation consisting of several units moving in line with one another.

Combat patrol – A patrol with the objective of finding and engaging the enemy.

Defilade – A position which protects against enemy gunfire or observation.

Det Cord – A flexible plastic cord with a hollow core filled with high explosive and used to detonate a main charge.

Direct fire – Fire which is aimed directly at an observable target.

Double Tap – A method of handgun fire in which two rounds are put into the target in quick succession.

DPM – Disruptive Pattern Material, the standard material of British Army uniforms.

DZ – Drop zone, the area in which parachutists aim to land.

E&E – Escape and Evasion.

Enfilade – Gunfire directed along a line from end to end.

ETA – Estimated Time of Arrival.

File – A unit formation in which all unit members walk in a single line, one man behind the other.

Fire-and-forget – A missile technology which guides a missile to a target after launching without post-launch control by the operator.

Fire-Direction Centre (FDC) – A command-and-control facility for artillery units.

Forward Observer (FO) – A frontline soldier responsible for adjusting and controlling artillery fire.

Fratricide – A term used to describe the accidental killing of soldiers by their own side.

Global Positioning Satellite (GPS) – A navigational system which allows an individual to compute his exact coordinates using orbiting military navigation satellites.

Grazing fire – Small-arms fire in which most of the rounds do not rise above 1m (3ft) from the ground.

HAHO – High Altitude High Opening, a parachuting technique. The parachutist opens his parachute after only a few seconds of free-fall, adopting parachute-retarded descent from a high altitude.

HALO – High Altitude Low Opening, a parachuting technique. The parachutist disembarks the aircraft and free-falls for about 95 per cent of the drop distance before deploying his parachute. This technique requires precision timing.

Hammer-and-anvil – Offensive manoeuvre aimed at trapping enemy forces between advancing units (the hammer) and static units (the anvil).

High Explosives – Explosives which instantly transform into gas upon detonation, producing an extremely powerful explosion.

HR – Hostage Rescue.

HRU – Hostage-Rescue Unit.

Immediate CAS – Close Air Support requested in the immediate context of events on the battlefield.

Indirect fire – Fire from units which do not have visual contact with the enemy, usually directed onto target by an FO.

Infrared-Passive Sensor (IP) – A remote sensor which detects variations in surrounding temperature.

Interrogation Friend or Foe (IFF) – A device commonly fitted to aircraft and tanks which automatically confirms whether a possible target belongs to friendly or enemy forces.

IR – Infra-red.

Jamming – The activity of obscuring, inhibiting or prohibiting an enemy's radio communications.

Kill Zone – The area of an ambush designated for engaging and destroying the enemy.

Laser Designator – A device which illuminates a target with a laser beam, the beam acting as a target point for laser-guided munitions.

LAW – Light Anti-tank Weapon.

Linear ambush – An ambush formation in which the ambushers deploy parallel to the enemy's line of movement.

Linear Target – Any target between 200m (609ft) and 600m (1829ft) long.

Load-Carrying Equipment (LCE) – The system of webbing, pouches and packs which a soldier uses to carry his personal equipment.

Low Explosives – Explosives which burn slowly, most commonly used as propellants in ammunition.

LZ – Landing Zone.

Magnetic Sensor (MAG) – A remote sensor which detects variations in the surrounding magnetic field caused by vehicles and metallic objects.

MANPADS – Man Portable Air Defence System.

MBT – Main Battle Tank.

METT-TC – A US Army abbreviation denoting operational considerations: Mission, Enemy, Terrain and Weather, Troops, Time and Civilian Considerations.

Mils – A subdivision of a circle. There are 6400 mils in a circle.

Moving-Target Indicators (MTIs) – Radars which are capable of tracking moving targets on the ground.

MLRS – Multiple Launch Rocket System.

NATO – North Atlantic Treaty Organization.

NBC – Nuclear, Biological, Chemical.

Night-Vision Devices (NVDs) – Devices which enable a soldier to see in low-light or night-time conditions.

NIR – Near Infra-red.

Obscuration – A term used to describe any means applied to inhibit the enemy's vision, such as smoke bombs or blinding illumination.

OCOKA – A US military acronym denoting manoeuvre considerations. Stands for Observation and Fields of Fire; Cover and Concealment; Obstacles; Key Terrain; Avenues of Approach.

OP – Observation point.

OTH – Over-the-Horizon radar.

Permissive fire – Permissive-fire guidelines allow an observer to bring in any fire which he deems necessary within given locations.

Plunging fire – Small-arms fire in which the path of the rounds is higher than a standing man except in its beaten zone.

Point ambush – An ambush launched against a specific and limited location.

Point man – The man who occupies the lead position in a patrol unit or combat team.

Point Target – A single target less than 200m (609ft) wide.

Precision-Guided Munitions – Missiles or bombs which are guided precisely onto the target by advanced targeting systems.

Primary sector – An infantryman's fire sector which extends at an oblique angle from each corner of a trench, shooting around the edge of frontal cover.

Reconnaissance by fire – A crude process of discovering enemy locations by showering suspected positions with small-arms and artillery fire.

Reconnaissance patrol – A patrol conducted for the purposes of surveillance and information gathering.

Restrictive fire – Restrictive-fire guidelines prohibit calls for fire which are not part of the support-fire programme pre-agreed with the unit commander on the ground.

RO – Radio Operator.

RPG – Rocket-Propelled Grenade.

RPs – Rally Points.

SALUTE – An mnemonic for the elements which must be noted during surveillance of enemy positions: Size, Activity, Location, Unit, Time and Equipment.

SAM – Surface-to-Air Missile.

SATCOM – Satellite Communications.

Saturation patrolling – Patrolling by multiple small units on a 24-hour, seven-days-a-week basis.

Secondary sector – A fire zone directly in front of a soldier's position, targeted by angling the rifle around the frontal cover.

Sector stakes – Stakes set in the ground which mark out a soldier's fire sectors.

Seismic-Acoustic Sensor (SA) – A remote sensor which detects varia-

tions in surrounding noise levels or ground vibrations.

Sign – The term used in tracking for any evidence of environmental disturbance made by the passage of human or animal quarry.

SAW – Squad Automatic Weapon, a light machine gun.

Standard Operating Procedures (SOPs) – The basic operational methods taught to units.

Static-line – A method of parachute jumping in which the parachute is pulled from its pack by a line connected to the jump aircraft.

Stinger (UK) / Stop Strip (US) – Special strips of metallic spikes dragged across a road in front of a car to burst the tyres and stop the vehicle.

Stun grenade – A pyrotechnic device which emits a disorientating bang and flash, but no lethal fragmentation.

Submachine gun – A firearm capable of full-automatic fire but which fires pistol-calibre ammunition.

Support weapons – Any artillery or missile weapon which supports infantry manoeuvres.

Suppressive fire – Fire which inhibits enemy movement or their capacity to respond to attacks.

TOW – Tube-launched, Optically tracked, Wire-guided missile, a type of US anti-tank missile.

Tracking patrol – A patrol which tracks enemy movements.

Travelling – A unit manoeuvre consisting of two fire teams set in line with about 20m (61ft) between them. The two teams hold these positions during an advance to provide mutual fire support if necessary.

Travelling Overwatch – A unit manoeuvre which has the same structure as Travelling, but with about 50m (152ft) between the squads,

Wedge – A V-shaped unit formation.

Index

References in italics refer to illustration captions

Picture Credits

Aerospace Publishing: 68.

POPPERFOTO: 6-7, 12, 18 (both), 20, 22, 23 (both), 25, 26, 29 (both), 36, 38, 42, 46, 51, 57, 64, 74, 75, 80, 88, 90, 94, 96, 106, 107, 109, 140, 147, 151, 163, 172, 177, 181, 194, 196, 200, 201, 202, 209, 143.

TRH Pictures: 33, 45, 47, 49 (US Navy), 52 (US Marine Corps), 53, 58, 62, 71 (E. Nevill), 82, 86, 87, 89, 98, 101 (US Navy), 102 (US Army), 113, 114, 115, 121, 124 (US Army), 125 (US Army), 134 (US National Archives), 135, 136 (T A Davies), 139 (T A Davies), 142, 146, 150, 156 (US Navy), 159 (Mike Ingram), 160 (US National Archives), 168 (E. Nevill), 169 (US Army), 190, 199, 210, 212, 213, 216, 217, 218, 223, 229 (Yves Debay), 231, 232, 236 (USAF), 240, 248.

US Dept. of Defense: 8, 9, 10, 11, 60, 70, 78, 81, 92, 103, 104, 120, 122, 131, 133, 144, 161, 171, 178, 179, 185, 186, 187, 189, 228, 234, 247, 250, 253.

Illustrations: Tony Randell